MULTICULTURAL EDUCATION SERIES
James A. Banks, *Series Editor*

Measuring Race: Why Disaggregating Data Matters for Addressing Educational Inequality
  Robert T. Teranishi, Bach Mai Dolly Nguyen, Cynthia Maribel Alcantar, and Edward R. Curammeng

Campus Uprisings: How Student Activists and Collegiate Leaders Resist Racism and Create Hope
  Ty-Ron M. O. Douglas, Kmt G. Shockley, and Ivory Toldson

Transformative Ethnic Studies in Schools: Curriculum, Pedagogy, and Research
  Christine E. Sleeter and Miguel Zavala

Why Race and Culture Matter in Schools: Closing the Achievement Gap in America's Classrooms, 2nd Edition
  Tyrone C. Howard

Just Schools: Building Equitable Collaborations with Families and Communities
  Ann M. Ishimaru

Immigrant-Origin Students in Community College: Navigating Risk and Reward in Higher Education
  Carola Suárez-Orozco and Olivia Osei-Twumasi, Eds.

"We Dare Say Love": Supporting Achievement in the Educational Life of Black Boys
  Na'ilah Suad Nasir, Jarvis R. Givens, and Christopher P. Chatmon, Eds.

Teaching What *Really* Happened: How to Avoid the Tyranny of Textbooks and Get Students Excited About *Doing* History, 2nd Edition
  James W. Loewen

Culturally Responsive Teaching: Theory, Research, and Practice, 3rd Edition
  Geneva Gay

Music, Education, and Diversity: Bridging Cultures and Communities
  Patricia Shehan Campbell

Reaching and Teaching Students in Poverty: Strategies for Erasing the Opportunity Gap, 2nd Edition
  Paul C. Gorski

Deconstructing Race: Multicultural Education Beyond the Color-Bind
  Jabari Mahiri

Is Everyone Really Equal? An Introduction to Key Concepts in Social Justice Education, 2nd Edition
  Özlem Sensoy and Robin DiAngelo

Teaching for Equity in Complex Times: Negotiating Standards in a High-Performing Bilingual School
  Jamy Stillman and Lauren Anderson

Transforming Educational Pathways for Chicana/o Students: A Critical Race Feminista Praxis
  Dolores Delgado Bernal and Enrique Alemán, Jr.

Un-Standardizing Curriculum: Multicultural Teaching in the Standards-Based Classroom, 2nd Edition
  Christine E. Sleeter and Judith Flores Carmona

Global Migration, Diversity, and Civic Education: Improving Policy and Practice
  James A. Banks, Marcelo Suárez-Orozco, and Miriam Ben-Peretz, Eds.

Reclaiming the Multicultural Roots of U.S. Curriculum: Communities of Color and Official Knowledge in Education
  Wayne Au, Anthony L. Brown, and Dolores Calderón

Human Rights and Schooling: An Ethical Framework for Teaching for Social Justice
  Audrey Osler

We Can't Teach What We Don't Know: White Teachers, Multiracial Schools, 3rd Edition
  Gary R. Howard

Teaching and Learning on the Verge: Democratic Education in Action
  Shanti Elliott

Engaging the "Race Question": Accountability and Equity in U.S. Higher Education
  Alicia C. Dowd and Estela Mara Bensimon

Diversity and Education: A Critical Multicultural Approach
  Michael Vavrus

First Freire: Early Writings in Social Justice Education
  Carlos Alberto Torres

Mathematics for Equity: A Framework for Successful Practice
  Na'ilah Suad Nasir, Carlos Cabana, Barbara Shreve, Estelle Woodbury, and Nicole Louie, Eds.

Race, Empire, and English Language Teaching: Creating Responsible and Ethical Anti-Racist Practice
  Suhanthie Motha

Black Male(d): Peril and Promise in the Education of African American Males
  Tyrone C. Howard

LGBTQ Youth and Education: Policies and Practices
  Cris Mayo

(continued)

MULTICULTURAL EDUCATION SERIES, *continued*

Race Frameworks:
A Multidimensional Theory of Racism and Education
ZEUS LEONARDO

Class Rules
PETER W. COOKSON JR.

Teachers Without Borders? The Hidden Consequences of
International Teachers in U.S. Schools
ALYSSA HADLEY DUNN

Streetsmart Schoolsmart
GILBERTO Q. CONCHAS AND JAMES DIEGO VIGIL

Americans by Heart
WILLIAM PÉREZ

Achieving Equity for Latino Students
FRANCES CONTRERAS

Literacy Achievement and Diversity
KATHRYN H. AU

Understanding English Language Variation
in U.S. Schools
ANNE H. CHARITY HUDLEY AND CHRISTINE MALLINSON

Latino Children Learning English
GUADALUPE VALDÉS, SARAH CAPITELLI, AND LAURA ALVAREZ

Asians in the Ivory Tower
ROBERT T. TERANISHI

Our Worlds in Our Words
MARY DILG

Diversity and Equity in Science Education
OKHEE LEE AND CORY A. BUXTON

Forbidden Language
PATRICIA GÁNDARA AND MEGAN HOPKINS, EDS.

The Light in Their Eyes, 10th Anniversary Edition
SONIA NIETO

The Flat World and Education
LINDA DARLING-HAMMOND

Diversity and the New Teacher
CATHERINE CORNBLETH

Frogs into Princes: Writings on School Reform
LARRY CUBAN

Educating Citizens in a Multicultural Society, 2nd Edition
JAMES A. BANKS

Culture, Literacy, and Learning
CAROL D. LEE

Facing Accountability in Education
CHRISTINE E. SLEETER, ED.

Talkin Black Talk
H. SAMY ALIM AND JOHN BAUGH, EDS.

Improving Access to Mathematics
NA'ILAH SUAD NASIR AND PAUL COBB, EDS.

"To Remain an Indian"
K. TSIANINA LOMAWAIMA AND TERESA L. MCCARTY

Education Research in the Public Interest
GLORIA LADSON-BILLINGS AND WILLIAM F. TATE, EDS.

Multicultural Strategies for Education and Social Change
ARNETHA F. BALL

Beyond the Big House
GLORIA LADSON-BILLINGS

Teaching and Learning in Two Languages
EUGENE E. GARCÍA

Improving Multicultural Education
CHERRY A. MCGEE BANKS

Education Programs for Improving Intergroup Relations
WALTER G. STEPHAN AND W. PAUL VOGT, EDS.

City Schools and the American Dream
PEDRO A. NOGUERA

Thriving in the Multicultural Classroom
MARY DILG

Educating Teachers for Diversity
JACQUELINE JORDAN IRVINE

Teaching Democracy
WALTER C. PARKER

The Making—and Remaking—of a Multiculturalist
CARLOS E. CORTÉS

Transforming the Multicultural Education
of Teachers
MICHAEL VAVRUS

Learning to Teach for Social Justice
LINDA DARLING-HAMMOND, JENNIFER FRENCH, AND
SILVIA PALOMA GARCIA-LOPEZ, EDS.

Culture, Difference, and Power, Revised Edition
CHRISTINE E. SLEETER

Learning and Not Learning English
GUADALUPE VALDÉS

The Children Are Watching
CARLOS E. CORTÉS

Multicultural Education, Transformative Knowledge,
and Action
JAMES A. BANKS, ED.

Measuring Race

Why Disaggregating Data Matters for Addressing Educational Inequality

Edited by

Robert T. Teranishi
Bach Mai Dolly Nguyen
Cynthia M. Alcantar
Edward R. Curammeng

TEACHERS COLLEGE PRESS

TEACHERS COLLEGE | COLUMBIA UNIVERSITY
NEW YORK AND LONDON

Published by Teachers College Press,® 1234 Amsterdam Avenue, New York, NY 10027

Copyright © 2020 by Teachers College, Columbia University

Cover photo by OgnjenO / iStock by Getty Images.

All rights reserved. No part of this publication may be reproduced or transmitted in any form or by any means, electronic or mechanical, including photocopy, or any information storage and retrieval system, without permission from the publisher. For reprint permission and other subsidiary rights requests, please contact Teachers College Press, Rights Dept.: tcpressrights@tc.columbia.edu

Library of Congress Cataloging-in-Publication Data

Names: Teranishi, Robert T., editor. | Nguyen, Bach Mai Dolly, editor. | Alcantar, Cynthia M. editor. | Curammeng, Edward R., editor.
Title: Measuring race : why disaggregating data matters for addressing educational inequality / edited by Robert T. Teranishi, Bach Mai Dolly Nguyen, Cynthia Maribel Alcantar, Edward R. Curammeng.
Description: New York, NY : Teachers College Press, 2020. | Series: Multicultural education series | Includes bibliographical references and index.
Identifiers: LCCN 2020000699 (print) | LCCN 2020000700 (ebook) | ISBN 9780807763605 (paperback) | ISBN 9780807763612 (hardback) | ISBN 9780807778432 (ebook)
Subjects: LCSH: Educational equalization--United States. | Minorities—Education—United States. | Minority students—United States. | Group identity—United States. | Race awareness—United States. | Ethnicity—United States.
Classification: LCC LC213.2 .M448 2020 (print) | LCC LC213.2 (ebook) | DDC 379.2/60973—dc23
LC record available at https://lccn.loc.gov/2020000699
LC ebook record available at https://lccn.loc.gov/2020000700

ISBN 978-0-8077-6360-5 (paper)
ISBN 978-0-8077-6361-2 (hardcover)
ISBN 978-0-8077-7843-2 (ebook)

Printed on acid-free paper
Manufactured in the United States of America

Contents

Series Foreword   vii
    James A. Banks

Preface: Race: American Education's Inescapable Conundrum   xiii
    Walter R. Allen

1. **Introduction**   1
    Bach Mai Dolly Nguyen and Robert T. Teranishi

PART I: CONCEPTUAL CONSIDERATIONS OF RACIAL HETEROGENEITY

2. **Who's Black?**
   Hybridity, Complexity, and Fluidity in 21st-Century Racial Identity   15
   Gloria Ladson-Billings

3. **Latinos in the American Racial Hierarchy:**
   The Complexities of Identity and Group Formation   29
   Luis Ricardo Fraga and Nicole Perez

4. **Panethnicity and Ethnic Heterogeneity:**
   The Politics of Lumping and Disaggregating Asian Americans
   and Pacific Islanders in Educational Policy   46
   Michael Omi, Mike Hoa Nguyen, and Jason Chan

5. **The "Invisible" Minority: Finding a Sense of Belonging After**
   Imperialism, Colonialism, and (Im)migration for Native Hawaiian
   and Pacific Islanders in the United States   67
   'Inoke Hafoka, Kēhaulani Vaughn, Iosefa Aina, and Cynthia M. Alcantar

6. Draw Your Own Box? Further Complicating Racial Data
   for Multiracial/Two or More Races College Students — 84
   Marc P. Johnston-Guerrero and Karly Sarita Ford

PART II: UNMASKING EDUCATIONAL INEQUALITY THROUGH DISAGGREGATED DATA

7. Similar, But Not the Same: Considering the Intersections of
   Race, Ethnicity, and Immigrant Status in the Lives of Black Students — 103
   Kimberly A. Griffin and Chrystal A. George Mwangi

8. Beyond Reservations: Exploring Diverse Backgrounds and
   Tribal Citizenship Among Native College Students — 119
   Heather J. Shotton

9. The Mismeasure of Native American Students:
   Using Data Disaggregation to Promote Identity Safety — 131
   Laura M. Brady, Zoe Higheagle Strong, and Stephanie A. Fryberg

10. More Than Nuance: Recognizing and Serving
    the Diversity of the Latinx Community — 154
    Desiree D. Zerquera, Jasmine Haywood, and Martín De Mucha

11. Data Quality in the Evaluation of Latino Student Success — 170
    Stella M. Flores, Brian Holzman, and Leticia Oseguera

Conclusion — 195
   Robert T. Teranishi

About the Editors and Contributors — 202

Index — 207

Series Foreword

The prevailing, timely, and needed message of this informative book is that the differences within racial and ethnic groups must be identified and made explicit in order for various groups—and the subgroups within them—to attain equal educational opportunities. The editors as well as the authors contributing to this book give vivid, powerful, and sometimes disturbing examples of educational assumptions and practices that foster inequality when conjectures and conclusions are made about an ethnic or racial group that conceal the myriad diversity within it.

When viewed as a collectivity, African Americans have much lower college enrollment and completion rates than Whites and Asians. However, the 13% of Black college students in the United States who are immigrants, or the children of immigrants, have very high levels of academic achievement and college entrance and graduation rates. Many of these students attend one of the eight Ivy League colleges and universities. The chapter by Griffin and George Mwangi states that African immigrants have a higher level of educational attainment than Whites. In a 2007 article, Massey, Mooney, Torres, and Charles pointed out that "the representation of immigrant-origin [B]lacks at selective institutions was roughly double their share in the population" (p. 245). The overrepresentation of immigrants among African American college students at Ivy League colleges and universities has evoked deep concern and controversy among Black descendants of enslaved African Americans, which illuminates the *raison d'être* of this book. The chapters in this book detail the ways in which policies and practices that do not reflect the diversity within racial and ethnic groups can lead to unintended educational consequences. Affirmative action policies that were formulated to benefit the descendants of enslaved African Americans are disproportionately assisting Black immigrants in the nation's most prestigious colleges and universities.

Asian Americans are often called the "model minority" because of their high levels of academic achievement. However, this phrase obscures the low academic achievement and college admission and completion rates of many Southeast Asian and Pacific Islander students. *Students for Fair Admissions* (SFFA) *v. the President and Fellows of Harvard College*, the legal case filed in 2018 that challenged the Harvard College admission process that incorporates affirmative action, divided the Asian American community—some individuals and groups supported the Harvard admissions process and others strongly opposed it (Kang, 2019). The responses to this case revealed the deep divisions and views that often exist within panethnic groups such as Asian Americans, African Americans, and Latinxs.

This book consists of a group of trenchant and illuminating essays that were developed for the Racial Heterogeneity Project (RHP), an initiative that was designed to describe the diversity within racial and ethnic groups and the implications of *within-group diversity* for policy and practice in higher education. An important aim of the Racial Heterogeneity Project was to detail the challenges of depicting the diversity within racial and ethnic groups, suggest ways to wrestle with these challenges, and identify strategies and resources for enhancing educational equality for subpopulations within ethnic and racial group categories.

The incisive and engaging essays in this book about the diversity within racial and ethnic groups will help higher education scholars and practitioners to develop culturally responsive strategies and practices for the myriad diversity of the student population that is entering colleges and universities from the nation's schools. American classrooms are experiencing the largest influx of immigrant students since the beginning of the 20th century. Approximately 12.6 million new immigrants—documented and undocumented—settled in the United States in the years from 2000 to 2016 (Zong, Batalova, & Hallock, 2018). Less than 10% came from nations in Europe. Most came from Mexico, nations in South Asia, East Asia, Latin America, the Caribbean, and Central America. Although African immigrants make up a small part of the U.S. immigrant population (2,060 in 2015), they increased by 41% from 2000 to 2013 (Anderson, 2017). The largest number of immigrants to the United States today come from India and China, not Mexico. The influence of an increasingly diverse population on U.S. schools, colleges, and universities is and will continue to be enormous.

Schools in the United States are more diverse today than they have been since the early 1900s, when a multitude of immigrants entered the United States from Southern, Central, and Eastern Europe (Banks, 2005). In 2017, the National Center for Education Statistics (NCES) estimated that students from ethnic minority groups made up more than 52% of the students in pre-kindergarten through 12th grade in U. S. public schools, an increase from 39.2% in 2001 (National Center for Education Statistics, 2017). Latinxs made up 25% of the children in the United States in 2017, African Americans were 15%, Asian and Pacific Island children were 6%, and American Indians were 1% (Annie E. Casey Foundation, 2019).

Language and religious diversity is also increasing in the U.S. student population. A Center for Migration Studies publication estimated that 21.6% of Americans aged 5 and above (65.5 million) spoke a language other than English at home in 2016 (Camarota & Ziegler, 2017). This percentage has doubled since 1990, and almost tripled since 1980. The significant number of immigrants from nations such as India and China has also greatly increased religious diversity in the United States. Harvard professor Diana L. Eck (2001) calls the United States the "most religiously diverse nation on earth" (p. 4). Islam is now the fastest-growing religion in the United States, as well as in several European nations such as France, the United Kingdom, and the Netherlands (Banks, 2009; O'Brien, 2016).

The major purpose of the Multicultural Education Series is to provide preservice educators, practicing educators, graduate students, scholars, and policymakers with an interrelated and comprehensive set of books that summarizes and analyzes important research, theory, and practice related to the education of ethnic, racial, cultural, and linguistic groups in the United States and the education of mainstream students about diversity. The dimensions of multicultural education, developed by Banks (2004) and described in the *Handbook of Research on Multicultural Education* and in the *Encyclopedia of Diversity in Education* (Banks, 2012), provide the conceptual framework for the development of the publications in the Series. The dimensions are content integration, the knowledge construction process, prejudice reduction, equity pedagogy, and an empowering institutional culture and social structure. The books in the Multicultural Education Series provide research, theoretical, and practical knowledge about the behaviors and learning characteristics of students of color (Conchas & Vigil, 2012; Lee, 2007), language minority students (Gándara & Hopkins, 2010; Valdés, 2001; Valdés, Capitelli, & Alvarez, 2011), low-income students (Cookson, 2013; Gorski, 2018), and other minoritized population groups, such as students who speak different varieties of English (Charity Hudley & Mallinson, 2011), and LGBTQ youth (Mayo, 2014).

A number of other books in the Multicultural Education Series describe problems related to diversity in higher education and ways in which it can be reformed. These books include *Engaging the "Race Question": Accountability and Equity in U. S. Higher Education* by Alicia C. Dowd and Estela Mara Bensimon (2015); *Race, Empire, and English Language Teaching: Creating Responsible and Ethical Anti-Racist Practice* by Suhanthie Motha (2014); *Achieving Equity for Latino Students: Expanding the Pathway to Higher Education Through Public Policy* by Frances Contreras (2011); *Americans by Heart: Undocumented Latino Students and the Promise of Higher Education* by William Pérez (2011); *Asians in the Ivory Tower: Dilemmas of Racial Inequality in American Higher Education* by Robert T. Teranishi (2010); and *Immigrant-Origin Students in Community College: Navigating Risk and Reward in Higher Education*, edited by Carola Suárez-Orozco and Olivia Osei-Twumasi (2019).

The essays in this book describe the ways *panethnicity* and *ethnic heterogeneity* can create tensions and challenges for racial and ethnic groups as well as how these concepts are fluid and exemplified differently in varying contexts. Panethnic concepts, such as Latinx and Asian American, have been helpful to college student groups when they organized across ethnic lines to protest and to make demands from college administrators such as for more Latinx professors or for Asian American Studies programs. However, panethnic categories can and do result in the specific needs of groups such as Hmong American, Cambodian American, and Laotian American students being overlooked when they are viewed through the lens of Asian Americans. When educators are designing programs to promote educational equality for students from different racial and ethnic groups, they should be aware of and sensitive to the complex ways in which panethnic and heterogeneity concepts of groups can influence their self-identifications, how they are perceived by others, the extent to which they conceal within-group tensions, and their educational trajectories and experiences.

Because of the growing diversity of ethnic and immigrant groups in the United States and the increasing diversity within these groups—such as the rising number of multiracial people in the nation (Mahiri, 2017) and the expanding Black immigrant population (Anderson, 2017)—this book is both needed and timely. I am pleased to welcome it to the Multicultural Education Series and hope it will help higher education scholars and practitioners to develop a discerning and compassionate cultural eye for the enormous diversity across and within racial and ethnic groups when constructing policies and practices.

—*James A. Banks*

REFERENCES

Anderson, M. (2017, February 14). African immigrant population in the U.S. steadily climbs. Pew Research Center. Retrieved from www.pewresearch.org/fact-tank/2017/02/14/african-immigrant-population-in-u-s-steadily-climbs/

Annie E. Casey Foundation. (2019). *2019 kids count data book: State trends in child well-being*. Baltimore, MD: Author.

Banks, C. A. M. (2005). *Improving multicultural education: Lessons from the intergroup education movement*. New York, NY: Teachers College Press.

Banks, J. A. (2004). Multicultural education: Historical development, dimensions, and practice. In J. A. Banks & C. A. M. Banks (Eds.). *Handbook of research on multicultural education* (2nd ed., pp. 3–29). San Francisco, CA: Jossey-Bass.

Banks, J. A. (Ed.). (2009). *The Routledge international companion to multicultural education*. New York, NY & London, UK: Routledge.

Banks, J. A. (2012). Multicultural education: Dimensions of. In J. A. Banks (Ed) *Encyclopedia of diversity in education* (vol. 3, pp. 1538–1547). Thousand Oaks, CA: Sage Publications.

Camarota, S. A., & Ziegler, K. (2017, October). 65.5 million U.S. residents spoke a foreign language at home in 2016. *The Center for Immigration Studies*.

Retrieved from cis.org/Report/655-Million-US-Residents-Spoke-Foreign-Language-Home-2016
Charity Hudley, A. H., & Mallinson, C. (2011). *Understanding language variation in U.S. schools.* New York, NY: Teachers College Press.
Conchas, G. Q., & Vigil, J. D. (2012). *Streetsmart schoolsmart: Urban poverty and the education of adolescent boys.* New York, NY: Teachers College Press.
Contreras, F. (2011). *Achieving equity for Latino students: Expanding the pathway to higher education through public policy.* New York, NY: Teachers College Press.
Cookson, P. W., Jr. (2013). *Class rules: Exposing inequality in American high schools.* New York, NY: Teachers College Press.
Dowd, A. C., & Bensimon, E. M. (2015). *Engaging the "race question": Accountability and equity in U.S. higher education.* New York, NY: Teachers College Press.
Eck, D. L. (2001). *A new religious America: How a "Christian country" has become the world's most religiously diverse nation.* New York, NY: HarperCollins.
Gándara, P., & Hopkins, M. (Eds.). (2010). *Forbidden language: English language learners and restrictive language policies.* New York, NY: Teachers College Press.
Gorski, P. C. (2018). *Reaching and teaching students in poverty: Strategies for erasing the opportunity gap* (2nd ed.). New York, NY: Teachers College Press.
Kang, J. C. (2019, September 1). Where does affirmative action leave Asian-Americans? *The New York Times Magazine.* Retrieved from www.nytimes.com/2019/08/28/magazine/affirmative-action-asian-american-harvard.html
Lee, C. D. (2007). *Culture, literacy, and learning: Taking bloom in the midst of the whirlwind.* New York, NY: Teachers College Press.
Mahiri, J. (2017). *Deconstructing race: Multicultural education beyond the color-bind.* New York, NY: Teachers College Press.
Massey, D. S., Mooney, M., Torres, K. C., & Charles, C. Z. (2007). Black immigrants and Black natives attending selective colleges and universities in the United States. *American Journal of Education, 113*(2), 243–271.
Mayo, C. (2014). *LGBTQ youth and education: Policies and practices.* New York, NY: Teachers College Press.
Motha, S. (2014). *Race, empire, and English language teaching: Creating responsible and ethical anti-racist practice.* New York, NY: Teachers College Press.
National Center for Education Statistics. (2017). *Enrollment and percentage distribution of enrollment in public elementary and secondary schools, by race/ethnicity and region: Selected years, fall 1995 through fall 2025.* Retrieved from nces.ed.gov/programs/digest/d15/tables/dt15_203.50.asp
O'Brien, P. (2016). *The Muslim question in Europe: Political controversies and public philosophies.* Philadelphia, PA: Temple University Press.
Pérez, W. (2011). *Americans by heart: Undocumented Latino students and the promise of higher education.* New York, NY: Teachers College Press.
Suárez-Orozco, C., & Osei-Twumasi, O. (2019). *Immigrant-origin students in community college: Navigating risk and reward in higher education.* New York, NY: Teachers College Press.
Teranishi, R. T. (2010). *Asians in the ivory tower: Dilemmas of racial inequality in American higher education.* New York, NY: Teachers College Press.

Valdés, G. (2001). *Learning and not learning English: Latino students in American schools*. New York, NY: Teachers College Press.

Valdés, G., Capitelli, S., & Alvarez, L. (2011). *Latino children learning English: Steps in the journey*. New York, NY: Teachers College Press.

Zong, J., Batalova, J., & Hallock, J. (2018, February). *Frequently requested statistics on immigrants and immigration in the United States*. The Migration Policy Institute. Retrieved from www.migrationpolicy.org/article/frequently-requested-statistics-immigrants-and-immigration-united-states#Demographic

Preface
Race: American Education's Inescapable Conundrum

Walter R. Allen

Race matters in America. This fact, true at the nation's founding, is as true today. Many despair that race, racism, racial discrimination, and racial inequality are written into the DNA of our society. They believe these elements are immutable, permanent features of America's very fabric. The U.S. Constitution explicitly established a *racial democracy* where Whites were free and Blacks were enslaved; where Indians were foreigners, but Whites were citizens. Notions of white supremacy, fixed in the national imagination, codified by laws, and enforced by state power, form the bedrock of a racial hierarchy that penetrates all aspects of life.

Relentless demographic and cultural changes demand that education address the increased racial–ethnic diversity in our dynamic society. Despite our rapidly changing global society, outdated misconceptions, ideas, and policies about race and ethnicity are stubbornly persistent. These antiquated perspectives fail to adequately address the changing landscape of education and the students enrolled in our schools and colleges. Teranishi, Nguyen, Alcantar and Curammeng intentionally problematize race in order to better understand this elusive but extremely powerful identity. They forcefully declare that *race matters* for economic viability and quality of life in America. In particular, this book critically interrogates the complex relationships between race and inequality in U.S. education. Readers are challenged to unpack the complexity that is race in America by challenging common assumptions, critically re-evaluating "settled" research findings and considering alternative perspectives, evidence, and conclusions. The book asks *What? How?* and *Why?* questions in order to elucidate the relevance of race for education. *What* is race—what are key definitions and measures? *How* is race correlated with educational opportunities and outcomes? *Why* does racial inequality in educational access and success stubbornly persist across the American ethos?

RACIAL FORMATION

The racial and ethnic classification of individuals and groups dates to the origins of the United States. As such, these taxonomies embody underlying, preconceived notions of biological and cultural differences in human beings. Omi and Winant (2014) see race as a social construction used to create, organize, and validate a social order. Race and ethnicity operate as tools to create distinctions between who is "the norm" and who is "the other," outside of "the norm"—a perspective also known as "racial formation." Omi and Winant (2014) contend that *"race is a master category*—a fundamental concept that has profoundly shaped, and continues to shape, the history, polity, economic structure, and culture of the United States" (p. 106, emphasis in original). How racial and ethnic categories are defined holds immense significance, helping to validate social hierarchies and distribute power.

Racial and ethnic categories are arbitrary constructions that are formulated through social, political, legal, historical, and cultural temporal conditions, which implicate racial formation or the racialization process. Ladson-Billings (1998) states: "Although racial categories in the U.S. census have fluctuated over time, two categories have remained stable—Black and White. And, while the creation of the category does not reveal what constitutes within it, it does create for us a sense of polar opposites that posits a cultural ranking designed to tell us who is White or, perhaps more pointedly, who is not White!" (p. 8). The characteristics prescribing who fits within each racial category may change; what remains consistent is the utilization of racial categories to define Whiteness and uphold the dominant position of Whites. The U.S. Census originated as a tool of White domination, control, and power—or white supremacy; thus the 1790 classification options were: free White men (both over and under 16 years of age), free White women (both men and women were described as heads of families), all other free persons, and slaves (Charles, 2014).

RACE, ETHNICITY, AND U.S. EDUCATION

Education serves various functions, including educating the public, creating new knowledge, enhancing civic engagement, and opening avenues for social mobility. However, the educational system has also advanced racist ideas and created racial inequality. White dominance is the product of centuries of racial violence, including: Black slavery, genocide against Indigenous people, exploitation of Chinese labor, conquest of Mexican lands, Japanese internment, and Jim Crow segregation. Not only is the ideology and reality of White domination normative throughout the fabric of U.S. institutions, it is also the norm in education, from primary to postsecondary.

The very founding of American public education was built upon a foundation of racism: In the late 1700s, Thomas Jefferson "endorsed free elementary schools for all white children, including girls, funded by the state" (Reese, 2007, p. 223). By the 19th century, when the first public schools were opened in Boston, Massachusetts, Black and Native children were explicitly excluded (Hochschild & Scovronick, 2003). The inclusion of Native students was motivated only due to the "belief that assimilation would occur more rapidly if Indian students were integrated with non-Indian students" (Deyhle & Swisher, 1997, pp. 114–115). Racial discrimination has continued to mar American public education, as evidenced by *Brown v. Board of Education* and the exclusion of Chinese children in San Francisco schools (Low, 1982).

Higher education has fared no better. Historically, college was reserved for propertied White men; women and non-Whites were denied access. These colleges graduated "Masters of the Universe" who were trained to establish and operate institutions systems that entrenched White power (Patton, 2016). Despite a half century of equal opportunity and affirmative action policies, Blacks and Latinos continue to be drastically underrepresented as students, faculty, and administrators on the nation's campuses (Allen, McLewis, Jones, & Harris, 2018; NCES, 2017). Although White women and Asian American students are better represented in U.S. higher education, they are also mostly underrepresented in the most powerful and prestigious spaces of academe.

RACIAL AND ETHNIC CATEGORIZATION IN EDUCATION

Racial and ethnic categorization is common practice in education, apparent in the many forms students complete, in classroom discussions, and in the assignment and occupation of school and campus geographic spaces. Data on race and ethnicity are routinely gathered by staff, analyzed by researchers and used by administrators. Rarely, if ever, are these racial and ethnic categories critiqued as problematic, arbitrary misrepresentations of the diversity between *and* among the students sorted into the different, monolithic boxes (Allen, Jones and McLewis, 2019). Although racial and ethnic categories may be unrepresentative, they exert tremendous power over lives. Reified illusions of race and ethnicity determine assessments of student intellect, understandings of institutional types, patterns of federal funding, and student composition (Griffin & Hurtado, 2011).

As an example, racial and ethnic categories inform knowledge about institutional types and determine federal designations (Conrad and Gasman, 2015). For instance, colleges and universities recognized as Hispanic-Serving Institutions (HSIs) under the Higher Education Act of 1965 have a minimum 25% full-time equivalent (FTE) Hispanic undergraduates (20

U.S.C. 1101a). Similarly, Predominantly Black Institutions (PBIs) must enroll at least 40% Black students (20 U.S.C. 1059e).

Eligibility for both HSIs and PBIs also includes a financial requirement that at least half the students must receive need-based assistance or be low-income. HSIs, PBIs, and Historically Black Colleges and Universities (HBCUs) generally have lower retention and graduation rates than Predominantly White (PWI) and elite institutions. As a rule, these institutions generally serve student populations from disadvantaged educational and economic backgrounds. By comparison, PWIs, especially elite institutions, have considerably greater resources and funding. PWIs also enroll students with significantly stronger academic and financial backgrounds.

Racial essentialism, tied to racial–ethnic categorization in education, can fuel stereotypes or the "belief that all people perceived to be in a single group think, act, and believe the same things in the same ways. Such thinking leads to considerable misunderstanding and stereotyping" (Ladson-Billings, 2013, p. 40). With respect to race and ethnicity, education, both primary and postsecondary, face challenges over how best to: (1) categorize students, (2) analyze student and school/institutional data, (3) interpret student experiences and outcomes, and (4) implement or evaluate academic policies. Simply put, racial and ethnic categorization attaches socially constructed meanings to groups of people, from which policies, practices, ideologies, and laws are developed, at times with devastating consequences (Nguyen, Noguera, Adkins & Teranishi, 2019; Park, 2018).

Drawing from federal sources like the U.S. Census, unexamined, stereotypic classifications of race have sometimes been uncritically applied by education institutions (Espinosa, Turk, Taylor, & Chessman, 2019). For example, under federal regulations, the classification of underrepresented minority (URM) students in the University of California system only includes African American, Hispanic/Latino(a), or American Indian students (UCOP, n.d.). This operationalization of URM does not take into account the historical sociocultural diversity among Asian American and Pacific Islander (AAPI) students (e.g., Hmong compared to Japanese students). Similarly, in Washington State, Asian American is excluded in the URM grouping for public education (Washington Student Achievement Council, 2013). By contrast, the City University of New York (CUNY) defines URM faculty as Asian, Black/African American, Hispanic/Latino(a) and separately defines underrepresented groups (URG) as Asian, Black/African American, Hispanic/Latino(a), Italian Americans, and women (CUNY, 2012).

That the terms Latino and Hispanic, or Native American and American Indian, are in use at the same time indicates that official designations of race and ethnicity are unsettled, even contested (Tatum, 2017). Racial and ethnic categories have shifted over time depending on social, political and economic considerations. At different moments, for example, Mexicans have been categorized in the U.S. Census as racially White or ethnically Hispanic.

RACIAL AND ETHNIC CATEGORIZATION IN EDUCATION RESEARCH

The accepted practice in educational research of aggregating racial and ethnic data often results in misrepresentative categories. Groupings such as Black, Latinx, Asian American and Pacific Islander, and Indigenous may ultimately obscure their contents (e.g., erasing the differences between Black students from Nigeria and from South Carolina). When these classifications are operationalized by schools and institutions, another frequent result is the omission of Indigenous populations, as seen above in the definitions of URM. Generalizations from the analysis of aggregated data can contribute to the development of deficit narratives and assumptions about Black and other underrepresented students of color (Park, 2018).

Racial classification also influences surveys and student metrics, where racial and ethnic categories are often conflated when used to classify student groups (Garcia & Mayorga, 2018). Generally, research design, data analysis, and interpretation of findings rely on overarching categories that reduce rich diversity to simple categories or units of analysis. However, as many scholars note, the aggregation of students—particularly students of color—can distort observed results and lead to incorrect conclusions (Allen, Suh, González, & Yang, 2008). The aggregation of students in research data can also lead to the adoption of policies that further marginalize and penalize disadvantaged groups. Chang, Nguyen, and Chandler (2015) identify policy blind spots that often omit Native Hawaiian or other students based solely on small sample sizes. This unfortunately leads to statistically erasing populations, as they literally do not appear in the data. For this reason, many scholars call for disaggregation of racial and ethnic categories, greater nuance and more granular narratives about student outcomes, experiences, and backgrounds (Chang et al., 2015; Garcia & Mayorga, 2018; Teranishi, 2007). For example, when Asian American students are disaggregated, the myth of the model minority collapses, given significant within-category differences (e.g., Pacific Islanders vs. Koreans) (Teranishi, 2007).

Student identity development models reveal much about student experiences and outcomes. However, most student development frameworks ignore the complexity of racial and ethnic identity (Harper, 2012). For example, the often-cited Chickering and Reisser (1993) model of student development lists challenges students must navigate (e.g., developing competency, managing emotions); yet this model overlooks race and racism (Patton, McEwen, Rendón, & Howard-Hamilton, 2007). Kodama, McEwen, Liang, and Lee (2002) concluded the model provided inadequate explanation of student development pathways among Asian Americans. Patton et al. (2007) conclude that most student development theories are "raceless." In this respect, Harris (1993) argues that the default position of "race neutral" perspectives is "Whiteness" (absent explicit identification as "non-White"). Further, the origins and influences of most prominent psychosocial theories are overwhelmingly grounded in raceless and/or racist materials as demonstrated, for example, by Erikson, (1968).

RACIAL AND ETHNIC CATEGORIZATION IN EDUCATION POLICY

Affirmative action policies that sit at the intersection, or the point of transition, between primary and postsecondary education are controversial. Policies that seek to address persistent educational disadvantage for Blacks and other historically underrepresented groups have often faced court challenges (e.g. *Regents of the University of California v. Bakke* [1978], *Grutter v. Bollinger* [2003], *Gratz v. Bollinger* [2003], *Fisher v. University of Texas at Austin* [2016]). Affirmative action has also been banned by voters in some states (e.g. California, Proposition 209; Michigan, Proposal 2) and compromised by giving priority to the educational benefits of diversity for all students (e.g., Rehnquist dissent in *Grutter v. Bollinger,* [2003]). The consideration of race in higher education admissions decisions has prompted questions about what is Constitutional, what is just, what is equitable, and whom should benefit.

Some narratives frame affirmative action and race-conscious policies as "racial preferences" in a supposedly "colorblind society"; or as "reverse discrimination" against White Americans (Crenshaw, 2006). Opponents suggest college admissions should be based on merit and blind to color (Bonilla-Silva, 2017). Yet opponents of race-conscious policies rely on racial stereotypes to discount the achievements of Black, Indigenous, and Latinx students (Crenshaw, 2006) and to misrepresent Asian Americans as the "model minority" in order to justify resistance to race-conscious policies (Chang, 2011; Moses, Maeda, & Paguyo, 2018). All the while, Black, Indigenous, and Latinx students—and some AAPI subgroups (e.g., Filipino and Southeast Asian students)—continue to be dramatically underrepresented at selective, four-year institutions (Tatum, 2017). Also obscured are other educational inequities, such as K–12 racial segregation, lower high school completion rates, financial aid shortfalls, and limited transfer opportunities (Chang, 2011; Teranishi, 2007).

More recently, a court case charging Harvard University with racial discrimination against Asian Americans highlights how racial classifications can be weaponized to mask and protect White privilege. Like the Grutter, Gratz, and Fisher cases, this case obscures how affirmative action policies have benefitted Southeast Asians and Pacific Islanders (or for that matter White females, who are the greatest beneficiaries of equal opportunity and affirmative action policies) (Park, 2018). The Harvard University case also masks the true goal of dismantling affirmative action in university admissions to the ultimate benefit of White applicants (Moses, Maeda, & Paguyo, 2018). Suits at Harvard University, the University of North Carolina, and the University of Texas give continual witness to systemic efforts to position race and ethnicity in a manner that preserves White advantages in U.S. education.

DISCUSSION AND CONCLUSION

Racial and ethnic categories have been used to reproduce attitudes, policies, and practices that create, perpetuate, and preserve white advantage in U.S. education. Ultimately, these constructs undergird and reproduce white supremacy. As education expands, diversifies, and seeks to serve a broader, more complex constituency, we must accept "that educational institutions operate in contradictory ways, with their potential to oppress and marginalize coexisting with their potential to emancipate and empower" (Solórzano & Yosso, 2002, p. 26). This volume faces painful truths squarely, in order to assist our quest for solutions by better understanding the complex forces that undergird the racialization of the education system.

The history and power of racial and ethnic categorization in education demands we resist status quo racial dominance and subjugation. This requires systematic examination of how these categories are created and deployed, and toward what end. We must acknowledge historical and contemporary relationships between racial categories and racial hierarchies in order to disrupt false notions of racelessness in education. Substantial evidence in research, theory, practices, and policies confirms that American education is not "colorblind" (nor is the larger society) (Jayakumar, 2015; Reese, 2007). Educators must have many more difficult conversations and demonstrate commitment to concrete actions if fundamental change is truly the goal. We must bring renewed energy and nuance to challenge outdated ideas; to do this requires that we recognize race and ethnic categories as arbitrary sociopolitical constructs. At the same time, it is necessary to recognize the Thomas theorem's conception that what people perceive as real becomes real in its consequences. We must not lose sight of the conundrum that while race is an ephemeral, elusive, imaginary construct (Allen, Jones and McLewis, 2019), it has profoundly real, lived consequences for students who are assigned to the different boxes.

Teranishi, Nguyen, Alcantar and Curammeng offer perspectives and tools to systematically challenge the design, purpose, and consequences of racial and ethnic categories. How well do these categories apply to multiracial and/or multiethnic individuals? How do racial and ethnic categories impact students who are born and socialized outside the United States? What are some significant within-group differences that must be considered (e.g., language, phenotype, region, age cohort, gender, social class)? It is also not sufficient to simply interrogate racial and ethnic categories; we must also examine how these categories intersect with other signal social identities, like class, gender, sexuality, immigration status, and religion (Collins & Bilge, 2016). Above all else, we must stay focused on the ultimate goals of inclusive diversity and academic excellence as we struggle to bridge the stubborn gap between educational ideals and practice. The future of our nation literally hangs in the balance.

NOTE

This Preface draws upon and expands ideas from Allen, Jones, & McLewis (2019), *The problematic nature of racial and ethnic categories in higher education* (in Espinosa, Turk, Taylor, & Chessman, 2019), *Race and ethnicity in higher education: A status report*. Washington, DC: American Council on Education).

REFERENCES

Allen, W., Jones, C., and McLewis, C. (2019). The problematic nature of racial and ethnic categories in higher education. In L. L. Espinosa, J. M. Turk, M. Taylor, & H. M. Chessman, *Race and ethnicity in higher education: A status report*. Washington, DC: American Council on Education. Retrieved from www.equityinhighered.org/resources/report-downloads/

Allen, W., McLewis, C., Jones, C., & Harris, D. (2018). From Bakke to Fisher: Black students in U.S. higher education over forty years. In S. T. Gooden & S. L. Myers Jr. (Eds.), *The fiftieth anniversary of the Kerner commission report* (pp. 41–72). New York, NY: Russell Sage Foundation.

Allen, W. R., Suh, S. A., González, G., & Yang, J. (2008). Qui bono? Explaining—or defending—winners and losers in the competition for educational achievement. In T. Zuberi & E. Bonilla-Silva (Eds.), *White logic, White methods* (pp. 217–238). Lanham, MD: Rowman & Littlefield Publishers, Inc.

Bonilla-Silva, E. (2017). *Racism without racists: Color-blind racism and the persistence of racial inequality in America* (5th ed.). Lanham, MD: Rowman & Littlefield Publishers, Inc.

Chang, M. J. (2011). Battle hymn of the model minority myth. *Amerasia Journal*, *37*(2), 137–143.

Chang, M. J., Nguyen, M. H., & Chandler, K. L. (2015). Can data disaggregation resolve blind spots in policy making? Examining a case for native Hawaiians. *AAPI Nexus: Policy, Practice and Community*, *13*(1), 295–320.

Charles, C. (2014). *The representations of race in the decennial censuses of the United States from 1970–2010*. Retrieved from papers.ssrn.com/sol3/papers.cfm?abstract_id=2529562

Chickering, A.W., & Reisser, L. (1993). *Education and identity* (2nd ed.). San Francisco, CA: John Wiley & Sons, Inc.

City University of New York. (2012). *Building on a strong foundation: A strategy of enhancing CUNY's leadership in the areas of faculty diversity and inclusion*. Retreived from www.cuny.edu/wp-content/uploads/sites/4/page-assets/

about/administration/offices/hr/diversity-and-recruitment/DiversityAction-Plan09_17_14.pdf
Collins, P. H., & Bilge, S. (2016). *Intersectionality*. Malden, MA: Polity Press.
Conrad, C., & Gasman, M. (2015). *Educating a diverse nation: Lessons from minority serving institutions*. Cambridge, MA: Harvard University Press.
Crenshaw, K. W. (2006). Framing affirmative action. *Michigan Law Review First Impressions, 105*(1), 123–133.
Deyhle, D., & Swisher, K. (1997). Chapter 3: Research in American Indian and Alaska Native education: From assimilation to self-determination. *Review of Research in Education, 22*(1), 113–194.
Erikson, E. H. (1968). *Identity: Youth and crisis*. New York, NY: W.W. Norton & Company.
Espinosa, L. L., Turk, J. M., Taylor, M., & Chessman, H. (2019). *Race and ethnicity in higher education: A status report*. Washington, DC: American Council on Education.
Fisher v. University of Texas at Austin, 579 U.S. (2016).
Garcia, N. M., & Mayorga, O. J. (2018). The threat of unexamined secondary data: a critical race transformative convergent mixed methods. *Race, Ethnicity and Education, 21*(2), 231–252.
Gratz v. Bollinger, 539 U.S. 244 (2003).
Griffin, K. A. & Hurtado, S. (2011). Institutional variety in American higher education. In J. H. Schuh, S. R. Jones, S. R. Harper, & Associates (Eds), *Student services: A handbook for the profession* (pp. 24–42). San Francisco, CA: John Wiley & Sons.
Grutter v. Bollinger, 539 US 306 (2003).
Harper, S. (2012). Race without racism: How higher education scholars minimize racist institutional norms. *Review of Higher Education, 36*(1), 9–29.
Harris, C. I. (1993). Whiteness as property. *Harvard Law Review, 106*(8), 1707–1709.
Hochschild, J. L., & Scovronick, N. (2003). *The American dream and the public schools*. Oxford, UK: Oxford University Press.
Jayakumar, U. M. (2015). The shaping of postcollege colorblind orientation among Whites: Residential segregation and campus diversity experiences. *Harvard Educational Review, 85*(4), 609–645.
Kodama, C., McEwen, M. K., Liang, C. T., & Lee, S. (2002). An Asian American perspective on psychosocial student development theory. *New Directions for Student Services, 2002*(97), 45–60.
Ladson-Billings, G. (1998). Just what is critical race theory and what's it doing in a nice field like education? *International Journal of Qualitative Studies in Education, 11*(1), 7–24.
Ladson-Billings, G. (2013). Critical race theory—what it is not! In M. Lynn & A. D. Dixson (Eds.), *Handbook of critical race theory in education* (pp. 34–47). New York, NY: Routledge.
Low, V. (1982). *The unimpressible race. A century of educational struggle by the Chinese in San Francisco*. San Francisco, CA: East West Publishing Company.
Moses, M. S., Maeda, D. J., & Paguyo, C. H. (2018). Racial politics, resentment, and affirmative action: Asian Americans as "model" college applicants. *The Journal of Higher Education, 90*(20), 1–26.

National Center for Education Statistics. (2017). Race/ethnicity of college faculty. *The Condition of Education 2017 (NCES 2017-144)*. Retrieved from nces.ed.gov/fastfacts/display.asp?id=61

Nguyen, B. M. D., Noguera, P., Adkins, N., & Teranishi, R. T. (2019). Ethnic discipline gap: Unseen dimensions of racial disproportionality in school discipline. *American Educational Research Journal, 56*(5), 1973–2003.

Omi, M., & Winant, H. (2014). *Racial formation in the United States* (3rd ed.). New York, NY: Routledge.

Park, J. J. (2018). *Race on campus: Debunking myths with data*. Cambridge, MA: Harvard Education Press.

Patton, L. D. (2016). Disrupting postsecondary prose: Toward a critical race theory of higher education. *Urban Education, 51*(3), 315–342.

Patton, L. D., McEwen, M., Rendón, L., & Howard-Hamilton, M. F. (2007). Critical race perspectives on theory in student affairs. *New Directions for Student Services, 2007*(120), 39–53.

Regents of the University of California v. Bakke, 438 U.S. 265 (1978).

Reese, W. J. (2007). Why Americans love to reform the public schools. In *History, education, and the schools* (pp. 159–171). New York, NY: Palgrave Macmillan.

Solórzano, D. G., & Yosso, T. J. (2002). Critical race methodology: Counter-storytelling as an analytical framework for education research. *Qualitative Inquiry, 8*(1), 23–44.

Tatum, B. D. (2017). *Why are all the Black kids sitting together in the cafeteria?: And other conversations about race*. New York, NY: Basic Books.

Teranishi, R. T. (2007). Race, ethnicity, and higher education policy: The use of critical quantitative research. *New Directions for Institutional Research, 2007*(133), 37–49.

University of California Office of the President. (n.d.). CA's freshman diversity pipeline to UC. Retrieved from www.universityofcalifornia.edu/infocenter/ca-hs-pipeline

Washington Student Achievement Council. (2013). *Educational attainment for all: Diversity and equity in Washington State higher education*. Olympia, WA: Authors. Retrieved from www.wsac.wa.gov/sites/default/files/DiversityReport.FINAL.Revised.07-2013_0.pdf

CHAPTER 1

Introduction

Bach Mai Dolly Nguyen and Robert T. Teranishi

The nation is changing. Americans are more diverse now than ever before, and this trend of diversification is projected to continue. Minority groups will constitute a new majority sometime between now and 2044, by which time Whites will comprise under half of the total population (Colby & Ortman, 2015). By 2060, one in five individuals will be considered foreign born, which is already true of primary school children (Colby & Ortman, 2015). In that same time frame, the Asian American and Latino populations will each increase by over 100%, with Native Hawaiians' and Pacific Islanders' growth following closely behind (Colby & Ortman, 2015). And just five years beyond that mark, in 2065, immigration is predicted to be one of the greatest stimulators to the changing face of America (Cohn, 2015).

These immense, and rapid, demographic shifts affect education as racial stratification continues to challenge educational equity. Although overall rates of high school completion and college access have increased beginning in the 1900s, marked gaps remain between racial groups (Kena et al., 2016). Although the percentage of Latino college enrollment rose by 11% between 1976 and 2012, the percentage of Black enrollment grew by 5%, and the rate of enrollment of Asian Americans and Pacific Islanders increased by 4%, enrollment stratification between racial groups persists (Ross et al., 2012). An NCES report that examined the gaps in higher education access found that among 2004 high school graduates, lower proportions of Black and Latino students were enrolled in college than their White and Asian peers, two years following their graduation (Ross et al., 2012). Larger proportions of Asian (66%) and White (47%) individuals between the ages of 18 and 24 years were enrolled in college or graduate school than were their Native Hawaiian and Pacific Islander (39%), Black (37%), and Latino (31%) counterparts (Ross et al., 2012, p. 162). Although the gaps are narrowing, these data point to the enduring racial stratification of postsecondary enrollment. The racial disparities are even more severe when considering degree attainment. In an examination of the national college completion landscape, for example, the College Board notes the severe disparities in six-year graduation rates of bachelor's degree-seeking students, where 68.5%

of White and 76.6% of Asian students have obtained a degree, as compared to only 46.4% of Black, 52.2% of American Indian, and 61.1% of Latinos who have achieved that same level of success (Hughes, 2012).

The search for explanations for these disparate patterns is extensive, ranging from family responsibilities (Pascarella & Terenzeni, 1997), to cultural mismatch (Armstrong & Hamilton, 2013), to lack of institutional role models (Rendon, 1994). Scholarship paints an empirically established and generally accepted picture of unequal access to and distribution of resources that have maintained and perpetuated racial inequality in American education (Kao & Thompson, 2003). Gaps remain even when resources are redistributed to racial groups who are experiencing the lowest rates of achievement.

While there are likely a myriad of explanations for this (e.g., not enough resources to address deficits; inequitable school policies; racist and discriminatory school and campus environments), we suggest that one source that is driving inequality is our inaccurate understanding of the complexity of race, and thus misguided distribution of resources, particularly as the demography of the nation rapidly diversifies. Although broader racial categories largely remain the categorical markers for distilling opportunity gaps between groups (which we do not dispute as a valid practice), there is a deeper level of analysis that requires the attention of the education field as emerging research begins to articulate the depth of racial inequality.

INVISIBLE INEQUALITY

In a *Washington Post* editorial on the nation's changing demography, the authors conclude, "America's complexion is changing, literally" (*Washington Post*, 2012, para. 8). A primary driving force of this change is immigration, which has brought a multitude of different people representing vast regions, and varied languages, cultures, and histories into the United States (Cohn, 2015; Colby & Ortman, 2015). Although deeply heterogeneous, these groups have been pushed into a rigid categorical system that inaccurately defines their experiences and forces individuals to grapple with the consequences of that labeling, which at times emerges as invisibility and at others as discrimination and racism. To call for ethnicity data is one way to push back on unrepresentative categorization.

Today, the U.S. Census collects data on six categories: American Indian and Alaska Native, Asian, Black, Latino, Native Hawaiian and Pacific Islander (NHPI), and White. Although the most recent amendment to those groupings was the separation of Asian from NHPI in 1997, the U.S. Census has considerably, albeit slowly, changed. The shift in the U.S. Census ethnic categories reflects the remarkable increase in diversity within American demography, and it also highlights the need for disaggregated data that more accurately captures that change. Scholarship using the disaggregated data that does exist already reveals patterns of otherwise invisible inequality.

Hidden opportunity gaps are a central concern for the vastly diverse Asian American and Pacific Islander (AAPI) communities and have prompted a decades-long push to collect data disaggregated by ethnic group (Endo, 1980). Since Hune and Chan (1997) offered the first scholarly argument for AAPI data disaggregation, many others have followed with their own studies demonstrating the need for acknowledging within-AAPI group heterogeneity (Gomez et. al., 2010; Hune et al., 2008; Kim, 2011; Ong & Ishikawa, 2006; Ponce, 2011; Um, 2003). The scholarship collectively points out that while Asian Americans are among the highest-achieving racial groups when aggregated (as demonstrated by their 49% rate of college degree attainment in the population, as compared to 28% among all U.S. adults), this statistic can be misleading when applied to particular subgroups (Pew Research Center, 2012). The aggregation of heterogeneous ethnic groups into a single racial category masks the starkly different educational realities of Asian Americans: While a high proportion of Taiwanese (74.1%), Asian Indians (71.1%), and Koreans (52.7%) have attained a bachelor's degree or higher, the reverse is true for Lao (12.4%), Cambodian (14.1%), and Hmong (14.7%) individuals (National Commission on Asian American and Pacific Islander Research in Education [CARE], 2013). Additionally, these statistical portraits erase the severely dissimilar educational experiences of NHPIs, for whom the consequence of aggregation is invisibility (Empowering Pacific Islander Communities [EPIC] & Asian Americans Advancing Justice [AAAJ], 2014).

Studies that delve deeper into the nuances of the AAPI educational experience help to shape a more accurate narrative about their academic success. In a study of the campus experiences of AAPI students at the University of California, Los Angeles (UCLA), for example, a close examination of within-group diversity by ethnicity revealed that AAPI students expressed a range of opinions regarding their satisfaction with their college experiences (National Commission on Asian American and Pacific Islander Research in Education [CARE], 2016). For example, a statistically significant difference was found between the 31.9% of Southeast Asian students—a historically underrepresented group in higher education—who expressed dissatisfaction with their overall academic experience, as compared to only 24.8% of East Asians, who represent the majority of AAPIs enrolled in the postsecondary sector (CARE, 2016). A different study on factors that influence Asian American academic performance found that while there are instances when Asian Americans do perform exceedingly well—Chinese, Korean, and Southeast Asian students earn higher math grades than comparable White students—"Asians are not uniformly advantaged educationally and economically, but [. . .] compositional differences account for differences in skill development and most of the variation in grades" (Kao, 1995, p.

151). These examples demonstrate that while the distinctions between ethnic groups do not always lead to similar conclusions about where gaps exist, they do lay the groundwork for a deeper analysis of how to make sense of the complexity within the AAPI category, which scholarship suggests can be achieved through the examination of ethnicity.

Similarly, ethnicity is important for understanding the Latino racial group for whom *panethnicity* is an area of focus in research (Duany, 2003; Itzigsohn, 2004; Jones-Correa & Leal, 1996). Lopez and Espiritu (1990) write that panethnicity is "the development of bridging organizations and the generalization of solidarity among ethnic subgroups" (p. 198). This theoretical solidarity, however, is a point of contestation, as even in the effort to cultivate unity there are varying levels of attachment to the broader "Hispanic" or "Latino" categories among ethnic groups (Calderón, 1992; Feliciano, 2009). In fact, comparing to Asian Americans and Indo Americans, Lopez and Espiritu (1990) conclude that "Latinos, the set of subgroups which is culturally the most homogenous, but which also shares the least in terms of structural characteristics and apparent common interests, are clearly the least panethnic" (p. 218). Although we neither confirm nor deny this assertion, as it is beyond the scope of the book, it points to how challenging it is to make sense of the complexity that is layered within a single category.

Oboler's (1995) foundational book, *Ethnic Labels, Latino Lives: Identity and the Politics of (re)presentation in the United States,* similarly discusses the risks related to using a monolithic label in her interviews with ethnically diverse individuals who fall into the Latino category. She finds that her participants ascribed different meanings and social values to their categorization, thus testing the reliability of using racial groupings without attention to the variation within. Latino ethnic groups are represented by one racial grouping, yet their experiences vary widely (Newby & Dowling, 2007; Ricourt & Danta, 2003). Household income, for example, is stratified by ethnicity, with Argentines, Chileans, Costa Ricans, and Cubans earning higher incomes than Mexicans, Puerto Ricans, and Dominicans, which (research suggests) is a byproduct of colorism (Bonilla-Silva & Glover, 2004). In these disparities, and in the factors that play a role in producing them, we can see that understanding racial heterogeneity goes beyond simply disaggregating by ethnicity. It requires us to acknowledge the within-group characteristics, unique to each racial group, that produce gaps in experiences and outcomes.

For Black Americans, generational status is a prominent factor for consideration, as research shows globalization and migration have complicated the constructs of race for both native-born Blacks and Black immigrants in the United States (George Mwangi, 2014), for whom outcomes are vastly different. In earnings, for example, it is found that African immigrants make more than Caribbean immigrants, who out-earn African Americans (Dodoo, 1997). Although it is not conclusive as to what drives the disparities between groups—differential levels of discrimination and opportunity (Waters, 1994), variance in racial group identity (Benson, 2006), or dissimilar parental levels of education (Haynie, 2002), to list a few ideas—research on Black racial heterogeneity establishes that different generational groups vary in how they grapple with race.

In their qualitative study on perspectives on campus diversity and racial climate, for example, Griffin, Cunningham and George Mwangi (2016) ascertain that while native-born, first, second, and 2.5 generation Black students uniformly report issues of negative perceptions and stereotypes of Black students, their conceptualizations of those experiences are different. For example, whereas second and 2.5 generation Black students perceived negative interactions mostly in academic settings, native-born Black students encountered feelings of marginalization, discrimination, and racism outside the classroom. The differences, while subtle, reveal the distinctions that emerge by ethnicity and generational status. This conclusion also serves as the focal motivation for Celious and Oyserman's (2001) heterogeneous race model, wherein they offer a frame through which to acknowledge that Black Americans do not experience race in only one way. Rather, the authors find that individuals falling into the Black racial category distinguish themselves by a range of characteristics, including gender, socioeconomic status, and physical features. Their study emphasizes that race must be viewed as a heterogeneous construction.

As is evident by the literature on each racial group, attention must be paid to the complexity of race as heterogeneity emerges in many forms from ethnicity to generational status. For Native Americans, tribal affiliation is particularly important (Caldwell, Davis, Du Bois, and Echo-Hawk, 2005). Although there is very little research that explores Native American people at all, let alone by tribe, some studies have affirmed the need to examine within-group heterogeneity more closely. Scholars of the educational pathways of Native students say that "While combining American Indians and Alaska Natives provides useful data, it can also serve to mask important social and economic differences that significantly impact the overall well-being and life outcomes of individuals from the two groups" (Faircloth, Alcantar & Stage, 2015, p. 5). In a similar reflection, Tachine, Cabrera, and Yellow Bird's (2017) study on Native students' senses of belonging discussed the heterogeneity in the experiences of those in their small sample, and the need to further explore the variations among Native students.

Collectively, the literature that either examines or calls for examinations of racial heterogeneity asserts that singular and monolithic views of race mask inequalities that exist within racial groups. Although race categories remain a significant marker for understanding disparities, there are opportunity gaps that could be wholly overlooked when viewing race from such a perspective. As the racial and ethnic composition of the nation rapidly diversifies, the question at the heart of this book becomes increasingly significant: *Can institutions address educational inequality if the beliefs they hold about students—based on current racial categorizations—are inaccurate?* In short, the answer is that they cannot.

As such, there is an urgent need to closely examine data practices responsible for the representation of our rapidly changing national demography. In considering how to broach the difficult task of collecting data on complex racial and ethnic identities, it is important to consider whether the racial categories that currently exist accurately represent the individuals who fall into those groupings. Put another way, what are the limitations for aggregated data, which may conceal a great deal of diversity within these groups? Are there benefits to disaggregating data further to examine within-group diversity? What can be revealed when racial groups are reorganized and re-examined? It is with this context that we raise the relevance of racial heterogeneity and the need to further examine within-group differences in order to address educational inequities.

Within the educational context, obtaining good data is especially critical, as there is a surge of activity to establish a culture of inquiry and design decisionmaking processes, with implications for how we understand and respond to the particular needs of specific student groups. As a RAND study on data-driven decisionmaking shows, however, having data does not mean it will be used appropriately (Marsh, Pane, & Hamilton, 2006). As the authors of the report suggest, "equal attention needs to be paid to *analyzing data* and *taking action based on data*" and, we would add, to how data is collected (Marsh et al., 2006, p. 10). In more carefully discerning how data is collected, analyzed, and applied, institutions, organizations and government agencies may gain a clearer picture of the populations they serve, and unmask inequities that are hidden in the practice of aggregation.

Data disaggregation is a tool for addressing inequality because it sheds light on ways to mitigate disparities in educational outcomes and improve support for the most marginalized and vulnerable populations. Data disaggregated for individual student subgroups raises awareness about issues and challenges that impact those subgroups disproportionately. If racial heterogeneity were a sandbox through which we frame our understanding of the complexity of race and the changing demography, data disaggregation is the shovel that digs into that complexity to discover what lies under the surface. As the research cited in this chapter has shown, the investigation of within-group difference is a significant step in better understanding racial inequality, as it ensures that the most disenfranchised populations are seen and represented.

RACIAL FORMATION

This book is grounded in the theoretical approach of *racial formation*, which postulates that race is a socially and politically constructed concept that is malleable and can fluctuate as it absorbs the circumstances of its time (Omi & Winant, 2014). Said differently, the concept of race—particularly as it pertains to racial categorization—represents a complex process through which individuals are grouped by the conditions of politicization. The theorizations of racial formation are discernable when reflecting upon the many changes within the U. S. Census racial categories. In the 1930 census, for example, "Mexican" emerged on the form as an individual racial category, separating individuals identifying as ethnically Mexican from the White population for the first time in census history. Advocates within the Mexican community saw that the categorical separation from White signaled a risk of segregation, discrimination, and "symbolic exclusion" (Schor, 2005, p. 93). Accordingly, the Mexican American community, including advocacy organizations and the Mexican government itself, mobilized to pressure the U.S. State Department to remove the category, which was achieved a decade later, reaggregating Mexican with White. Keeping in mind that these changes redefine the racial positioning of entire populations of people with respect to policy decisions, allocation of resources, and symbolic racialization, the categorization process is far from mere labeling.

Moreover, it is important to understand how changes in racial categories impact not only a single group, but also its relationship with other racial groups, as it reimagines the boundaries of racialization. In the reaggregation of "Mexican" with White, for example, not only are self-identified Mexicans impacted by the change, so too is the White racial category redefined and its relationship to other racial groups transformed. As such, it is as imperative to understand single racial groups as it is to comprehend the relationship between groups to make sense of changing demographics and the increasing complexity of race.

As it pertains to racial heterogeneity in education, racial formation offers a lens through which to examine racial diversity and the changing context of race. As this book argues for the deeper investigation of within-group variation through the use of disaggregated data, racial formation allows for stretching the theoretical boundaries of racial categorization, admittedly drawing from the rapidly changing sociopolitical landscape that comes with a changing demography, which now calls for the recognition of the diversity within each racial group.

THE RACIAL HETEROGENEITY PROJECT

In response to the need for closer attention to racial heterogeneity, the Institute for Immigration, Globalization, and Education at the University of California, Los Angeles (UCLA), with generous support from ACT, initiated the Racial Heterogeneity Project (RHP). This collaborative effort focuses on identifying and targeting attention and resources to improve the experiences and outcomes of underrepresented communities—Asian American, Black,

Latino, Native American, and Pacific Islander. There are three primary questions of interest for RHP:

1. What unique challenges does each racial/ethnic population in the United States face in terms of its racial heterogeneity?
2. Have inaccurate data practices hindered the ability of scholars, practitioners, and policymakers to understand and respond to the unique needs of each racial/ethnic population?
3. What conceptual approaches or practical strategies should be considered to better support each racial/ethnic population?

We assembled a group of scholars and advocates to collaborate in a discussion considering and responding to these questions. This convening was a critical space for scholars to share work on racial heterogeneity for the racial groups in which they conduct their research, but more importantly, it was an opportunity for dialogue across racial boundaries—an insightful and fruitful conversation that led to the chapters in this volume.

ROADMAP FOR THE BOOK

The contributions of RHP scholars are divided into two distinct sections—the conceptual and the applied. The chapters within the first part of the volume lay a foundation for understanding, exploring, and critiquing race and ethnicity. Fusing historical and contemporary conceptions of race, Part I, Conceptual Considerations of Racial Heterogeneity, opens with Gloria Ladson-Billings's chapter, wherein she offers a landscape for discussing the "hybridity, complexity, and fluidity" of Blackness, which foregrounds the evolving complexity of race. The part then dives further into explaining that complexity through the examination of Latinos and their place in the racial hierarchy. Extending the ethnoracial framework, Luis Ricardo Fraga and Nicole Perez discuss how a rearticulated view of race and ethnicity can allow for the simultaneous recognition of group distinctions, and the maintained sense of panethnic solidarity. Also exploring the concepts of panethnicity and the ethnoracial framework, Michael Omi, Mike Hoa Nguyen, and Jason Chan's chapter discusses how the Asian American and Pacific Islander communities have straddled these seemingly binary states as forms of advocacy, offering that careful attention must be paid to how categories are "understood, interpreted, contested, and redefined." Turning greater attention to the Pacific Islander portion of AAPIs, the section moves to 'Inoke Hafoka, Kēhaulani Vaughn, Iosefa Aina, and Cynthia M. Alcantar's chapter, which discusses how colonialism and (im)migration have shaped the Native Hawaiian and Pacific Islander categorization. Finally, section one closes with Marc P. Johnston-Guerrero and Karly Sarita Ford's consideration of multiraciality, a conception that is relevant to a rapidly growing population of individuals. Putting together the tapestry of frameworks and concepts from panethnicity to colonialism, to racial formation, Part I is the backdrop to understanding racial heterogeneity and its implications.

Part II, Unmasking Educational Inequality Through Disaggregated Data, illuminates the concepts previously covered by applying disaggregated data to the field of education. Beginning with chapters by Kimberly A. Griffin and Chrystal A. George Mwangi and by Heather J. Shotton, the section opens by revealing the fluidity of how race is represented in data, demonstrating that disaggregation of not just ethnicity, but also generational status and tribal affiliation, is illuminating for understanding within-group heterogeneity of Black and Native students, respectively. The continued practice of aggregation, Laura M. Brady, Zoe Higheagle Strong, and Stephanie A. Fryberg point out, can be detrimental to Native students who experience *identity threat*—a sense that one's group is viewed negatively in a given context. These perceptions of being unseen or seen negatively, Desiree D. Zerquera, Jasmine Haywood, and Martín De Mucha Flores's chapter can be patterned along the lines of geography, ethnicity, and race, each of which have implications for students navigating their educational trajectories. Their recommendations include the call for better data, foregrounding Stella M. Flores, Brian Holzman, and Leticia Oseguera's chapter examining the strengths and gaps in federal and state datasets and offering practical insights for how these data can better capture Latino students' diversity. The volume concludes with a final chapter that details our insights on how we move forward in both conceptualizing racial heterogeneity and applying disaggregated data to reveal and address racial inequities in aggregation.

REFERENCES

Armstrong, E. A., & Hamilton, L. T. (2013). *Paying for the party*. Boston, MA: Harvard University Press.

Benson, J. E. (2006, June). Exploring the racial identities of black immigrants in the United States. *Sociological Forum, 21*(2), 219–247.

Bonilla-Silva, E., & Glover, K. S. (2004). "We are all Americans": The Latin Americanization of race relations in the United States. In M. Krysan & A. E. Lewis (Eds.), *The changing terrain of race and ethnicity* (pp. 149–183). New York, NY: Russell Sage Foundation.

Calderón, J. (1992). "Hispanic" and "Latino": The viability of categories for panethnic unity. *Latin American Perspectives, 19*(4), 37–44.

Caldwell, J. Y., Davis, J. D., Du Bois, B., & Echo-Hawk, H. (2005). Culturally competent research with American Indians and Alaska natives: Findings and recommendations of the first symposium of the work group on American Indian research and program evaluation methodology. *American Indian and Alaska Native Mental Health Research, 12*(1), 1–21.

Celious, A., & Oyserman, D. (2001). Race from the inside: An emerging heterogeneous race model. *Journal of Social Issues, 57*(1), 149–165.

Cohn, D. (2015). *Future immigration will change the face of America by 2065.* Washington, DC: Pew Research Center. Retrieved from www.pewresearch.org/fact-tank/2015/10/05/future-immigration-will-change-the-face-of-america-by-2065/

Colby, S., & Ortman, J. (2015). *Projections of the size and composition of the U.S. population: 2014-2060.* Washington, DC: U.S. Census Bureau. Retrieved from census.gov/content/dam/Census/library/publications/2015/demo/p25-1143.pdf

Dodoo, F. N. A. (1997). Assimilation differences among Africans in America. *Social Forces, 76*(2), 527–546.

Duany, J. (2003). Puerto Rican, Hispanic, or Latino? Recent debates on national and pan-ethnic identities. *Centro Journal, 15*(2), 256–267.

Empowering Pacific Islander Communities (EPIC) & Asian Americans Advancing Justice. (2014). *Native Hawaiian and Pacific Islanders: A community of contrasts in the United States.* Washington, DC: Author. Retrieved from www.empoweredpi.org/uploads/1/1/4/1/114188135/a_community_of_contrasts_nhpi_us_2014-1.pdf

Endo, R. (1980). Asian Americans and higher education. *Phylon (1960–), 41*(4), 367–378.

Faircloth, S. C., Alcantar, C. M., & Stage, F. K. (2015). Use of large-scale data sets to study educational pathways of American Indian and Alaska Native students. *New Directions for Institutional Research, 2014*(163), 5–24.

Feliciano, C. (2009). Education and ethnic identity formation among children of Latin American and Caribbean immigrants. *Sociological Perspectives, 52*(2), 135–158.

George Mwangi, C. A. (2014). Complicating Blackness: Black immigrants & racial positioning in U.S. higher education. *Journal of Critical Thought and Praxis, 3*(2), 1–27.

Gomez, S. L., Quach, T., Horn-Ross, P. L., Pham, J. T., Cockburn, M., Chang, E. T., & Clarke, C. A. (2010). Hidden breast cancer disparities in Asian women: Disaggregating incidence rates by ethnicity and migrant status. *Journal Information, 100*(S1), S125–S131.

Griffin, K. A., Cunningham, E. L., & George Mwangi, C. A. (2016). Defining diversity: Ethnic differences in Black students' perceptions of racial climate. *Journal of Diversity in Higher Education, 9*(1), 34–49.

Haynie, A. C. (2002). Not "just black" policy considerations: The influence of ethnicity on pathways to academic success amongst black undergraduates at Harvard University. *Journal of Public and International Affairs, 13*, 40–62.

Hughes, K. (2012). *The college completion agenda 2012: Progress report.* Washington, DC: College Board. Retrieved from media.collegeboard.com/digitalServices/pdf/advocacy/policycenter/college-completion-agenda-2012-progress-report.pdf

Hune, S., & Chan, K. S. (1997). Special focus: Asian Pacific American demographic and educational trends. In D. J. Carter & R. Wilson (Eds.), *Minorities in higher education: Fifteenth annual status report*, 39–67. Washington, DC: American Council on Education.

Hune, S., Takeuchi, D., Hong, S., Kang, J., Redmond, M. A., & Yeo, J. J. (2008). *Asian Americans in Washington State: Closing their hidden achievement gaps.* Seattle, WA: University of Washington.

Itzigsohn, J. (2004). The formation of Latino and Latina panethnic identities. In N. Foner & G. M. Frederickson (Eds.), *Not just black and white: Historical and contemporary perspectives on immigration, race, and ethnicity in the United States* (pp. 197–216). New York, NY: Russell Sage Foundation.

Jones-Correa, M., & Leal, D. L. (1996). Becoming "Hispanic": Secondary panethnic identification among Latin American-origin populations in the United States. *Hispanic Journal of Behavioral Sciences, 18*(2), 214–254.

Kao, G. (1995). Asian Americans as model minorities? A look at their academic performance. *American Journal of Education, 103*(2), 121–159.

Kao, G., & Thompson, J. S. (2003). Racial and ethnic stratification in educational achievement and attainment. *Annual Review of Sociology, 29*, 417–442.

Kena, G., Hussar, W., McFarland, J., de Brey, C., Musu-Gillette, L., Wang, X., Zhang, J., Rathbun, A., Wilkinson-Flicker, S., Diliberti, M., Barmer, A., Bullock Mann, F., and Dunlop Velez, E. (2016). *The condition of education 2016.* Washington, DC: National Center for Education Statistics. Retrieved from nces.ed.gov/pubs2016/2016144.pdf

Kim, M. (2011). Asian Americans and Pacific Islanders: Employment issues in the United States. *AAPI Nexus, 9*(1&2), 58–69.

Lopez, D., & Espiritu, Y. (1990). Panethnicity in the United States: A theoretical framework. *Ethnic and Racial Studies, 13*(2), 198–224.

Marsh, J., Pane, J., & Hamilton, L. (2006). *Making sense of data-driven decision making in education: Evidence from recent RAND research.* Santa Monica, CA: RAND Corporation. Retrieved from www.rand.org/pubs/occasional_papers/OP170.html

National Commission on Asian American and Pacific Islander Research in Education. (2013). *iCount: A data quality movement for Asian Americans and Pacific Islanders in higher education.* New York, NY: CARE Project.

National Commission on Asian American and Pacific Islander Research in Education. (2016). *The racialized experiences of Asian American and Pacific Islander students: An examination of campus racial climate at the University of California, Los Angeles.* Los Angeles, CA: CARE Project.

Newby, C. A., & Dowling, J. A. (2007). Black and Hispanic: The racial identification of Afro-Cuban immigrants in the southwest. *Sociological Perspectives, 50*(3), 343–366.

Oboler, S. (1995). *Ethnic labels, Latino lives: Identity and the politics of (re)presentation in the United States.* Minneapolis, MN: University of Minnesota Press.

Omi, M., & Winant, H. (2014). *Racial formation in the United States* (3rd ed.). New York, NY: Routledge.

Ong, P. M., & Ishikawa, H. (2006). *A Research Agenda: Impacts of welfare reform on Asian Americans and Pacific Islanders (AAPIs).* Los Angeles, CA: UCLA School of Public Affairs Conference.

Pascarella, E. T., & Terenzini, P. T. (1997). Studying college students in the 21st century: Meeting new challenges. *The Review of Higher Education, 21*(2), 151–165.

Pew Research Center. (2012). *The rise of Asian Americans.* Washington, DC: Pew Research Center.

Ponce, N. (2011). What a difference a data set and advocacy make for AAPI health. *AAPI Nexus, 9*(1), 159–162.

Rendon, L. I. (1994). Validating culturally diverse students: Toward a new model of learning and student development. *Innovative Higher Education, 19*(1), 33–51.

Ricourt, M., & Danta, R. (2003). *Hispanas de Queens: Latino Panethnicity in a New York City Neighborhood*. Ithaca, NY: Cornell University Press.

Ross, T., Kena, G., Rathbun, A., KewalRamani, A., Zhang, J., Kristoapovich, P. & Manning, E. (2012). *Higher education: Gaps in access and persistence study*. Washington, DC: U.S. Department of Education. Retrieved from nces.ed.gov/pubs2012/2012046.pdf

Schor, P. (2005). Mobilising for pure prestige? Challenging federal census ethnic categories in the USA (1850–1940). *International Social Science Journal, 57*(183), 89–101.

Tachine, A. R., Cabrera, N. L., & Yellow Bird, E. (2017). Home away from home: Native American students' sense of belonging during their first year in college. *The Journal of Higher Education, 88*(5), 785–807.

Um, K. (2003). *A dream denied: Educational experiences of Southeast Asian American youth: Issues and recommendations*. Washington, DC: Southeast Asia Resource Action Center.

Washington Post Editorial Board (2012). *America's changing demographics should mean changes in policies*. Retrieved from www.washingtonpost.com/opinions/americas-changing-demographics-should-mean-changes-in-policies/2012/05/17/gIQAUo1pWU_story.html

Waters, M. C. (1994). Ethnic and racial identities of second-generation Black immigrants in New York City. *International Migration Review, 28*(4), 795–820.

PART I

CONCEPTUAL CONSIDERATIONS OF RACIAL HETEROGENEITY

CHAPTER 2

Who's Black?
Hybridity, Complexity, and Fluidity in 21st-Century Racial Identity

Gloria Ladson-Billings

> Bill Clinton is our first Black president.
>
> —Toni Morrison

In 2008, the nation (indeed the world) was abuzz with the possibility of a U.S. Senator from Illinois, Barack Hussein Obama, winning the election that would make him the 44th President of the United States. The story is almost a fairy tale. A young boy born in Hawai'i of a White American mother and a Black Kenyan father, raised in Indonesia, Hawai'i, and Kansas, makes his way to Ivy League universities, where he becomes editor of the Harvard Law Review; he later interns in Chicago where he meets a beautiful and equally talented Black woman whom he marries. On the surface this is just the kind of story America should love. It is the kind of story that proves the American Dream narrative. However, many other narratives were spun out of these events.

One narrative that emerged on the left was that the country had become "postracial." Barack Obama was able to assemble a broad coalition of supporters—Blacks, Latinos, Asian Americans, American Indians, youth, and White middle class. After his election some argued that there was no longer any reason to engage race since we were now "postracial." The claim of "postracial" is that we are no longer bound by the racial labels of the past because there is seeming boundary breaking and transcending based on the emergence of mixed race identities and cultural sharing across racial lines. Others, from a rightist perspective, declared that we could no longer consider race as a determining factor of difference because Obama's election proved we were "colorblind." This discourse made its way into the national media. Newsmagazines and papers ran stories with cover stories like "Is Obama the End of Black Politics?" (Bai, *New York Times Magazine*, 2008), and "The End of White America?" (Hsu, *The Atlantic*, 2009). Each article intimated that the election of Barack Obama signaled the declining significance of race in American life and culture.

A very different narrative grew up at the same time among some African Americans. In this narrative people began to ask the question, "Is Barack Obama really Black?" or more specifically, "Is Barack Obama Black *enough*?" These questions pointed to the complexity of Black identities, and they were not posed solely by African Americans. Then-presidential candidate Senator Joe Biden described his primary opponent as a special kind of African American. In his words, "I mean, you got the first mainstream African-American who is articulate and bright and clean and a nice-looking guy" (Thai & Barrett, 2007). Similarly, then Senator Majority Leader Harry Reid said Barack Obama was electable because of his, "light-skinned appearance and speaking patterns with no Negro dialect, unless he wanted to have one" (Preston, 2010). Although Biden and Reid were forced to apologize for their remarks, in closed Black spaces similar conversations were occurring. Black people recognized that unlike Shirley Chisholm, Jesse Jackson, and Al Sharpton, Barack Obama seemed to represent a different kind of Black person and might indeed be the "Magic Negro" capable of winning a national election.

Those who are wedded to "respectability politics" saw Barack Obama as somehow able to transcend Blackness. Those for whom being Black is a daily fact of life wondered if Barack Obama was really Black. Although Black people understood the genetic reality of Obama's race they also saw him as having been raised with experiences that made him other than "culturally black." In truth, Barack Obama was never able to transcend race. Even in the highly optimistic era of the 2008 election, closer analysis of the election revealed an electorate that divided along urban/rural and racial/ethnic lines. Although more states ended up in the "blue" (Democratic) column, the county-by-county results indicated that urban, densely populated areas voted for Democratic candidates, while rural, less densely populated areas continued to vote for the Republican candidates. Sixty-seven percent of Latinos voted for Obama, 62 percent of Asians voted for him, 66 percent of those designated as "other" voted for him, and 95 percent of Blacks voted for him. Fifty-five percent of Whites voted for John McCain and Sarah Palin.

We saw race play out throughout the Obama Administration. From his first State of the Union Address where a Southern Congressman yelled out, "You lie," to the regular challenges to his citizenship and religious affiliation, to the open hostility to his legislative initiatives (e.g., health care, immigration) and nominees (e.g., Attorney General, Supreme Court), race was a subtext of all 8 years. On some level we can argue that this opposition was predictable. We should not have expected the first person of color in the history of the nation to assume its highest office to have an easy go of it.

A previous president, Bill Clinton—a White man—was described as our "first Black president" by Nobel Laureate Toni Morrison (1998). However, journalist Ta-Nehisi Coates (2015) argues that Morrison's assertion was not a compliment. A closer reading of Morrison's assertion about Clinton deploys every trope attributed to Blackness—single-parent upbringing, born poor, working class, saxophone-playing, McDonald's junk food–eating, sexually immoral boy from Arkansas—as a way to ascribe Blackness to Clinton. Coates reminds us, "Race has never been much about skin color, or physical features, so much as the need to name someone before doing something to them. Race is not a sober-minded description of peoples. It is casus belli" (Coates, 2015). But in addition to the realm of the political we are seeing anti-Black racism in an area that often considers itself "beyond race"—popular entertainment.

On the night before the 2016 Super Bowl American football championship game, mega-star Beyoncé released a song and video, "Formation," that rocked the nation. The song is outspoken about Beyoncé's pride in her Black heritage—her father from Alabama and her mother from Louisiana—and her desire to keep that heritage alive in her baby daughter. In it, she celebrates her daughter's nose and natural hair. But she also addresses the poor treatment of Black people in New Orleans in the aftermath of Hurricane Katrina. During the Super Bowl performance Beyoncé evoked the image of the Black Panthers. A critical firestorm ensued. Police officers from some cities claimed that they would not provide security for her upcoming tour because they read her song and performance as anti-police and perhaps anti-White. In a brilliant spoof of White reaction to Beyoncé's song and video, NBC's *Saturday Night Live* ran a skit where White people view the music video and "discover" that Beyoncé is Black (www.etonline.com/news/182286_saturday_night_live_cast_gets_formation_for_hilarious_beyonce_spoof/). Beyoncé, like Michael Jackson, Michael Jordan, and Tiger Woods, had appeared to "transcend" race, and her decision to produce a song that overtly embraced her Black heritage was an affront to the "honorary whiteness" she had been accorded.

Another example of the complexity of racial identity comes in the form of a woman from Spokane, WA, named Rachel Dolezal. Ms. Dolezal is a 38-year-old White woman who has spent many years representing herself as a Black woman. The age-old notion of "passing" is common in the Black community. It refers to African Americans with complexions light enough and hair straight enough to make them appear White. People who chose to pass did it to avoid the pain and disadvantage that racism produced. However, deciding to go from White to Black seems unique (except for journalistic or research purposes). Ms. Dolezal wore darker make-up, styled her hair like an African American woman (braids, twists, Afros) and was active in the African American community, including serving as president of her local National Association for the Advancement of Colored People (NAACP).

When asked whether she was Black she claimed not to understand the question. She taught classes in African American studies and earned an MFA from historically Black Howard University. Ms. Dolezal was not a person with one White and one Black parent who opted to identify with the Black identity. Both of her parents are White. She appropriated an African American identity and once again complicated our notions of Blackness.

A more social-scientific approach to complicating Blackness emerges in the work of social psychologist James Jackson. Jackson studied the increasing diversity within Black America (2000). In his study of American life and culture, Jackson disaggregated a robust Black data set that did more than over-sample Harlem.[1] Jackson's group drew samples from every state in the nation where there was a representative number of Blacks. Then, the study disaggregated the sample to examine domestic Blacks (African Americans), African Blacks (immigrants and children of immigrants from the continent of Africa), and Caribbean Blacks. This third category was further disaggregated to look at English speakers, Spanish speakers, and Haitians. Jackson's research discovered that each of these groups were having a different experience in the United States. Spanish-speaking Blacks felt it was important to maintain their native tongue because it seemed to provide a bit of a buffer against the more pernicious aspects of American racism. Haitians experienced deep racism linked to perceptions of them as carriers of HIV-AIDS and as economic rather than political refugees. Jackson's study also pointed to the importance of global media in forming what might be seen as a "Black identity." Instead of allowing the processes of acculturation and assimilation to create these identities, rapid global, technological aspects of culture quickly tell new immigrants how to be Black in this society.

CRITICAL RACE THEORY IN OUR UNDERSTANDING OF RACE

The primary way I understand race and our response to it is through the theoretical lens of Critical Race Theory (CRT). Critical Race Theory began as a set of legal theories to explain the ways race is figured in our legal system. Over the past 20 years scholars in education, gender studies, sociology, anthropology, and other social sciences have appropriated CRT to explain racial inequity in their specific areas. CRT emerged from the dissatisfaction of legal scholars of color who felt that both the law and the newly developing Critical Legal Studies (CLS) failed to place issues of race and racism at the center of their analysis of inequity. One of the champions of a more racialized approach to the law was Derrick Bell (2008), the first African American tenure track professor at Harvard Law School. Along with Bell were legal scholars and students, including Kimberlé Crenshaw, Richard Delgado, Patricia Williams, Linda Green, and others. The primary tenets of

CRT include: Acknowledgment of the permanence of racism in U.S. society, use of critical social science, development of counter-stories, a resistance to claims of objectivity and neutrality, and a critique of liberalism.

CRT flies in the face of most conventional approaches to race, equality, and civil rights. For example, liberal approaches to race relations presume progress in a steady but gradual way. Thus, we tell a historical story of steady progress toward racial equality. What is not included in the narrative are the deliberate, intentional ways inequitable structures have been planned to ensure that race would be a permanent dividing line between Whites and those not designated as White.

An example of a CRT analysis can be seen in its approach to racial housing policy. The standard narrative regarding how our nation became so racially segregated begins in the passive voice where Whites "just happen" to find themselves in the suburbs and Blacks find themselves in the cities' urban cores. This narrative is offered as an unplanned, unintentional set of incidents where Whites decided to move to the suburbs and that led to racial housing segregation. Liberal analysis calls this *de facto* segregation. CRT scholars challenge the very existence of *de facto* segregation and argue that it is all *de jure*.

Left out of most stories about urban housing is the fact that in the late 1940s and early 50s Blacks and Whites did live in the same neighborhoods or at least in nearby neighborhoods. While they may not have always been next-door neighbors, most people knew that a block or two away from them lived people of another race. People were not living in racial isolation where they never saw people of another race. Racial isolation in the North came about because of direct intervention of the government. Two actions—the creation of the interstate highway system and the development of Levittown homes—sped up housing segregation. The development of Levittown is particularly interesting.

Levittown was an attempt to make the American Dream of home ownership a reality for White working-class veterans after World War II. While White GIs could come back from the war to the pride of home ownership, their Black counterparts were relegated to tenements and other substandard housing. This was not a subtle form of discrimination. Clause 25 in the standard lease for the first Levitt house, which included an option to buy, stated that the home could not "be used or occupied by any person other than members of the Caucasian race" (Lambert, 1997). By 1953, 70,000 people lived in Levitt homes—not one of them was Black. Those early Levittown homes cost $6,000. With no money down and $60 a month a White veteran could become a homeowner for less than it cost to rent an apartment in urban centers like Chicago, New York, or Philadelphia. Today, a Levittown home in suburban New York can go for over $700,000. The ability of working-class Whites to accumulate wealth was facilitated by commercial developers and the federal government. William Levitt built 17,000 homes in Bucks County, PA. It would not have been possible for him to finance that many homes without help from the federal government through its favorable financing rates. For CRT scholars, the connections between disadvantage and race are evident. But how do we get to a place where race is such an important identifying human characteristic—so important that we decide to organize our entire society around it?

BUT WHAT IS RACE[2]?

The entire practice of dividing human beings into racial categories has been debunked as scientifically vacuous, yet it persists in our society (Sussman, 2014). We need to ask: What purpose does the concept of race serve? If we need to find some way to divide people, we could use geopolitical identities or linguistic groups. The primary reason for deploying the concept of race appears to have been to create a way to rank people so that some groups can be seen as superior and deserving of more power and privilege. In a country like the United States that declared itself to be founded on democratic principles of equality and justice, racial divisions are philosophically incompatible. In order to justify hierarchy, those in power have to suggest a less than human status for those who do not fit into their racial group. And the boundaries of that racial group must be tightly guarded. For example, in 1923, in the case of *U.S. v. Bhagat Singh Thind,* the Supreme Court deemed Asian Indians ineligible for citizenship because U.S. law allowed only free Whites to become naturalized citizens. The court conceded that Indians were "Caucasians" but argued, "the average man knows perfectly well that there are unmistakable and profound differences." (*History Matters*, 1998). The *Thind* decision also led to successful efforts to denaturalize some who had previously become citizens.

The challenge of working with a concept as amorphous as race is that despite the contention of natural scientists that it does not exist and that of social scientists that it is a social construction, it is regularly deployed in the everyday lived experiences of people throughout our nation and the world. Nobel Laureate Toni Morrison (1992) declared:

> Race has become metaphorical—a way of referring to and disguising forces, events, classes, and expressions of social decay and economic division far more threatening to the body politic than biological "race" ever was.
>
> Expensively kept, economically unsound, a spurious and useless political asset in election campaigns, racism is as healthy today as it was during the Enlightenment. It seems that it has a utility far beyond economy, beyond the sequestering of classes from one another, and has assumed a metaphorical life so completely embedded in daily discourse that it is perhaps more necessary and more on display than ever before (p. 63).

But how do we determine who is a part of what race? In 1806 a jurist by the name of Tucker imposed a racial determination test on three generations of women—a daughter, grandmother, and mother. These women could not prove that they were descendants from a free maternal ancestor which, at that time, was the determiner as to who was White, and their owner, a Mr. Hudgins, could not prove that they were descendants from a female enslaved African (Lopez, 1995). To determine whether the Wrights were Black (and thus slaves) or American Indian (and allegedly free), Judge Tucker of the Virginia courts insisted that in addition to skin color, there were two markers of Blackness that endured over many generations. Those markers were the flatness of the nose and the coarse texture of the hair.

> Nature has stampt upon the African and his descendants two characteristic marks, besides the difference of complexion, which often remain visible long after the characteristic distinction of colour either disappears or becomes doubtful; a flat nose and woolly head of hair. The latter of these disappears the last of all; and so strong an ingredient in the African constitution is this latter characteristic, that it predominates uniformly where the party is in equal degree descended from parents of different complexions, whether white or Indians. *(Hudgins v. Wright*, 11 Va 134, Sup. Ct. App. 1806, cited in Lopez, 1995, p. 1910)

By this standard, Judge Tucker looked at the long, straight hair of Hannah Wright and judged the women to be not of African descent and, therefore, free. The full ruling includes an operationalized definition of race that declared that one single African ancestor, a "flat nose," or a "woolly head of hair" made one Black. Almost 200 years later this perception of who is Black remains.

The concept of race, although prefigured in early history by notions of civilization and barbarity (Snowden, 1983) or citizen and slave (Hannaford, 1996), is, according to Winant (2000), a modern one. Along with his colleague Michael Omi, Howard Winant (2014) points out that there is no biological basis for race and even the sociohistorical categories we use to differentiate among groups are both imprecise and arbitrary. Winant (2000) asserts that the concept of race as we now know it began to form "with the rise of a world political economy" (p. 172). As nation-states begin to participate in a worldwide economy—seaborne empires, conquest of the Americas, and the rise of the Atlantic slave trade—we see the development of race as a practical project to create an "Other" whose threat could be integrated and deployed in every aspect of society. Such an Other justified not only the conquering of militarily defenseless nations, but its existence was mapped onto an entire set of symbol systems and rationalities that made them seem natural and normal.

Over the past few years we have come to see how race matters, despite its ambiguity of meaning. The series of police and citizen shootings of unarmed Black citizens have created a discourse about the worth and value of Black lives that has made it clear that the society has less concern for Black people. The headline case was that of Trayvon Martin. To briefly recap, 17-year-old Trayvon Martin was visiting his father in Sanford, FL, on the weekend of the NBA AllStar game. During halftime he decided to go to the store for a snack. On his way back to his dad's home he noticed a White man following him. This man, later identified as George Zimmerman, was a member of the neighborhood watch and reported Martin as a suspicious character. He called the police and was directed to stop following Martin. Martin was on the phone with a friend, Rachel Jeantel, and described Zimmerman as "creepy." At some point Martin and Zimmerman ended up in a confrontation that left Martin dead. The subsequent actions—the lag in arresting Zimmerman, the community protests, and trial—were all racialized performances.

One of the more significant aspects of the trial came when Martin's friend Rachel Jeantel was called to the stand. Instead of a focus on the facts of the case the entire narrative became all about Jeantel's illiteracy and "ghetto" affect. As a Black, overweight, seemingly inarticulate teenaged woman, Jeantel became the joke of the trial and an ineffective witness for the prosecution. Jeantel's Blackness cancelled out her intellect.

In the case of Tamir Rice, the Cleveland teen who was playing with a toy gun, we see how his Blackness cancelled out his childhood. Rice was a 12-year-old who was shot within 5 seconds of the police's arrival on the scene. The officers reportedly thought Rice was a 20-year-old. Although the caller to the dispatch said on at least 2 occasions that Rice's gun was "probably a fake" the officers quickly swooped down on the 12-year-old and shot him. Rice's shooter was a police officer who had lost a similar position in a suburban police force where he was determined to be "unstable and unfit for duty."

In Texas, Sandra Bland was stopped for apparently changing lanes in her car without using her signal lights. The traffic stop escalated to an arrest when the officer told Bland to put out her cigarette and Bland refused because she was sitting in her own car. Next, the officer insisted that Bland come out of her car where she was roughed up, handcuffed, and taken to jail. Bland never left the jail because she was found dead in her cell. Her Blackness made her vulnerable to police surveillance.

According to the website Mapping Police Violence (www.mappingpoliceviolence.org), police killed 102 unarmed Black people in 2015, five times the rate of any other racial group. This perception of Black people as a threat or dangerous has fueled an anti-Black racism that is more than a minor inconvenience in the way Black people are forced to live their daily lives. Everything from parenting to shopping to driving requires Black people to carefully monitor their actions in hopes of avoiding an unfortunate confrontation with police. Anti-Black racism, for which justice cannot be found through the legal system, has helped to fuel a new form of activism with a foundation generated by the youth culture phenomenon known as hip hop.

HYBRIDITY, COMPLEXITY, AND FLUIDITY

Although notions of racial hybridity, complexity, and fluidity are threaded throughout this paper it is important to specifically identify them, to underscore the degree to which these concepts reflect the condition of Blackness in our nation and throughout the world. *Hybridity* is a term borrowed from biology that refers to the mixing of two separate (and allegedly distinct) races or ethnicities. Most "hybrid" people are assigned the status of the more subordinate group. So a person with a Black parent and a White parent, although considered mixed-race, is likely to experience life in this country as a Black person.

Complexity refers to the issue of multiple identities that include but may transcend race. For example, a Black person who is transgendered may feel that their sexual identity is the most salient aspect of their identity or at least the part of their identity that is most threatened in the society. In one of my graduate courses I show my students a *60 Minutes* interview with the late Rev. Peter Gomes, who served as the chaplain at Harvard University. Mr. Gomes was Black, male, gay, a Christian in the New England Baptist tradition, Republican, and conservative. In the interview he claimed all of those identities and declared that the hardest one to publicly acknowledge was Republican (see www.cbsnews.com/videos/a-harvard-man/). Gomes maintained a complex set of identities and his life at Harvard insulated him from many of the life experiences of most Black people in the United States.

Finally, the notion of *fluidity* also comes from science. It refers to the viscosity of an amorphous, continuous substance that assumes the shape of its container (as is true of a liquid or gas). In racial identity, fluidity refers to an individual's ability to move comfortably across identity categories. A Black Puerto Rican might see herself as Black when she is with her Black sorority sisters, but Puerto Rican when she is visiting her *abuela* in New York. The spaces in which she expresses her identities allow for her fluid conceptions of self. National Basketball Association player Tony Parker was Black and French. He was once married to Latina actress Eva Longoria. If Parker and Longoria had children they could be hybrid, complex, and fluid or they could have more fixed identities assigned to them.

In his 2002 volume, *The World is a Ghetto: Race and Democracy Since World War II*, Howard Winant describes the reconstruction of race in several geographic spaces—the United States, the United Kingdom, Brazil, and South Africa—and how Blackness was reconfigured as a universally denigrated subject position. South Africa was perhaps the most proscriptive of the nations in determining Blackness. People who were not White were required to carry passbooks when they traveled outside of their homeland (state or community) to identify their racial classifications. Some non-Whites were considered Black and others were considered "coloureds." Arabs, Indians, people of other Asian descent, and mixed-race people typically were considered coloureds. While they had a few more rights than Blacks, they also experienced discrimination. South Africa worked hard to create strict rules determining Whiteness and non-Whiteness.

Similarly, the UK seemed to lump all non-Whites into the category of Black. Indeed, before the attack on the World Trade Center in New York and the Pentagon in Washington, DC, many in the UK referred to Pakistani and Indian-descent residents as Black. Now these people are regularly known as "Muslim" (whether or not they are). Many racially Black citizens and residents of the UK have heritage connections on the continent of Africa and throughout the Caribbean, all as a result of the UK's historical empire-building. Their national identities are subsumed under the category of Black. Rather than being seen as Nigerian or Jamaican, their all-encompassing identity category is Black.

In Brazil there is a more complex notion of race that looks at Indigenous, White, Black, and what it calls "yellow" (Asian). Any combinations of these broad categorizations is known as "Pardo" or mixed race. More specifically, a Black/White mix is "Mulatto." A Black/Indian mix is "Cafuzo." A White/Indian mix is "Caboclo." A Black/Indian/White mix is called "Juçara." And a White/Japanese mix is called "Ainocô." Of course, mathematically four categories can create 24 permutations and Brazil is a country that now includes many more than four groups of people. This constant coding and recoding of human racial identities underscores how difficult it is to make sense of hybrid, complex, and fluid identities in our 21st century environments.

The United States, which is the focus of my work, has been especially interesting when it comes to the work it makes race do. Historically, Blacks were aligned with poor Whites in the subject position of indentured servitude. However, once slavery became an institution this "free" nation embraced, race became the all-encompassing category that gave rise to legally cordoning off one group of people based on perceived biological deficits linked to skin color. Arguments about who is and is not Black have raged throughout the nation's history. The Napoleonic system that reigned in the Louisiana Territory took the position that "one drop" of "Black blood" made one Black. Somewhat like the Brazilian system, this code made fine distinctions of Black, Mulatto, Quadroon, and Octaroon to trace "Black ancestry" back over several generations. People like President Obama, Mariah Carey, Lenny Kravitz, or Alicia Keys, now called mixed race, would have been considered mulatto. However, growing up in the United States has shaped their identities by a Black experience that excluded them from privileges associated with Whiteness.

Although the culture is finding new ways to think about and consider racial hybridity, complexity, and fluidity, official records such as the U.S. Census and state documents (e.g., driver licenses, college applications, prison records) remain locked in fairly rigid categorical spaces that demand that respondents make forced choices. The U.S. Census has attempted to break out race and ethnicity and allows respondents to select "mixed race," but those choices do not help us make sense of the experiences of people. For example, someone can be Spanish-speaking and Black and not clearly identify with either category, or identify strongly with both. How is that person accounted for as a part of the political process? Are they Black? Latinx? Both?

Increasingly, aspects of youth culture blend and blur racial lines in new and interesting ways. In the next section I focus on the ways hip hop culture creatively takes on and rearticulates race for 21st-century youth.

BLACK LIVES MATTER TO HIP HOP

After the death of teenager Michael Brown in Ferguson, MO, the face and form of activism on behalf of Black people changed radically. No longer content merely to march as their Civil Rights foreparents had done, a new brand of activism emerged from the millenial generation that was bolder, angrier, and more aggressive. It was confrontational and brash. It was not content to follow the rules of past civil rights efforts with what John Brown Childs (1993) called "vanguard leadership." Vanguard leadership depends on a strong and charismatic leader. Booker T. Washington and W. E. B. DuBois were early vanguard leaders. Later, both Martin Luther King, Jr., and Malcolm X were vanguard leaders. But, Childs argues, there are also "grassroots leaders" who motivate and energize movements by helping groups of people organize so that they decide for themselves the direction of change they want to effect. People like Harriet Tubman, Sojourner Truth, and Marcus Garvey were considered grassroots leaders.

The Black Lives Matter organizers, Alicia Garza, Opel Tometi, and Patrisse Cullors, are in the tradition of grassroots leadership. According to the group's website, www.blacklivesmatter.com, the group was organized in 2012 after George Zimmerman's acquittal for the murder of Trayvon Martin. Unlike previous civil rights movements, Black Lives Matter expanded the racial paradigm to include Black queer, trans, disabled, and undocumented people. The organizers declare their movement "centers those that have been marginalized *within* [emphasis added] Black liberation movements." The powerful youth cultural form known as *hip hop* also works to expand Black identity.

Hip hop culture influences the dress, language, and art forms of today's youth. Although some consider hip hop a Black art form, Hahn (2014) argues that it is not merely the anomaly of Eminem that marks White participation in hip hop, but Mr. Freeze, Third Base, the Beastie Boys, and Iggy Azalea have also achieved success in the genre. More significantly, market analysis suggests that White suburban teenagers consume about 80% of all hip hop. Of course there are powerful arguments against hip hop for racist, sexist, mysogynist, violent, drug-glorifying lyrics, but those songs and artists represent a particular genre of hip hop, not all of it. It is as if someone decided never to go to the movies because they somehow stumbled into an X-rated film and now declare that all movies are pornographic. There is a wide range of hip hop including east coast, west coast, southern, gangsta, crunk, alternative, conscious, battle, and world scene. The work of activists like Black Lives Matter emanates primarily from the *conscious* genre. This is the music of Public Enemy, Lauryn Hill, Talib Kweli, Lupe Fiasco, KRS-One, Immortal Technique, and of course Kendrick Lamar. (There are many more artists in this category who are not named here.)

Kendrick Lamar has become what *Billboard Magazine* calls the "thinking man's rapper." I would contend that Lamar is the archetypical conscious hip hop artist who is less concerned with commercial success than with critical acclaim that initiates activism. His album *To Pimp a Butterfly* (2015) is a powerful example of how hip hop artists deploy race politically (Guinier & Torres, 2003). Tracks like "Complexion," "The Blacker the Berry," and "Mortal Man" all speak to the ways that race both defines and confines human existence. However, Lamar works to turn the racial paradigm on its head and make race a tool for challenging the dominant discourse. This work is in the tradition of early hip hop such as that of Grandmaster Flash and the Furious Five in their iconic track "The Message" that spoke of the structural inequities that are a part of everyday life for Black people. Also, Public Enemy's declaration "Fight the Power" became an anthem of Black dissatisfaction with the agents of oppression. Other artists like Mos Def (Yasiin Bey), Lauryn Hill, and Common have also created politically targeted lyrics designed to speak to social inequity.

Many of the underground artists like Dead Prez, Wise Intelligence, and Jasiri X work hard to trouble the notion that there is one Black identity that defines what it means to be Black. Even commercially successful artists like Jay-Z and Kanye West have attempted to push the envelope about what Black identities we are able to recruit and deploy. For example, their mega hit *Watch the Throne* (2011) with the best selling "N**gas in Paris" can be read less as a paean to excess than a way to describe a wider and broader representation of Black identity. For those who have not seen the accompanying video, there is a re-made French flag with a black stripe in the place of the blue one. Jay-Z, a collector of Basquiat's art, represents a decidedly different notion of what America thinks of when it imagines a Black man from the Marcy Housing Projects of Brooklyn, New York.

The entire hip hop movement works actively against labels and static conceptions of identities. It is deeply immersed in a digital world that relies on instant communication and cultural sampling and mash-ups. A decade or more ago when we referenced the "digital divide" we pointed to the way social status, for example, class, race, or ethnicity, kept some students from accessing electronic information. However, with the advent of smart technologies—phones, tablets, and other mobile devices—electronic communication has become ubiquitous. Even in developing nations mobile devices provide access to information, global communication, and financial transactions. The new digital divide is that which exists between generations.

Our digitally savvy young people do not fit neatly into rigid categories of race, class, gender, language groups, or national origin that older generations have relied upon to make distinctions and create hierarchy. Their sports heroes and heroines include LeBron James and J J Watt, Serena Williams and Mia Hamm. They listen to Bruno Mars, Beyoncé, and Justin Timberlake. They are more likely to endorse same-sex marriage and are unperturbed by Will Smith's son Jaden wearing a skirt. They also recognize that this culture they have created is a mash-up with permeable boundaries. They engage with a culture that is simultaneously sacred and profane. They have deep religious convictions and embrace all things secular. This flexible understanding of their experiences has allowed them to take on a more flexible outlook toward their identity—including a flexible approach to their racial identities.

NOTES

1. Often studies of Blacks in America use Harlem as a proxy for all Blacks in the nation.
2. Portions of this section come from an unpublished manuscript by Gloria Ladson-Billings, *The Social Funding of Race* (2004).

REFERENCES

Bai, M. (2008, August 6). Is Obama the end of black politics? *New York Times Magazine*. Retrieved from www.nytimes.com/2008/08/10/magazine/10politics-t.html

Bell, D. (2008). *Race, racism and American law* (6th edition). The Netherlands: Aspen Publishers.

Childs, J. B. (1993). *Leadership, conflict and cooperation in Afro-American social thought*. Philadelphia, PA: Temple University Press.

Coates, T. (2015, August 27). It was no compliment to call Bill Clinton "The first Black president." *The Atlantic*. Retrieved from www.theatlantic.com/notes/2015/08/toni-morrison-wasnt-giving-bill-clinton-a-compliment/402517/

Guinier, L., & Torres, G. (2003). *The miner's canary: Enlisting race, resisting power, transforming democracy*. Cambridge, MA: Harvard University Press.

Hahn, J. (2014, June 8). The politics of race in rap. *Harvard Political Review*. Retrieved from harvardpolitics.com/books-arts/politics-race-rap/

Hannaford, I. (1996). *Race. The history of an idea in the West.* Washington, DC: Woodrow Wilson Centre Press; Baltimore: Johns Hopkins University Press.

History Matters (1998). Not all Caucasians are White. Retrieved from historymatters.gmu.edu/d/5076/

Hsu, H. (2009, January/February). The end of White America? *The Atlantic.* Retrieved from www.theatlantic.com/magazine/archive/2009/01/the-end-of-white-america/307208/

Jackson, J. (2000). *New Directions: African Americans in a diversifying nation.* Ann Arbor, MI: Program for Research on Black Americans, University of Michigan.

Lambert, B. (1997, December 28). At 50, Levittown contends with its legacy of bias. *New York Times.* Retrieved from www.nytimes.com/1997/12/28/nyregion/at-50-levittown-contends-with-its-legacy-of-bias.html?pagewanted=all

Lopez, I. H. (1995). The social construction of race. In R. Delgado (Ed.), *Critical race theory: The cutting edge* (pp. 191–203). Philadelphia, PA: Temple University Press.

Morrison, T. (1992). *Playing in the dark: Whiteness and the literary imagination.* Cambridge, MA: Harvard University Press.

Morrison, T. (1998, October 5). Comment. *The New Yorker.* Retrieved from www.newyorker.com/magazine/1998/10/05/comment-6543

Omi, M., & Winant, H. (2014). *Racial formation in the United States* (3rd ed.). New York, NY: Routledge.

Preston, M. (2010, January 9). Reid apologizes for racial remarks about Obama during campaign. Retrieved from www.cnn.com/2010/POLITICS/01/09/obama.reid/

Snowden, F. M. (1983). *Before color prejudice: The ancient views of Blacks.* Cambridge, MA: Harvard University Press.

Sussman, R. W. (2014). *The myth of race: The troubling persistence of an unscientific idea.* Cambridge, MA: Harvard University Press.

Thai, X., & Barrett, T. (2007, February 9). Biden's description of Obama draws scrutiny. Retrieved from www.cnn.com/2007/POLITICS/01/31/biden.obama/

Winant, H. (2000). Race and race theory. *Annual Review of Sociology, 26,* 169–185.

Winant, H. (2002). *The world is a ghetto: Race and democracy since World War II.* New York, NY: Basic Books.

CHAPTER 3

Latinos in the American Racial Hierarchy
The Complexities of Identity and Group Formation

Luis Ricardo Fraga and Nicole Perez

Among the most intriguing questions confronting scholars of group relations in the United States is the following: How does the presence and diversity of the country's growing Latino population affect America's traditional racial hierarchy? We address this question in several parts. First, we identify the consequences associated with America's racial hierarchy for both Whites and non-Whites and patterns of race relations. Second, we consider the distinction between racial groups and ethnic groups. We argue that although some scholars have consistently stated that there is a clear distinction between the two, focusing on the fundamental similarities in the conceptualization of the groups lets us see better how Latinos fit within America's evolving racial hierarchy. We use the term *ethnoracial hierarchy* for this system of group relations. Third, we examine several dimensions of current Latino subgroup and Latino panethnic group formation. We focus specifically on how national origin affects group formation among Latinos and find, counterintuitively and in contrast to earlier research, that the most significant predictor of strong levels of national origin identity among Latinos is the extent to which they simultaneously identify in panethnic terms. Strong national origin identification and panethnic identification exist at the same time and are not in competition with one another. This is consistent with our view of the presence of an ethnoracial hierarchy in the United States. Fourth, we conclude with a consideration of the position of Latinos in the U.S. racial hierarchy for the ever-evolving nature of the ethnoracial hierarchy of group relations in the United States. Consistent with recent theory, we argue that Latinos as a panethnic group are detrimentally affected by, and must mobilize to challenge, the unfavorable consequences of their ascribed and self-identified position.

AMERICA'S EVOLVING RACIAL HIERARCHY

Previous discussions in this volume specify how racial classifications are socially constructed to serve two primary purposes: (1) to marginalize non-White peoples by limiting their opportunities, resources, status, prestige, and power, and (2) in this way to establish systems of white privilege that serve to advantage members of this group to better access and benefit from the asymmetrical distribution of those opportunities, resources, status, prestige, and power. These processes in turn can have direct implications for the educational opportunities and disadvantages communities of color confront. Given the changing demographics of the United States, such as the growth in the Latino population, and the implications these changes can have for the country's color lines (Lee & Bean, 2004), scholars have posited alternative racial hierarchies. One new hierarchy, for example, posits "nonblack" and "black" populations with the multiracial population fitting within a residual or middle category (Yancey, 2003). This hierarchy is not solely based on color or other physical features but also on a distinction between undeserving and deserving races. Other scholars are going "beyond black and white" by utilizing a "racial triangulation" framework in order to understand, for example, where Asian Americans fit within racialization processes (Kim, 1999). Another triracial order proposes a racial hierarchy where Whites are at the top, with an intermediary group of "honorary Whites" and a non-White group or the "collective black" at the bottom (Bonilla-Silva, 2004). These emerging racial stratification systems suggest various ways that white supremacy can be maintained within an increasingly diversifying society. In these alternative conceptualizations of racial hierarchies, it is apparent how the social construction of race and its associated corporeal elements can work to maintain racial hierarchies that reinforce white privilege.

Where do Latinos fit within the traditional Black–White paradigm? Once a mainly biracial society with a large White and smaller African American minority (with a largely overlooked Native, indigenous population)—and a historical color line dividing these groups—following the post-1965 waves of immigration from Latin American and Asia, the United States is now a society composed of multiple easily identifiable racial and ethnic groups (Lee & Bean, 2004). The Black–White dichotomy has also dominated education research seeking to understand the Black–White achievement gap (Jencks & Phillips, 2011; Porter, 1974; Portes & Wilson, 1976). This body of research also linked achievement differences to racial attitudes and identity (Fordham & Ogbu, 1986; Mickelson, 1990; Ogbu, 1978). Latinos pose a conundrum for racial classification because despite largely originating from common geographical areas and having cultural similarities, they are most often not considered a race because they do not share a particular biological or genetic makeup (Alcoff, 2000). As a racially heterogeneous group with White, Indigenous, Black, and even Asian origins, Latinos do not fit into any of the traditionally recognized U.S. racial categories (Morning, 2011; Rodriguez, 2000).

Beyond locating the Latino community within existing racial hierarchies, Latino educational outcomes have also been implicated in understanding how variation in assimilation processes leads to educational success (Kao & Tienda, 1995; Neidert & Farley, 1985; Rumberger & Larson, 1998; Velez, 1989). In discussions of the Black–White achievement gap, Latino youth generally are located in the "racial middle"—they aren't excelling at the same rates as Whites but on average tend to perform better than Black students (Goldsmith, 2004; Madrid, 2011). Some research has looked into why Latino students excel even if assimilation is not occurring and it suggests that "immigrant optimism" offers an opportunity to increase educational achievement (Kao & Tienda, 1995). And yet another body of research has identified institutional barriers that prevent educational attainment in the third and fourth generation (Telles & Ortiz, 2008).

George M. Fredrickson (1988) has defined race as a "consciousness of status and identity based on ancestry and color" (p. 12). If we delete the color criterion from this definition, there is a workable definition of ethnicity. Applying these definitions to racial/ethnic groups in the United States, Blacks are treated as a racial group. In the cases of the growing Latino and Asian groups, however, the term "race" does not by itself serve as an all-encompassing label because it is not clear that "color" is (or is becoming) an attribute that is always ascribed to peoples with origins in Latin America and Asia, at least on a consistent basis. For example, some Latinos view themselves and are seen by others as White, some as mestizo, and a few as Black (Lee & Bean, 2004).

Racial/ethnic categorization provides insight into how broad processes such as migration trends and political shifts lead to the establishment of new categories and subsequently locate Latinos within the Black–White paradigm. For example, G. Cristina Mora (2014) delineates how the label *Hispanic* came into existence: As late as 1969, Latinos were largely categorized as part of the White racial group by the Census Bureau. In the 1980s the bureau instituted a new Hispanic[1] category that sorted persons of Latin American descent into their own panethnic classification. The census does not yet treat Hispanics as a separate racial category, but Lee and Bean (2004) suggest that they should be so treated for two reasons: first, Latinos often see themselves as a separate category—many choose the "some other race" category when it is offered (e.g., in the 2000 U.S. Census 47.9% of Hispanics chose the "some other race" category while in the 2010 Census the figure was 36.7%); and second, they have been legally treated as a separate group, often as a racial/ethnic minority group that qualifies for and receives benefits from federal programs designed to assist disadvantaged minorities.

This dynamic also influenced consideration of altering the 2020 U.S. Census to allow Latinos to identify as a group through the combined race/

ethnicity question. This approach considerably increases the Hispanic response rates on the race question without depressing the count of the Hispanic population (National Advisory Committee on Racial, Ethnic and Other Populations, 2014). The results from the focus groups used to test the combined race/ethnicity question indicated that it appropriately fits the way Americans—both Hispanics and others—think of the main population groups and may better capture the preferences that Latinos express for self-identification. (The Census Bureau ultimately decided not to integrate the Hispanic question within the race question.)

Within sociological research, race and ethnicity are treated as two distinct analytical categories where the former is associated with hierarchical and ascribed processes while the latter is assumed to be mobilized and agentic. Despite these differences, race and ethnicity both require a structural and contextual framework to track the ways in which boundaries are constructed and maintained, or fluid and permeable. Ethnic boundaries are patterns of social interaction that give rise to, and subsequently reinforce, in-group members' self-identification and outsiders' confirmation of group distinctions (Sanders, 2002). The ways that insiders and outsiders go about characterizing a group, and thereby positioning its members in the larger society, are responsive to the social and historical context of the intergroup interactions (Nagel, 1994; Waters, 1990). Consequently, ethnic identities are fluid across time and social contexts and can even allow for "ethnic switching" (Alba, 1999; Nagel, 1995). Ethnic identity, then, is the result of a dialectical process involving internal and external opinions and processes, as well as the individual's self-identification and outsiders' ethnic designations—what you think your ethnicity is, and what others think your ethnicity is. Since ethnicity changes situationally, the individual carries a portfolio of ethnic identities that are more or less salient in various situations and contexts, and vis-à-vis various audiences (Nagel, 1994).

Within this conceptual framework, ethnic and racial identities are the products of particular events, relationships, and processes—with groups themselves playing an active role in identity construction. Once created, many ethnic and racial identities have a life and impact of their own, operating as a lens through which people interpret and make sense of the world around them (Cornell & Hartmann, 1998). There is a dialectical process between imposition and embracement of racial and ethnic identities: "[t]o understand race and ethnicity, we have to study both composition and context. We have to look at what groups bring with them to their encounters with other people and with the world around them, and what the world that they encounter consists of" (Cornell & Hartmann, 1998, pp. 12–13). This framework applies to the ways in which U.S. Latinos have embraced terms that were originally imposed panethnic labels (e.g., Hispanic) or intended as derogatory (e.g., Chicano).

Along with ethnic identity, immigrant generation status also factors into how fluid ethnic identity options are. In addition, ethnic identity for Latinos also matters across geographic spaces—for example established or immigrant gateways versus new immigrant destinations. The presence or absence of a coethnic enclave has implications for youth and parents in how they approach various institutional spaces, such as schools, and make sense of their ethnoracial identities. For example, immigrant youth are incorporated into the school system while their parents are incorporated into the labor market (Gleeson & Gonzales, 2012). These divergent institutional spaces provide unique contexts for Latinos to develop and understand their positionality within the ethnoracial hierarchy. Thus, there are important generational differences between Latino immigrant parents and youth as they progress within the educational pipeline and develop their ethnoracial identities across space and time.

While the majority of the Latino population migrates, settles, and has historically resided in immigrant gateway cities, since the 1990s "new immigrant destinations" within the Southern and Midwestern regions of the United States have rapidly increased. Variation in local contexts of reception (Portes & Rumbaut, 2001) and racial hierarchies also matter for the Latino population and their identity processes because the Los Angeles School District varies drastically from a smaller new immigrant community such Elkhart County in Indiana. Youth in the latter context attend schools with a majority White student demographic and, depending on the curricular tracking regimes, Latinx identity is either supported or rejected. However, Latino youth within Elkhart County who previously rejected their Latino identity accepted that aspect of themselves as they approached postsecondary education (Perez, 2019). Institutional spaces like schools along with local ethnoracial hierarchies matter for youth as they come of age and make sense of their identity options.

To further understand how Latinos fit within the American racial hierarchy, we suggest that the intersection between ethnicity and immigration is formative to how group identities are now created and maintained. Governments routinely shape their internal ethnic maps by their immigration policies. Immigration is a major engine of new ethnic group production as immigrant groups transition to ethnic and ethnic-derived groups. This worked in a straightforward manner for most ethnic Whites, as Irish and Italian immigrants became White at the turn of the 20th century; however, this process has yet to be reality for most Latinos. Unlike European immigrant groups, Latinos' realities can become conditioned by "ethnic replenishment" where continual immigration flows from Latin America and the physical border between the United States and Mexico dictates how the U.S. Latino diaspora is viewed and rendered as immigrants (Jimenez, 2010).

The divide between race and ethnicity literature also leads to the divide between racialization and panethnicity. The race literature focuses on racialization processes, whereas ethnicity encompasses panethnic processes. Specifically, racialization research focuses on macrolevel institutions that shape racial change such as the census and national policies (Lee, 2002; Ngai, 2004; Rodriguez, 2000), while panethnicity is occupied with more micro- and meso-level institutions leading to group formation processes (Espiritu, 2003; Lopez & Espiritu, 1990; Okamoto, 2003). To ameliorate this inherent divide in past research, Brown and Jones (2015) propose an *ethnoracialization* model to show how the concept of panethnicity can be reconfigured to develop a robust account of group formation and to bridge the divide between race and immigration research. From our historical and contemporary understandings of U.S. Latinos, they argue, both race and immigration need to be positioned in a dialectical relationship to identify changes in ethnoracial identification processes over time. Thus, linking panethnicity to both immigration and racialization processes can unearth the mutually reinforcing relationship between ascription and identification (sometimes in the form or for the purposes of ethnic mobilization) (Brown & Jones, 2015).

Ultimately, the ethnoracialization framework is critical to "divert attention from group-specific lines of inquiry and direct it toward the political, economic, and social–psychological processes that disrupt, reinforce, dampen and amplify group formation and mobilization" (Brown & Jones, 2015, pp. 187–188). At the policy and practice levels, ethnoracial frameworks are important because they allow for a complete understanding of group formation processes across time and space, highlighting the relational aspects between agency and ascription. This approach is useful for accurately understanding Latino identity formation for the purposes of data (dis)aggregation because it tracks the ways in which changes in individual and group formation and related identification occur.

THE COMPLEXITIES OF LATINO NATIONAL ORIGIN, PANETHNICITY, AND GROUP FORMATION

How do Latinos fit within an ethnoracial framework for understanding group relations in the United States? To address this question, we examine the complexities of national origin, panethnicity, and group formation among Latinos. Recent data on the distribution of Latinos in the United States by country of origin estimates that Latinos of Mexican origin comprise 64% of all Latinos in the United States, Puerto Ricans 9.6%, Salvadorans 3.8%, Cubans 3.7%, Dominicans 3.2%, and all other Latino subgroups are below 3%. There is considerable national origin diversity among Latinos. (See Fraga et al., 2010, and Fraga et al., 2012, for a fuller discussion of the growing diversity of Latinos in the United States.)

We use data from the Latino National Survey (LNS) (Fraga et al., 2006) for our empirical examination of the relationship between national origin and panethnicity with direct implications for the analytical utility of using an ethnoracial framework for understanding Latinos in the United States.[2]

Fraga et al. (2012) present a comprehensive discussion of the bivariate relationships between national origin, panethnicity, and a series of attitudinal and behavioral characteristics including being foreign-born, generation, time in the United States, language preference, sense of linked fate, formal education, gender, and panethnicity. It is clear that many of these variables affect national origin simultaneously. In this essay, we construct a dependent variable that we term *strength of national origin identification*, with distinct values, and then generate ordered logit multivariate models to further examine national origin identity and panethnicity. The independent variables are a set of attitudinal, behavioral, demographic, and contextual factors that are related to strength of national origin identification. Tables 3.1, 3.2, and 3.3 display the ordered logit coefficients and standard errors for three models: all respondents, the foreign-born, and the U.S.-born. Independent variables that achieved significance at the .05 level are then used to generate predicted probabilities.

Across all respondents, expression of a strong panethnic identity was the factor that most significantly correlated with an increase in strong national origin identification.

Moving from the lowest to highest identification as a Latino or Hispanic increases the likelihood of strong national identification by 29%. Other key predictors include cultural affinity, which yields a 20% increase in national origin identification across the range of that scale; moving Latino solidarity from the lowest to highest value increases national origin identification by 12%. Also, a dense Hispanic household increases the likelihood of strong national identification by 25%.

For U.S.-born respondents, one of the factors that most increases the probability that a respondent will identify strongly with national origin is again strength of panethnic identity, which increases the probability by 27%. High levels of cultural affinity also increase national origin identification significantly (by 23%), as again does Latino solidarity (by 19%). Living in a high-density area increases the strength of national origin identification by 32%. Other factors associated with increased national origin identification were higher rates of transnational contact (9% increase), belief in Latino hard work (6%), belief that Latinos are a separate race (4%), the percent Cuban in the neighborhood (21%), and percent Mexican in the neighborhood (15%). Being a homeowner (-4%), or a second (-6%), third (-9%) or fourth (-10%) generation Latino decreases the probability that Latinos will identify strongly with national origin.

Foreign-born respondents differ in some ways from the full group and from U.S.-born respondents. Again, strength of panethnic identity increases the likelihood that a foreign-born respondent will identify strongly with their national origin; the probability increases by 30%. Cultural affinity and Latino solidarity again are significant but at noticeably smaller magnitudes; affinity increases the probability by 14% and Latino solidarity by only 1%. The relative magnitudes of increasing the probability of a foreign-born respondent indicating strong national origin identification for the remaining variables are transnational contact (6%), interest in home country politics (5%), belief in self-reliance (3%), believing that Latinos can get ahead if they work hard (7%), believing that Latinos are a separate race (3%), and the percent foreign-born in the dataset (11%). Three factors decrease the probability that one will identify strongly with national origin for the foreign-born: frequency of sending remittances (-3%), number of dependents (-10%), as well as percent African American in the dataset (-8%).

Our empirical analysis allows us to reach several significant conclusions. First, Latinos have very strong levels of national origin identification. A majority of both U.S.-born and foreign-born Latinos report very strong identification with their national origin. Second, panethnic Latino/Hispanic identity and national origin identification are very closely related to one another. Although at one time scholars argued that panethnic identity was best understood as distinct from national origin identity (de la Garza, DeSipio, Garcia, Garcia, & Falcon, 1992), this is no longer the case. The strongest and most consistent effect on the strength of national origin identification, for all respondents, the foreign-born, and the U.S.-born, is strength of panethnic identity. One cannot fully understand Latinos in the United States today, including immigrants, unless one appreciates the way that national origin identification and panethnic identification are additive and not subtractive. They may even be mutually reinforcing.

Third, strength of national origin identification is substantially related to cultural affinity. Language, social networks, and maintaining a distinct culture are very highly related to strength of national identity. Interestingly, this is more the case for the U.S.-born than for the foreign-born. This is an unexpected result, but one for which we can offer a plausible explanation. Although U.S.-born Latinos are less likely to speak Spanish and are more distant from other elements of cultural practices from their home countries, those U.S.-born Latinos who value language and cultural maintenance and who have Latino-dominant social networks are the ones more likely to demonstrate very strong levels of national origin identification.

Fourth, a stronger sense of Latino shared interests is also very highly related to national origin identification. A stronger sense of Latino solidarity regarding jobs, education, and politics is associated with stronger levels of national origin identification. Again, this is the case for all Latinos, but this is especially the case for the U.S.-born. A greater sense of commonality is related to a higher sense of national origin.

Fifth, our multivariate analysis also reveals that generation is an important factor. Although our examination did reveal some differences among the first generation as compared to the second, third and fourth, these differences are not as relevant as Latino/Hispanic panethnic identification, cultural affinity, and Latino solidarity. A Latino's strength of national origin identification is not determined so much by how long you have been in the United States or whether your parents or grandparents were born here, or whether you are a citizen, as much as by how you see yourself and your coethnics within American society.

Sixth, among the broad set of beliefs and values examined, only those related to the benefits provided by hard work, the importance of being self-reliant, and seeing Latinos as a distinct race were associated with strong national origin identification, especially for the foreign-born. A heightened sense of self-worth, faith in the system, and seeing oneself as racially distinct were associated with stronger national origin identification.

Seventh, certain characteristics of individual background and social context also matter. For U.S.-born Latinos, being a homeowner and, for foreign-born Latinos, sending remittances are associated with decreases in strong identification with national origin. Having a large number of dependents to care for is associated with decreases in strong identification with national origin for both groups. For foreign-born Latinos, the only contextual factors that are associated with national origin identification are percent foreign-born and percent African American respondents in the dataset. Percent foreign-born is associated with a decrease in strength of national origin identification, and percent African American decreases the propensity to identify with national origin. Interestingly, for U.S.-born Latinos, the percent Cuban is associated with an increase in the likelihood of strong national origin identity.

LATINOS AND AMERICA'S EVOLVING ETHNORACIAL HIERARCHY

The growing presence and diversity of Latino communities in the United States allows us to reach several counterintuitive conclusions. Incorporating Latinos within America's traditional racial hierarchy is easily achieved through the concept of ethnoraciality. The long presence of some Latinos in the United States, the challenges many in these communities continue to face regarding access to and inclusion in institutions that determine power, prestige, status, and resources, and the interplay of ascription by others and their self-identification as a group largely distinct from those who most often control those institutions, places Latinos as more similar to than different from African American communities upon whom America's traditional racial hierarchy is grounded. Moreover, continued immigration from countries in Latin America, and the ways that many of these immigrants continue to face challenges of access and inclusion, only reinforce the analytical utility of understanding fundamental components of group relations in the United States as constituting an ethnoracial hierarchy. As such, the rich history of the traditional Black–White racial hierarchy is maintained, and, we suggest, further enriched by broadening the paradigm through the application of ethnoraciality. Stated differently, the ethnoracial framework both incorporates America's racialized past *and* facilitates understanding its nuanced manifestations to include the reality of many Latino communities in the present day and in the future.

Additionally, our empirical analysis of Latino group identity reveals that the diversity of Latinos by country of origin, generation, time in the United States, and other demographic dimensions is present and yet it coexists with high levels of panethnic identity as well. Strong national origin identification is fully compatible with high levels of panethnic Latino identification. They are not subtractive, but additive. It is simultaneity that best characterizes how Latinos can at the same time display noticeable distinctions from one another, and yet maintain a sense of shared culture and solidarity. Differences among Latinos matter, but so does their perceived common position relative to mainstream institutions and their leaders. Latinos understand themselves in the United States as panethnic brothers and sisters with linked fates and common destinies at the same time that they identify strongly with their countries of origin. Ethnoraciality, again, allows this reality to be captured and thus studied and understood. Although elements of the evolution of Latino and Hispanic panethnicity may have been driven by lobbyists, government officials, and media executives as Mora (2014) helps us understand, what characterized all of these elite efforts to promote panethnicity was a common desire for inclusion into avenues of upward political, social, and economic mobility in the United States for large numbers of Latinos. These efforts are perhaps best understood not as manipulations to develop a false consciousness of panethnicity, but rather as manifestations of efforts to promote greater access and inclusion, a fundamental component of identity formation as understood through the lens of ethnoraciality.

Survey data further verifies this conclusion. The Latino National Survey in 2006 revealed that 65% of all adults of Latin American origin in the United States identify "very strongly" as Hispanic or Latino. In fact, 35% prefer the term Hispanic, 14% prefer Latino, and 51% have no preference between the two (Fraga et al., 2012, pp. 79–81). Additionally, when asked the specific question "In the U.S., we use a number of categories to describe ourselves racially. Do you feel that Latinos/Hispanics make up a distinctive racial group in America?" 52% of respondents said "yes." These percentages varied substantially by immigration and generational status: 37% of noncitizens answered yes to this question, 53% of naturalized citizens, and 74% of those respondents who were born in the United States (Fraga et al.,

2012, p. 82). Sizeable numbers of Latinos see themselves as a racial group, and the proportion increases substantially if a Latino is born in the United States. Ethnoraciality is a part of the lived identities of Latinos, especially for those who have lived most of their lives in the U.S. Recent research further corroborates these findings among Latino millennials, and Flores-González (2017) specifically finds that ancestry, skin color and phenotype, social class, education, gender, language, and aspects of culture factor into how respondents experience and navigate everyday racialization. Latino millennials are thus racialized through three major processes: "as an ethnorace, as a racial middle, and as not 'real' Americans—these youths remain outside of the boundaries of 'America'" (Flores-González, 2017, p. 7). Acknowledging citizenship without identifying as "American" has implications for everyday racialization processes, the ethnoracial hierarchy, and belonging.

Finally, we suggest that our analysis and discussion reveal that there is an undoubted complexity to ethnoracial group relations in the United States with regard to the diversity of Latino communities, but that complexity coexists with a clarity of their sense of panethnic identity. It may be the case that just as privilege and related access, such as in education, have always coexisted with sustained efforts to limit access and inclusion, so too does diversity within Latino communities coexist with a simultaneous sense of shared position as manifested in panethnic group identity. The framework of an ethnoracial hierarchy is analytically rich enough to allow these manifestations to exist simultaneously, and it keeps us focused on understanding the skewed distribution of power, privilege, status, opportunity, and resources in the United States.

NOTES

1. Although we use the term "Latino" throughout our chapter, "Hispanic" is the term used by the federal government to describe any persons from Latin America and other Spanish-speaking countries.

2. A full discussion of the data, constructed indices, and methodology is available from the authors.

Table 3.1. Strength of National Origin Identity, All Respondents

Variable	B	SE	Pr (min-max)
Americanness	-0.027	0.052	-0.01
Panethnic Identity	1.352***	0.055	0.29
Latino Diversity	-0.127	0.020	-0.01
Remittances	-0.035	0.019	-0.02
Transnational Contact	0.207***	0.033	0.07
Home Country Politics	0.154***	0.029	0.05
Latino Solidarity	0.353***	0.050	0.12
Inegalitarianism	-0.037	0.027	-0.01
Political Liberties	0.025	0.042	0.01
Self Reliance	0.068*	0.030	0.02
Latino Hard Work	0.138**	0.046	0.05
Home Ownership	-0.095	0.064	-0.01
Formal Education	0.024	0.019	0.02
Female	0.001	0.060	0
U.S. Citizen	0.653**	0.203	0.07
Naturalized Citizen	-0.728***	0.205	-0.08
Second Generation	-0.558**	0.208	-0.06
Third Generation	-0.963***	0.215	-0.11
Fourth Generation	-1.067***	0.218	-0.12
Latino Race	0.290***	0.065	0.03
Cultural Affinity	0.586***	0.080	0.20
Dependents	-0.043*	0.018	-0.08
Hispanic Household Density	<0.000*	<0.000	0.25
Percent Foreign-Born	0.202	0.118	0.07
Percent Puerto Rican	0.391	0.505	0.03
Percent Cuban	<0.000	<0.000	0.11
Percent Mexican	<0.000	<0.000	0.08
Percent Salvadoran	<0.000	<0.000	0.04
Percent Dominican	<0.000	<0.000	0.05
Percent Central American	0.125	0.084	0.12
Percent South American	0.084	0.061	0.08
Percent Black	-0.003	0.002	-0.04
Total N	5696		

*** $p \leq 0.001$, ** $p \leq 0.01$, * $p \leq 0.05$

Table 3.2. Strength of National Origin Identity, Foreign-Born

Variable	B	SE	Pr (min-max)
Americanness	-0.071	0.066	-0.01
Panethnic Identity	1.412***	0.075	0.30
Latino Diversity	-0.308*	0.132	-0.03
Remittances	-0.061*	0.024	-0.03
Transnational Contact	0.179***	0.046	0.06
Home Country Politics	0.176***	0.038	0.05
Latino Solidarity	0.164*	0.068	0.01
Inegalitarianism	-0.044	0.036	-0.01
Political Liberties	0.040	0.053	0.01
Self Reliance	0.094*	0.038	0.03
Latino Hard Work	0.207**	0.072	0.07
Home Ownership	0.040	0.091	0
Formal Education	0.021	0.024	0.01
Female	0.035	0.081	0
U.S. Citizen	-0.145	0.102	-0.01
Latino Race	0.297***	0.083	0.03
Cultural Affinity	0.499***	0.122	0.14
Dependents	-0.062*	0.026	-0.10
Hispanic Household Density	<0.000	<0.000	0.11
Percent Foreign-Born	0.404**	0.156	0.11
Percent Puerto Rican	0.738	0.754	0.05
Percent Cuban	<0.000	<0.000	0.03
Percent Mexican	<0.000	<0.000	0
Percent Salvadoran	<0.000	<0.000	0.01
Percent Dominican	<0.000	<0.000	0.01
Percent Central American	0.125	0.099	0.11
Percent South American	0.047	0.074	0.04
Percent Black	-0.007**	0.002	-0.08
Years in United States	-0.030	0.047	-0.01
Total N	3505		

*** $p \leq 0.001$, ** $p \leq 0.01$, * $p \leq 0.05$

Table 3.3. Strength of National Origin Identity, U.S.-Born

Variable	B	SE	Pr (min-max)
Americanness	0.051	0.093	0.01
Panethnic Identity	1.285***	0.087	0.27
Latino Diversity	0.120	0.158	0.01
Remittances	0.011	0.037	0.01
Transnational Contact	0.250***	0.051	0.09
Home Country Politics	0.097	0.05	0.03
Latino Solidarity	0.534***	0.081	0.19
Inegalitarianism	-0.034	0.045	0.01
Political Liberties	-0.017	0.077	-0.01
Self Reliance	0.032	0.051	0.01
Latino Hard Work	0.156**	0.066	0.06
Home Ownership	-0.306**	0.101	-0.04
Formal Education	0.013	0.033	0.01
Female	-0.113	0.096	-0.01
Second Generation	-0.474*	0.221	-0.06
Third Generation	-0.760**	0.234	-0.09
Fourth Generation	-0831***	0.238	-0.10
Latino Race	0.300**	0.110	0.04
Cultural Affinity	0.655***	0.114	0.23
Dependents	-0.021	0.028	-0.04
Hispanic Household Density	<0.000*	<0.000	0.32
Percent Foreign-Born	<0.073	0.204	0.03
Percent Puerto Rican	0.109	0.751	0.01
Percent Cuban	0.001*	<0.000	0.21
Percent Mexican	<0.000	<0.000	0.15
Percent Salvadoran	<0.000	0.001	0.01
Percent Dominican	<0.000	<0.000	0.09
Percent Central American	0.193	0.182	0.08
Percent South American	0.156	0.116	0.09
Percent Black	0.004	0.003	0.05
Total N	2013		

*** p ≤ 0.001, ** p ≤ 0.01, * p ≤ 0.05

REFERENCES

Alba, R. (1999). Immigration and the American realities of assimilation and multiculturalism. *Sociological Forum, 14*(1), 3–25.
Alcoff, L. M. (2000). Who's afraid of identity politics? In P. Moya & M. R. Hames-Garcia (Eds.), *Reclaiming identity: Realist theory and the predicament of postmodernism* (pp. 312–44). Oakland, CA: University of California Press.
Bonilla-Silva, E. (2004). From bi-racial to tri-racial: Towards a new system of racial stratification in the USA. *Ethnic and Racial Studies, 27*(6), 931–950.
Brown, H., & Jones, J. (2015). Rethinking panethnicity and the race-immigration divide. *Sociology of Race and Ethnicity, 1*(1), 181–191.
Cornell, S. E., & Hartmann, D. (1998). *Ethnicity and race: Making identities in a changing world*. Thousand Oaks, CA: Pine Forge Press.
de la Garza, R. O., DeSipio, L., Garcia, F. C., Garcia, J., & Falcon, A. (1992). *Latino voices: Mexican, Puerto Rican, and Cuban perspectives on American politics*. Boulder, CO: Westview Press.
Espiritu, Y. L. (2003). *Home bound: Filipino American lives across cultures, communities, and countries*. Berkeley, CA: University of California Press.
Flores-González, N. (2017). *Citizens but not Americans: Race and belonging among Latino millennials*. New York, NY: NYU Press.
Fordham, S., & Ogbu, J. U. (1986). Black students' school success: Coping with the burden of "acting white." *The Urban Review 18*(3), 176–206.
Fraga, L. R., Garcia, J. A., Hero, R. E., Jones-Correa, M., Martinez-Ebers, V., & Segura, G. M. (2006). *Latino National Survey* (LNS). ICPSR20862-v6. Ann Arbor, MI: Inter-university Consortium for Political and Social Research [distributor], 2013-06-05. doi.org/10.3886/ICPSR20862.v6.
Fraga, L. R., Garcia, J. A., Hero, R. E., Jones-Correa, M., Martinez-Ebers, V., & Segura., G. M. (2010). *Latino lives in America: Making it home*. Philadelphia, PA: Temple University Press.
Fraga, L. R., Garcia, J. A., Hero, R. E., Jones-Correa, M., Martinez-Ebers, V., & Segura, G. M. (2012). *Latinos in the new millennium: An almanac of opinion, behavior, and policy preferences*. New York, NY: Cambridge University Press.
Frederickson, G. M. (1988). *The arrogance of race: Historical perspectives on slavery, racism, and social inequality*. Middletown, CT: Wesleyan University Press.
Gleeson, S., & Gonzales, R. G. (2012). When do papers matter? An institutional analysis of undocumented life in the United States. *International Migration, 50*(4), 1–19.
Goldsmith, P. A. (2004). Schools' racial mix, students' optimism, and the Black-White and Latino-White achievement gaps. *Sociology of Education, 77*(2), 121–147.
Jencks, C., & Phillips, M. (Eds.). (2011). *The Black-White test score gap*. Washington, DC: Brookings Institution Press.
Jimenez, T. (2010). *Replenished ethnicity: Mexican Americans, immigration, and identity*. Berkeley, CA: University of California Press.
Kao, G., & Tienda, M. (1995). Optimism and achievement: The educational performance of immigrant youth. *Social Science Quarterly, 76*(1), 1–19.
Kim, C. (1999). The racial triangulation of Asian Americans. *Politics & Society, 27*(1), 105–138.

Lee, E. (2002). The Chinese Exclusion example: Race, immigration, and American gatekeeping, 1882–1924. *Journal of American Ethnic History, 21*(3), 36–62.

Lee, J., & Bean, F. D. (2004). America's changing color lines: Immigration, race/ethnicity, and multiracial identification. *Annual Review of Sociology, 30*, 221–242.

Lopez, D., & Espiritu, Y. (1990). Panethnicity in the United States: A theoretical framework. *Ethnic and Racial Studies, 13*(2), 198–224.

Madrid, E. M. (2011). The Latino achievement gap. *Multicultural Education, 19*(3), 7–12.

Mickelson, R. A. (1990). The attitude-achievement paradox among Black adolescents. *Sociology of Education, 63*(1), 44–61.

Mora, G. C. (2014). *Making Hispanics: How activists, bureaucrats and media constructed a new American*. Chicago, IL: University of Chicago Press.

Morning, A. (2011). *The nature of race: How scientists think and teach about human difference*. Berkeley, CA: University of California Press.

Nagel, J. (1994). Constructing ethnicity: Creating and recreating ethnic identity and culture. *Social Problems, 41*, 152–176.

Nagel, J. (1995). American Indian ethnic renewal: Politics and the resurgence of identity. *American Sociological Review, 60*, 947–965.

National Advisory Committee on Racial, Ethnic and Other Populations (2014). *2020 Census: Race and Hispanic origin working group final report*. Washington, DC: U.S. Census Bureau.

Neidert, L. J., & Farley, R. (1985). Assimilation in the United States: An analysis of ethnic and generation differences in status and achievement. *American Sociological Review, 50*(6), 840–850.

Ngai, M. (2004). *Impossible subjects: Illegal aliens and the making of modern America*. Princeton, NJ: Princeton University Press.

Ogbu, J. (1978). *Minority education and caste: The American system in crosscultural perspective*. New York, NY: Academic Press.

Okamoto, D. G. (2003). Toward a theory of panethnicity: Explaining Asian American collective action. *American Sociological Review, 68*(6), 811–842.

Perez, N. (2019). *At the crossroads of America: New Latino immigrants in Northern Indiana*. (Unpublished doctoral dissertation). University of Notre Dame, Notre Dame, IN.

Porter, J. N. (1974). Race, socialization and mobility in educational and early occupational attainment. *American Sociological Review, 39*(3), 303–316.

Portes, A., & Rumbaut, R. G. (2001). *Legacies: The story of the immigrant second generation*. Berkeley, CA: University of California Press.

Portes, A., & Wilson, K. L. (1976). Black-white differences in educational attainment. *American Sociological Review, 41*(3), 414–431.

Rodriguez, C. E. (2000). *Changing race: Latinos, the Census, and the history of ethnicity in the United States*. New York, NY: NYU Press.

Rumberger, R. W., & Larson, K. A. (1998). Toward explaining differences in educational achievement among Mexican American language-minority students. *Sociology of Education, 71*(1), 68–92.

Sanders, J. (2002). Ethnic boundaries and identity in plural societies. *Annual Review of Sociology, 28*, 327–57.

Telles, E. M., & Ortiz, V. (2008). *Generations of exclusion: Mexican-Americans, assimilation, and race.* New York: Russell Sage Foundation.

Velez, W. (1989). High school attrition among Hispanic and non-Hispanic white youths. *Sociology of Education, 62*(2), 119–133.

Waters, M. C. (1990). *Ethnic options: Choosing identities in America.* Berkeley, CA: University of California Press.

Yancey, G. A. (2003). *Who is White? Latinos, Asians, and the new Black/Nonblack divide.* Boulder, CO: Lynne Rienner.

CHAPTER 4

Panethnicity and Ethnic Heterogeneity

The Politics of Lumping and Disaggregating Asian Americans and Pacific Islanders in Educational Policy

Michael Omi, Mike Hoa Nguyen, and Jason Chan

On October 7, 2015, California Governor Jerry Brown vetoed Assembly Bill 176, legislation that would have required California public colleges and universities to collect and report detailed demographic information on Asian American and Pacific Islanders (AAPIs) by specific ethnic groups (e.g., Thai, Hmong, Bangladeshi, and Tongan). AB 176 had garnered strong political support prior to reaching the governor's desk. The bill passed unanimously in the state senate and drew just one dissenting vote in the assembly. The legislation had the overwhelming support of AAPI advocacy groups, who had long argued that more precise and detailed data was necessary to capture the diversity of the state's dramatically growing AAPI population. The practice of lumping disparate Asian ethnic groups under the racial category of "Asian," it was argued, prevented a fuller and more nuanced understanding of the socioeconomic status of different AAPI ethnic groups and hindered policy efforts to target specific needs, issues, and interests.

Such arguments and broad political support did not sway Governor Brown. In vetoing the bill, he argued, "I am wary of the ever growing desire to stratify. Dividing people into ethnic or other subcategories may yield more information, but not necessarily *greater wisdom* [emphasis added] about what actions should follow" (Brown, 2015). AAPI advocacy groups and their legislative supporters were shocked and dismayed by the substance and tone of the governor's veto letter. To some, his reasons for refusing to sign the bill into law seemed to resonate with the conservative critics of "identity politics" who have railed against what they claim is an unending expansion of group-specific categories for policy purposes. Regardless of what his motives might have been, Brown poses an important issue for reflection and consideration. What "greater wisdom" can be brought to bear on the issue of data disaggregation? What is gained and what is lost in policy and practice by disaggregating groups or, conversely, by lumping groups together?

In this chapter, we examine the politics of lumping and disaggregating the AAPI[1] groups for educational policy purposes. Our intent is to discern and deconstruct the political motives behind, and the policy implications of, lobbying for distinctive forms of racial/ethnic classification and data collection. The question of whether to aggregate or disaggregate AAPIs for educational policy purposes cannot be neatly framed and posed in a clear, binary manner. We argue that what is important is how the group categories themselves are understood, interpreted, contested, and redefined in specific political and legal contexts.

The use of different group categories is rooted in very different understandings of who AAPIs are, how they represent themselves, and how they are viewed and interpreted in the popular imagination. Lumping AAPIs together as a coherent racial category is reflective of two distinct forms of social representation. In one representation, AAPIs are tacitly assumed to constitute what Stacey Lee (1996) calls a "monolithic monotone" that conceals "ethnic, cultural, social-class, gender, language, sexual, generational, achievement, and other differences" (p. 6). Perhaps this is the most glaring and most often publicly discussed stereotype that AAPIs face—from casually expressed microaggressions about how all Asians "look alike" to deeper and more systemically ingrained beliefs that all AAPIs are "model minorities" who have achieved socioeconomic parity with Whites and who incur no social disadvantages by race. Lumping by race is also characteristic, from a very different vantage point, of panethnic identification and mobilization where AAPIs intentionally group themselves together to achieve social and political goals. More will be said about this.

In sharp contrast to perspectives that lump AAPIs together as a race, AAPIs can be socially constructed and represented as a diverse and heterogeneous group, with over 50 ethnic groups that include a plethora of distinct languages, cultures, immigration histories, and experiences. The problem of lumping by race, from this perspective, is that it ignores vast differences in socioeconomic status among AAPI groups. These differences manifest themselves in widely dissimilar Asian ethnic group profiles with respect to poverty rates, family income, educational attainment, and occupational distribution, among other social indicators.

These distinct representations and characterizations of the AAPI population can be understood as reflecting different conceptualizations by which the lives, experiences, and identities of AAPIs can be positioned for policy purposes. They need not be seen as irreconcilably in opposition to one another. They can potentially work in concert to provide a fuller portrait of the diversity and complexity that exists among AAPIs, as well as to help capture and situate the unique positioning of AAPIs in the broader patterns of racial stratification in the United States.

FRAMING THE ISSUE

In our discussion, we draw upon the theory of *racial formation* (Omi & Winant, 2014) to examine and interrogate the political claims advanced in the broader debate regarding appropriate racial/ethnic categories and the call for ethnic-specific data disaggregation. The theory of racial formation defines race as a sociohistorical process of "race making" and its impact throughout the social order. Racial categories and identities are neither static nor fixed, but are continually "created, lived out, transformed, and destroyed" (p. 109). Making race is often a process fraught with confusion, contradiction, and unintended consequences. Any definition of race can prove to be ephemeral as group boundaries shift, slippages occur, realignments become evident, and new collectivities emerge. State-based racial categories, as reflected in the census, are never stable and in recent decades have been subject to challenge by individuals and groups who contest existing categories, make claims for the recognition of new ones, or argue for ways to achieve more congruence and alignment between state definitions and individual/collective self-definitions (Espiritu & Omi, 2000).

Contestation over the definition and meaning of the categories themselves reflect different and competing *racial projects*. Omi and Winant (2014) define a racial project as "simultaneously an interpretation, representation, or explanation of racial identities and meanings, and an effort to organize and distribute resources (economic, political, cultural) along particular racial lines" (p. 125). Competing racial projects link structure and signification "not only in order to shape policy or exercise political influence, but also to organize our understanding of race as everyday 'common sense'" (Omi & Winant, 2014, p. 126).

Racial projects are evident in the varied ways the Asian American and Pacific Islander communities have negotiated questions of identity, specifically through the interrelated phenomena of *panethnicity* and *ethnoracialization*. Espiritu (1992) defines panethnicity as "the development of bridging organizations and solidarities among several ethnic and immigrant groups" (p. 14). Lumping by race, from this perspective, is shaped by the dominant racialization of AAPI ethnic groups from "above" and by AAPI responses from "below" to these racial representations. Espiritu argues that by "adopting the dominant group's categorization of them, Asian Americans have institutionalized pan-Asianism as their political instrument, thereby enlarging their own capacities to challenge and transform the existing structure of power" (Espiritu, 2008, p. 120).

Brown and Jones's (2015) concept of *ethnoracialization*, like panethnicity, refers to the dynamic process in which racial and ethnic identities change over time, and through forces both external and internal to the racial and ethnic communities being examined. Ethnoracialization considers ascription by others into a racial/ethnic category (i.e., census classification of "Asian American" or "Pacific Islander") and racial/ethnic self-identification (i.e., individual or group claims of an "Asian American" or "Pacific Islander" identity) as not sequential processes, but "mutually constitutive" (Brown & Jones, 2015, p. 186). In other words, both processes occur simultaneously and in relation to one another. Such a perspective is particularly relevant to the AAPI experience, as it allows us to capture in a dynamic fashion the emergence of regional subgroup identities (e.g., Southeast Asian, South Asian, Pacific Islander) that are distinct yet still a part of a broader social and political category of AAPIs.

Considered together, the concepts outlined above provide a framework by which to examine how AAPIs have strategically positioned themselves—while simultaneously navigating being positioned—within specific categories for political purposes. The decision to argue for an AAPI panethnic or ethnic-specific category cannot be advanced in the abstract outside of a particular policy context. It is also crucial to realize that these categories can be advanced in different contexts to suit widely different political claims and agendas. Key here is the concept of *rearticulation* that Omi and Winant (2014) define as "a practice of discursive reorganization or reinterpretation of ideological themes and interests . . . such that these elements obtain new meanings or coherence" (p. 165). Decisions to pursue AAPI panethnic or disaggregated categories for policy and data collection are continually subject to rearticulation by different political interests. Individuals and groups are making claims for specific forms of recognition that often are not simply reducible to, nor intelligible as, solely panethnic or group-specific identities and categories. Both forms of classification can be articulated and rearticulated to suit particular data needs and policy objectives. Again, what is important to observe and emphasize is how the categories themselves are understood, interpreted, contested, and redefined in specific political and legal contexts.

PANETHNICITY: LUMPING BY RACE

It can be argued that prior to the late 1960s, there were no "Asian Americans." Inspired by the civil rights and Black Power movements, distinct Asian ethnic groups—primarily Chinese, Japanese, Filipino, and Korean Americans—began to frame and assert their common identity as *Asian Americans*. The advancement of this social and political label reflected similar historical experiences of exclusionary immigration laws, restrictive naturalization rights, residential segregation, and economic discrimination that these groups encountered and shared. The racialization of Asian Americans involved muting the profound cultural and linguistic differences and minimizing the significant historical antagonisms that had existed among the distinct nationalities and ethnic groups of Asian origin. While acknowledging this diversity, Asian American activists found this political label a crucial rallying point for raising political consciousness about social problems, for creating coalitional efforts, and for asserting demands for recognition and resources from state institutions.

Espiritu (1992) argues that social factors as well as changing demographics after World War II played an important role in setting the stage for future coalition building by Americans with Asian heritage. Growth in population, the emergence of a second generation, as well as movements in and out of ethnic enclaves (in a cross-ethnic fashion) all contributed to Asian American panethnicity.[2] Although there were multiple arenas where panethnic solidarity and organizing emerged, college campuses were "ground zero" because inter-Asian interaction and communication were most pronounced at this site (Wong, 1972).

Panethnic identity and organization have always been contingent and contextually and strategically determined. Different Asian American ethnic groups have found that there are times when it is advantageous to be in a panethnic AAPI bloc, and times when it is more suitable to mobilize along specific ethnic group lines. In addition, the influx of new AAPI immigrant and refugee groups have made it increasingly difficult to speak of a "shared" historical experience and contemporary situation.[3] Distinct socioeconomic profiles, political attitudes, and residential patterns, among other variables, increasingly render a coherent notion of AAPI as a "community" problematic.

Espiritu (2008) observes that the challenge going forward "will be to identify and articulate shared interests and ideology within the socially and economically diverse Asian American community that can serve as the basis for pan-Asian identification and mobilization" (p. 136). But how are interests and issues defined as panethnic ones? How do individuals or collectivities define and take up a cause as panethnic, and who is included and excluded in this process? Inherent in panethnicity is a tension among and between ethnic groups, resulting from differences in socioeconomic status, culture, values, or political ideology. How might we engage this heterogeneity and its meaning for educational policy?

HETEROGENEITY AND DATA DISAGGREGATION

The formation of Asian American, Pacific Islander, and AAPI identities served strategic social and political purposes for ethnic groups facing similar experiences of racial oppression and discrimination by U.S. society. Over time, however, as these panethnic identities became codified in policies and constructed through social practices, the unique dimensions of individual ethnic groups' experiences have been rendered indistinct. Compounded by racial projects like the model minority myth (Lee, 2006; Museus & Kiang, 2009), a singular understanding of the AAPI experience has come to dominate public consciousness (Nakanishi & Yamano, 1995). The concept of the "model minority" undergirds the "notion that AAPIs achieve universal and unparalleled academic and occupational success" (Museus & Kiang, 2009, p. 6; Ngo & Lee, 2007), and politically serves to sustain anti-Black racism and White supremacy (Poon et al., 2016).

This monolithic definition has significant social and political implications for many within the AAPI population, particularly those whose experiences and needs are not captured by conventional understandings of the AAPI experience. Within the education realm, for example, it is commonly assumed and frequently reported that AAPIs have the highest levels of academic performance and educational attainment of all racial groups (see Pew Research Center, 2012). The prevailing popular belief is that AAPIs are "attending only the most selective four-year colleges and institutions and facing no challenges in attaining degrees" (Teranishi & Nguyen, 2012, p. 18). However, not all ethnic groups demonstrate the same levels of educational access and achievement; certain Southeast Asian and Pacific Islander communities, for example, are less likely to attend college and earn a bachelor's degree than their East Asian peers (National Commission on Asian American and Pacific Islander Research in Education [CARE], 2013; Ngo & Lee, 2007). This same phenomenon exists in data on income, employment, housing, health, and numerous other social and economic indicators (Asian Americans for Advancing Justice, 2011; Empowering Pacific Islander Communities & Asian Americans Advancing Justice, 2014), with AAPI ethnic groups representing a wide spectrum of experiences.

In response to this challenge of (mis)representation, AAPI community leaders, researchers, and policymakers have called for the disaggregation of data collected on the AAPI population, to more accurately reflect the heterogeneity of this population. These efforts, which have long been priorities for government and community leaders at both the local and national level, have recently been catalyzed by several key initiatives. In 2013, the National Commission on Asian American and Pacific Islander Research in Education (CARE), in conjunction with the White House Initiative on AAPIs (WHIAA-PI), launched iCount, a data disaggregation project that raises awareness of the "need for and benefits of collecting and reporting disaggregated data ... [and] implementing methods for collecting data that reflects the heterogeneity in the AAPI population" (National Commission on Asian American and Pacific Islander Research in Education, n.d.). Working in partnership with higher education institutions and federal and state agencies, iCount seeks to address and tackle existing disparities across AAPI ethnic groups by reforming the ways in which AAPI population data is collected and utilized. For example, iCount has successfully partnered with key leaders in the state of Washington to analyze disaggregated AAPI educational data, in order to better inform the development of educational policies and practices that support vulnerable AAPI student populations (CARE, 2015). Similar initiatives are underway in other regions of the United States and the Pacific Islands.

The efforts of iCount are part of a broader and decades-long movement regarding the heterogeneity of AAPIs, which is rooted in activism, advocacy, and legal battles. For example, in 1983, the San Francisco Unified School District (SFUSD) was subject to a court-ordered consent decree that grew out of litigation initiated by the NAACP to desegregate San Francisco's public schools. The consent decree disaggregated Asian Americans into four ethnic groups: Chinese, Japanese, Korean, and Filipino. Related, the *Ho v. SFUSD* lawsuit filed a decade later in 1994 argued that Chinese students were subject to a racial quota system that created differential admission requirements as they were "required to score a minimum of 66 out of a possible 69, while applicants who were Other White, Japanese, Korean, Filipino, American Indian, or Other Non-White were required to score only 59 and students who were Hispanic or African American were required to score 56" (cited in Robles, 2006, p. 41).

More recently, data disaggregation efforts focusing on educational disparities have gained traction at local, state, and national levels. In May 2016, AAPI grassroots and advocacy organizations secured passage and implementation of a data disaggregation resolution for the Oakland Unified School District that included categories (e.g., Tongan and Mien) not found on previous enrollment forms (AYPAL, 2016). Legislation mandating collection of disaggregated data has been introduced in cities like New York City (Ghosh, 2016) and states like California (Wang, 2016). Nationally, data disaggregation remains a top priority for the Congressional Asian Pacific American Caucus, where U.S. Congressman Mike Honda introduced legislation that would require state education agencies to collect and report disaggregated data "at the K–12 levels in annual state report cards, using the same race categories as the U.S. Census and including cross-tabulated data of student outcomes by gender and race/ethnicity. . . for better analysis of the experiences of all Asian Americans and Pacific Islanders" (Wang, 2014, para. 5). Furthermore, in May 2016, the federal Department of Education announced the creation of a $1 million grant designed to fund state and local initiatives that collect and evaluate disaggregated data on AAPIs, with the goal of identifying and funneling resources to underserved ethnic subgroups.

This increased recognition of the heterogeneity within the AAPI population is encouraging and has the potential to provide necessary resources to communities most in need. Supporters of such disaggregation efforts, however, must often walk a fine line between highlighting the diversity of the AAPI population and avoiding the fragmentation of AAPIs into disparate subgroups and rendering the very concept of an AAPI community problematic. This tension is manifest most tangibly in political contestation over specific policy initiatives and the interpretation of existing laws and practices, as the case studies in the following section illustrate.

CASE STUDIES

Although examples of the tension between the panethnicity and ethnic heterogeneity movements exist in the primary and secondary education sector, we choose to center our examination of these phenomena within the postsecondary educational realm, as both the panethnicity and ethnic heterogeneity movements were born out of AAPI activism on college campuses. This section thus details case studies in higher education where these binaries are opposed.

The first case study examines the movement for disaggregated data by focusing on two different initiatives: The University of California's Count Me In Campaign and California State Assembly Bill 176. The second case study looks at tensions that exists among AAPI groups regarding the practice of affirmative action. These case studies demonstrate how panethnicity and ethnic heterogeneity occur simultaneously and fuel each other to advance AAPI social and political initiatives, while providing a fuller portrait of the diversity and complexity that exists among AAPIs in the United States.

Case Study 1: Data Disaggregation Efforts

Due to its high concentrations of AAPI ethnic populations, California is often viewed as one of the states where AAPI data disaggregation efforts are the most advanced. And yet the majority of efforts in the state have been piecemeal and met with fierce opposition. Nonetheless, the uphill work to disaggregate educational data throughout California continues to be a top priority for AAPI advocacy groups and AAPI policymakers. The following section discusses two educational data disaggregation efforts in California: 1) the "Count Me In" campaign at the University of California, and 2) California State Assembly Bills 176 and 1726. These examples illustrate not only how AAPIs have chosen to position themselves as a panethnic social force at times and as a diverse set of ethnic groups at other times, but also the implications of these choices within the broader landscape of racial justice.

"Count Me In" Campaign at the University of California. In 2007, students at the University of California, Los Angeles (UCLA) engaged in a campaign to disaggregate AAPI student data. Led by the Asian Pacific Coalition, a student group comprised of students and campus leaders from different Asian American and Pacific Islander ethnic organizations at UCLA, the Count Me In campaign sought to address the lack of access to data on AAPI students' ethnic backgrounds. Because the larger University of California (UC) system lumped students of all AAPI ethnicities into a single racial category for data reporting purposes, administrative policy and general practice did not consider AAPI students to be underrepresented minorities. Southeast Asian and Pacific Islander students have long known that their numbers at UCLA were extremely low, but without access to disaggregated data there was little they could do to address and counter the misconception that they were not underrepresented on campus.

Having access to ethnic-specific data would allow Southeast Asian and Pacific Islander student organizations to more easily conduct targeted outreach, recruitment, and retention efforts to prospective and current students from similar ethnic backgrounds (e.g., Hmong students seeking out newly admitted Hmong students to join the Hmong Student Association), instead of manually reviewing student records from the Registrar's Office and identifying AAPI students' ethnicities by last name.

For better access to this information, as well as to urge the entire UC system to collect and utilize disaggregated data, AAPI students advocated for a change to the UC's policy on data collection for AAPI students. Through protests and rallies on campus, educational campaigns in classrooms and on social media, and coalitions with AAPI student organizations at other UC campuses, the Count Me In campaign caught the attention of students, faculty, and administrators across the UC system. They targeted their efforts towards Dr. Judy Sakaki, the then-newly appointed Vice President for Student Affairs for the entire UC system and one of the highest-ranking AAPI administrators within the UC Office of the President (UCOP), hoping that, as an Asian American, Sakaki would understand their issues and respond to their concerns. These efforts eventually paid off, as Sakaki announced at the end of 2017 that UC would begin collecting disaggregated data on AAPI students.

As CARE (2013) argued, the Count Me In campaign was an effort to rearticulate the meaning of race for AAPIs and, based on this new meaning, change the relationship of AAPI students with UC. In other words, this movement asserted the necessity for UC to understand AAPI students through not only a racial lens but also an ethnic one and, in doing so, move toward a more nuanced understanding of the utility of race and ethnicity in policy decisions. The campaign challenged the prevailing racialized view of AAPIs as a monolithic monotone, and through policy change, provided an alternative perspective that is inclusive of the diverse identities and experiences of AAPI ethnic groups. Without a doubt, the success of the Count Me In campaign came as a result of panethnic organizing by many different Asian American and Pacific Islander student groups across the UC system.

The name of the campaign, Count Me In, emphasized a simultaneous modality. AAPI students, as a panethnic coalition, shared the experience that they felt uncounted by UC. At the same time, students were working in coalition to demonstrate the heterogeneity of the AAPI community. In other words, students were strategically panethnic in order to successfully accomplish their goal of changing UC policy. Southeast Asian and Pacific Islander students in particular played a key role in the success of the campaign through their ability to demonstrate a panethnic AAPI identity while simultaneously calling attention to their invisibility within the AAPI racial category. Because their experiences are the ones most often lost within aggregated racial data (Krupnick, 2007; Lee, 2007; Mantle, 2016; Okamoto, 2007), it was the Southeast Asian and Pacific Islander students who were most vocal in the Count Me In campaign's arguments for data disaggregation.

The Count Me In campaign's victory, however, also highlights a critically important issue, which is the potential consequences of conducting data disaggregation efforts without incorporating a wider racial justice lens. As Poon, Dizon, and Squire (2017) described in their recounting of the campaign, the original impetus of the campaign was AAPI students' attempt to establish solidarity with the African American/Black students at UCLA, who were also calling attention to their extremely low representation on campus. As momentum for Count Me In grew, however, the broader focus on racial solidarity as a means of demanding racial equity from UCLA was replaced by a narrow emphasis on the educational disparities among AAPI ethnic groups (Poon et al., 2017). In other words, the push to illuminate the differences within the AAPI student community inadvertently overshadowed the experiences and efforts of the campus's Black student population. Thus, while UCLA (and the UC system), to a certain extent, now recognizes the diversity of the AAPI population through its data collection and reporting practices, racial equity and justice remain elusive on campus. Panethnicity and heterogeneity can be effective strategies for advocating for AAPI concerns, but when decoupled from larger racial justice issues, they can reinforce existing racial inequality for other communities of color.

California State Assembly Bills 176 and 1726. In 2015, California Assemblymember Rob Bonta authored AB 176, a bill that would require all three of California's higher public education systems not only to collect disaggregated data on their students in a uniform process, but also to release data and reports on an annual basis. The bill received little opposition in the California legislature, due to the intentional strategy of panethnic organizing among AAPI legislators and by AAPI advocacy organizations throughout California. However, as discussed in the introduction to this chapter, the bill was summarily vetoed by Governor Jerry Brown, who argued that AAPIs would lose their collective power if their data were disaggregated by ethnic ancestry. As Sacramento State Emeritus Professor of Communications

Barbara O'Connor contended, "I think [Governor Brown] really believes that minorities of all types are represented better when they're not stratified. Asians have more clout in Sacramento when they act as a caucus" (Shyong, 2015, para. 9). Such a perspective forces AAPIs into a binary: They must either be lumped together or, according to the perception of Governor Brown, needlessly divided. The extent of AAPI political clout in Sacramento seemed questionable given that non-AAPIs continued to dictate which choice would prevail in regards to educational data and public policy.

In 2016, Assemblymember Bonta introduced a second version of the bill: AB 1726. Also known as the Accounting for Health and Education in Asian Pacific Islander Demographics (AHEAD) Act, AB 1726 called for the collection and reporting of disaggregated AAPI data within state public health agencies and public educational institutions in California. AB 1726 would have facilitated the disaggregation of data on AAPI student admissions, enrollment, and graduation rates for the entire University of California, California State University, and California Community College systems.

Once again, a panethnic group of AAPI organizations at the local, state, and national level—led by the Southeast Asia Resource Action Center (SEARAC), the Asian & Pacific Islander American Health Forum, and Empowering Pacific Islander Communities (EPIC)—collectively intensified their lobbying and educational efforts to ensure that this legislation was signed into law (California State Assembly, n.d.). Proponents of AB 1726 argued that data disaggregation creates an inclusive AAPI community where all voices are heard and counted. As Assemblymember Bonta (2016) noted:

> [T]he Act is all about inclusion. By requiring that data be gathered regarding communities that have previously been rendered invisible, we will reveal hidden facts that could make our state and communities even stronger. The bill is supported by a broad, diverse and unified group of over 200 organizations representing the beautiful ethnic diversity of California. If you value the voices of every Californian and want accurate, inclusive data to ensure that those voices are counted, please stand with me! (para. 1–4).

Interestingly, AB 1726 did not enjoy full support from the entire AAPI community, a fact that underscores how the issue of disaggregation can be subject to rearticulation from different political perspectives. A number of AAPI individuals and groups largely comprised of conservative, wealthy Chinese immigrants (see Zhang, 2018, for a detailed discussion of this population's emerging political influence) organized in fierce opposition to AB 1726, claiming the bill to be racist against AAPIs in both its exclusive targeting of Asian Americans and its perceived intent to unnecessarily divide the AAPI community (Fuchs, 2016). Opponents of the bill even went as far as contending that data disaggregation was a gateway to racial profiling, and that the ability to single out specific ethnic groups would lead to events similar to the Chinese Exclusion Act or Japanese American incarceration during World War II (Fuchs, 2016). These arguments contributed to a different type of panethnic movement, one in which different AAPI groups came together to advocate for the homogenization—instead of the differentiation—of the AAPI community. This movement generated enough opposition to remove the educational provisions of AB 1726, leaving only public health–related data subject to disaggregation. Ultimately, and largely due to the panethnic advocacy efforts of the bill's supporters, the amended version of AB 1726 passed almost unanimously in both houses of the state legislature and was officially signed by Governor Brown in late September of 2016. Although the reasoning behind why Governor Brown approved AB 1726, compared to AB 176, remains unclear, AAPI legislators and panethnic organizers did redouble their efforts to lobby Brown.

AAPIs, as they have done in the past, continue to use panethnic organizing as "a symbol of pride and rallying point for mass mobilization" (Espiritu, 1992, p. 20) to achieve civil rights and public policy changes. However, when the goal or outcome is data disaggregation, AAPI panethnic movements must not only acknowledge the heterogeneity among AAPI ethnic groups and successfully articulate these differences to outsiders, but simultaneously be mindful of how AAPIs position themselves, and are positioned, within society's larger racial landscape. These dynamics are prominently at play in the area of affirmative action, where tensions have bubbled within the AAPI community over whom affirmative action programs are intended to serve and for what purpose. Both panethnicity and heterogeneity are central themes in this affirmative action debate, which we turn to next.

Case Study 2: Affirmative Action

The debate over affirmative action within higher education has long polarized the AAPI community. From the controversy over AAPI admissions at selective institutions during the 1980s (Takagi, 1993) and the passage of California's Proposition 209 in 1996 (Wu, 2002), to more contemporary discourse surrounding California's Senate Constitutional Amendment No. 5 (SCA-5; Fang, 2014), *Fisher vs. University of Texas* Supreme Court cases (Joshi, 2016), and the current lawsuits from Asian American plaintiffs against Harvard University, the AAPI population has championed multiple and often divergent stances on this contentious issue over the years. Representations of AAPIs are deeply embedded in the broader debate between supporters and opponents of affirmative action. In a study of the dominant racial narratives that are evoked in opposing sets of legal briefs in the *Fisher v. University of Texas* case, Chang (2015) observes that both sides rely on enduring cultural representations of Asian Americans as either a "model minority" or as a "yellow peril." He warns that unless Asian Americans and others concerned with advancing racial equity and justice dislodge these prevailing cultural tropes, "they will increasingly weaken their own collective capacity to shape the future of civil rights" (p. 146).

How have issues of panethnicity and heterogeneity been evoked in the broader debate? On one hand, there is a broad conceptualization that explicitly acknowledges the diversity of the population with regard to ethnicity, class, and experiences of racialization in the United States. On the other hand, there is a narrow definition that almost exclusively centers on a particular segment of the population, typically upper-middle-class, professional, Indian and Chinese Americans, and in some cases, Vietnamese Americans. Although representing different perspectives of what the term "Asian American" entails, each side of the affirmative action debate has invoked concepts of panethnicity and heterogeneity in their arguments, albeit in distinct ways and for distinct purposes.

Positions Utilized by Opponents of Affirmative Action. Opponents of affirmative action have used both panethnicity and heterogeneity, in some instances simultaneously, to defend their position against race-conscious admissions. Opponents frame Asian Americans through an individualistic, rather than ethnic-group, perspective. In other words, emphasis is on how the AAPI community is comprised of individuals with diverse interests and talents, rather than ethnic groups with different experiences of immigration, racialization, and oppression. For example, in their complaint against several elite universities' admissions practices, the Asian American Coalition for Education (AACE, 2016) expressed the following:

> [I]gnoring the diverse background of Asian-American applicants, admissions officers . . . often treat Asian-American applicants as a monolithic block rather than as individuals . . . The racial stereotypes that are applied to Asian-American applicants are patently false and are contradicted by the achievements of Asian-Americans in many diverse fields—12 Nobel laureates, many scientists and innovators, artists and designers, world-class musicians and performers, and entrepreneurs and business leaders. (p. 1)

The language put forth by this side of the debate also incorporates the notion of a panethnic AAPI identity, often mentioning common immigrant experiences and encounters with historical racism. AACE references the Chinese Exclusion Act of 1882 and the relocation and incarceration of Japanese Americans during World War II as examples of discriminatory acts taken against Asian Americans (AACE, 2015), in an attempt to portray a shared experience among the AAPI community. However, the purpose and effect of this argument is to homogenize the AAPI community, rather than to advocate for a panethnic identity representative of the diversity of experiences among the population. Recognition of the distinct experiences of Southeast Asian and Pacific Islander communities, for example, is notably absent from AACE's platform and advocacy efforts.

80-20 National Asian American PAC (80-20) is another organization that has played a significant role in the affirmative action debate. 80-20's advocacy approach also relies on panethnicity to defend their case against affirmative action. 80-20 (2018a) identifies itself as a "national, nonpartisan, Political Action Committee dedicated to winning equal opportunity and justice for all Asian Americans through a SWING bloc vote" (para. 1), and insists on their panethnic mission because "all laws and court decisions (for example regarding college admissions, equal opportunity and justice) apply equally to all Asian Americans. Therefore, all Asian Americans equally benefit from the activities of 80-20 Initiative" (80-20, 2018b, para. 4). In their amicus brief in the *Fisher* case, they state that 80-20 "speaks for the Asian American community with authority," and throughout their brief, Asian Americans are referred to as a single entity of victims, both historically and presently, of systematic discrimination. As Chang (2015) argues, in order to do this, 80-20 represents Asian Americans as a highly successful monolith that "must have significantly stronger high school records and test scores than other applications in order to gain admission to elite colleges" (p. 138). In other words, the manner in which 80-20 represents Asian Americans is not panethnic, but instead is a monolithic monotone that relies on the stereotype of all Asian Americans as a model minority.

In a similar vein, Asian Americans are also positioned as monolithic and heterogenetic by Students for Fair Admissions (SFFA), who have an active stake in affirmative action lawsuits before the federal courts. SFFA's (n.d.) "mission is to support and participate in litigation that will restore the original principles of our nation's civil rights movement: *A student's race and ethnicity should not be factors that either harm or help that student to gain admission to a competitive university* [emphasis in original]" (para. 1). More recently, SFFA has shifted its approach and recruited only Asian Americans as plaintiffs in its lawsuit against Harvard University. In an interview, SFFA's head, Edward Blum, was quick to note the heterogeneity of his coalition of "Asians"—the plaintiffs are "children of immigrant Chinese, children of first generation Korean and Vietnamese, and they have superlative academic records, I mean just startling so, perfect GPAs, perfect SATs and ACTs, active in sports, lots of volunteer efforts" (Abumrad, 2017).[4] Yet, in the same breath, Blum transforms his heterogenetic argument, by positioning Asian Americans as a monolithic model minority, who outperform all other students across all metrics. This overt usage of both heterogeneity and monolith, couched superficially as panethnicity, represents how opponents of affirmative action exploit both concepts simultaneously.

Positions Utilized by Proponents of Affirmative Action. On the other hand, proponents of affirmative action also utilize concepts of panethnicity and heterogeneity in arguing and organizing in favor of race-conscious admissions. For example, they often cite the heterogeneity of the AAPI population to argue that certain ethnic groups are disproportionately disadvantaged in the educational system. Specifically, Asian American Civil Rights (asianamericancivilrights.org), which advocates for the preservation of affirmative action, states: "Students of color, particularly African Americans, Latinos, Native Americans, *Pacific Islanders*, and *Southeast Asians*, are much more likely to attend under-resourced K–12 schools [emphasis added]" (Asian American Civil Rights, n.d.). The site builds upon this point to argue that affirmative action is beneficial for the AAPI community. While the main arguments of this side of the affirmative action debate rest on the premise of disaggregation, the building of panethnic coalitions has been central to their organizing strategy. The list of over 150 supporters includes both pan-Asian organizations (e.g., Asian American Legal Defense and Education Fund, Asian Pacific Americans for Progress) and ethnic-specific organizations (e.g., Filipino Migrant Center, Khmer Girls in Action, Pacific Islander Health Partnership).

In a similar manner, Asian Americans Advancing Justice (AAAJ) also emphasizes their panethnic coalitions to showcase how they reflect a broader alliance of AAPI ethnic groups in their efforts to defend race-conscious admissions. AAAJ (2011) states that its mission is to "promote a fair and equitable society for all by working for civil and human rights and empowering Asian Americans and Pacific Islanders ('AAPIs') and other underserved communities" (p. 1). AAAJ evokes panethnicity by arguing in their amicus brief in support of the University of Texas that affirmative action has supported and increased college access for AAPIs who have faced longstanding racial prejudice. At the same time, they also utilize heterogeneity by contending that specific AAPI subgroups require race-conscious admissions in order to promote their college access and student success. Thus, by addressing the common and problematic misconception that AAPIs are model minorities, one of AAAJ's primary arguments utilizes disaggregated AAPI data to show disparities in the educational experiences and outcomes on issues regarding school segregation, inadequate college preparation, college completion, and overall levels of attainment. In order to demonstrate support for their arguments, AAAJ lists a panethnic alliance of over 150 AAPI organizations as cosponsors of their amici brief. These organizations include pan-AAPI–focused groups (e.g., Asian Law Alliance, Association of Asian Pacific Community Health Organizations), subgroup/regional focused groups (e.g., Southeast Asian Coalition, South Asian Network), and ethnic-specific groups (e.g., Taulama for Tongans, Pilipino Workers' Center, Koreatown Immigrant Workers Alliance).

Unlike opponents of affirmative action, its proponents strategically deploy a concept of panethnicity that is not only more aligned with academic definitions of the term, but also with how AAPI groups have historically organized themselves in social movements that include a wider and more representative coalition of AAPIs (Espiritu, 1992). While both sides draw upon the concept of heterogeneity to advance their positions, proponents refer to the diversity within the AAPI population in order to underscore the disparities that exist for marginalized groups such as Southeast Asian and Pacific Islander students. Meanwhile, opponents utilize heterogeneity to perpetuate the model minority stereotype by cherry-picking evidence that AAPIs of different ethnicities experience the same discriminatory treatment.

The discourse over affirmative action offers an illustrative example of both the benefits and challenges that come from utilizing concepts of panethnicity and heterogeneity in conjunction with each other. Arguments in support of or in opposition to specific educational policies draw upon both concepts to define the issue and state their claims. As fluid concepts, panethnicity and heterogeneity are both subject to rearticulation to advance different interests of the AAPI population.

CONCLUSION

The case studies presented illustrate how groups strategically utilize and deploy specific understandings of the AAPI category to advance social and political initiatives. Their claims regarding the importance and utility of panethnic or disaggregated group categories can be seen as "racial projects." These projects advance claims for specific forms of recognition to suit particular data needs and policy objectives. As we have seen, what's important is how the categories themselves are understood, interpreted, contested, and redefined in specific political and legal contexts.

And context is indeed crucial. There is no inherent political meaning—as liberal or conservative, as progressive or regressive—behind the recognition and use of disaggregated categories. Any claim can be subject to rearticulation to serve very different political agendas. If we are not cautious about how notions of panethnicity and ethnic heterogeneity are embedded and advanced in specific policy claims and objectives, issues may be coopted in ways that undermine and subvert the goal of educational equity for not only AAPIs, but all communities of color as well.

A recent example is sobering and instructive. Justice Samuel Alito, in his minority opinion for *Fisher II*, declared that because "students labeled [as] 'Asian American,' seemingly include 'individuals of Chinese, Japanese, Korean, Vietnamese, Cambodian, Hmong, Indian and other backgrounds' . . . . It would be ludicrous to suggest that all of these students have similar backgrounds and similar ideas and experiences to share. So why has UT lumped them together and concluded that it is appropriate to discriminate against Asian-American students because they are 'overrepresented' in the UT student body?" (*Fisher v. University of Texas*, 2016, pp. 26–27). While Justice Alito's critique of the panethnic category of "Asian Americans" appears to be calling for data disaggregation and the recognition of distinct subgroups to create a more diverse and inclusive admissions policy, in actuality he is using the heterogeneity of AAPIs in order to critique and challenge the continued use of racial and ethnic categories altogether. Any forms of racial and ethnic classification in his eyes are illegitimate and suspect. Justice Alito contends that the University of Texas utilizes "crude, overly simplistic, racial and ethnic categories" and rejects their use to create both "favored" and "disfavored" groups for admissions purposes (p. 26).

A dramatically different take on the use of disaggregated categories is evident in the All Students Count Act passed by the Rhode Island House of Representatives in June 2017. This legislation requires the state's Department of Elementary and Secondary Education to collect data on specific groups including Cambodian, Filipino, and Vietnamese (Yam, 2017). Previously, students from different Asian subgroups were lumped together under the Asian and Pacific Islander category. Data disaggregation in this instance will assist educational policymakers and AAPI advocacy groups to assess and grapple with the differences in educational access, resources, and outcomes that are experienced by distinct AAPI subgroups.

Given that the call for AAPI data disaggregation can be susceptible to rearticulation to suit very different political and policy agendas, what can we conclude? What "greater wisdom," to evoke California Governor Brown's phrase, can be brought to bear on the issue? In the end, we believe that the litmus test to evaluate calls for the use of AAPI disaggregated categories and data will be whether their use hinders or advances the broader goal of achieving racial equity in educational settings.

NOTES

1. Scholars, practitioners, and policymakers often use different terminology when referring to Asian Americans and Pacific Islanders (AAPI). In this chapter, we aim to be straightforward and succinct when referring to those who would identify or be categorized as AAPIs by the current census. Thus, we define Asian American as any individuals who would identify with the ethnic categories that make up this racial group in the U.S. Census. Similarly, we define Pacific Islander as referring to all those who identify with the ethnic categories of the Pacific Islander racial group in the U.S. Census. Asian American and Pacific Islander (AAPI) refers to individuals from both categories.

2. Admittedly, what is noticeably absent is attention and scholarship that examines the important role of Pacific Islanders in panethnic movements. Nonetheless, limited scholarship does exist on Pacific Islander panethnicity (e.g., Aoki & Nakanishi, 2001; Espiritu 1992; McGavin, 2014).

3. More recently, scholars have begun studying subgroup or regional panethnicity within the AAPI community (e.g., Museus, Nguyen, Vue, & Yeung, 2013), which at the moment appears to be a phenomenon unique to AAPIs. For example, a Southeast Asian panethnic identity has emerged and advanced to a point where college student groups, community agencies, and national advocacy organizations

geared toward advancing the priorities of those who identify as Southeast Asian are commonplace. Southeast Asians, typically understood as those who identify as Hmong, Laotian, Cambodian, and Vietnamese, share a similar refugee history.

4. Blum notes in this interview that a federal judge has placed under seal the identities and number of Asian American plaintiffs that are suing Harvard University.

REFERENCES

80-20 National Asian American PAC. (2018a). *Mission*. Retrieved from www.80-20initiative.net/

80-20 National Asian American PAC. (2018b). *Who is an Asian American?* Retrieved from www.80-20initiative.net/about/who-is-an-asian-american.asp

Abumrad, J. (Host). (2017, December 6). *The Architect*. [Audio podcast]. Retrieved from www.wnycstudios.org/story/architect-edward-blum

Aoki, A., & Nakanishi, D. (2001). Asian Pacific Americans and the new minority politics. *PS: Political Science and Politics, 34*(3), 605–610.

Asian American Civil Rights. (n.d.). Overview. Retrieved from asianamericancivilrights.org/overview

Asian American Coalition for Education (AACE). (2015). Discrimination in college admissions. Retrieved from asianamericanforeducation.org/en/issue/discrimination-on-admissions

Asian American Coalition for Education. (2016). *Executive summary: Complaint of the Asian American Coalition for Education v. Yale University, Brown University, and Dartmouth College*. Livingston, NJ: Author.

Asian Americans for Advancing Justice (2011). *A community of contrasts: Asian Americans in the United States: 2011*. Washington, DC: Author.

AYPAL. (2016). *We passed a historic data resolution!* Retrieved from aypal.org/2019/01/we-passed-a-historical-data-resolution/

Bonta, R. (2016, August 10). *Facebook post*. Retrieved from www.facebook.com/RobBontaCA/posts/1160790104005507:0

Brief of Amici Curiae Members of Asian Americans for Advancing Justice et al., in Support of Respondents, *Fisher v. University of Texas*, 579 U.S. ___ (2016). Retrieved from www.advancingjustice-alc.org/wp-content/uploads/2015/11/Fisher-final-14-981-bsac-AAAJ.pdf

Brown, E. G. (2015). *Assembly Bill 176 Veto Message*. Retrieved from www.ca.gov/archive/gov39/wp-content/uploads/2017/09/AB_176_Veto_Message.pdf

Brown, H., & Jones, J. A. (2015). Rethinking panethnicity and the race-immigration divide: An ethnoracialization model of group formation. *Sociology of Race and Ethnicity, 1*(1), 181–191.

California State Assembly. (n.d.). AB 1726 (Bonta) [fact sheet]. Accounting for Health and Education in API Demographics, The AHEAD Act. Sacramento, CA: Author.

Chang, M. J. (2015). Amplifying Asian American presence: Contending with dominant racial narratives in *Fisher*. In U. M. Jayakumar & L. M. Garces (Eds.), *Affirmative action and racial equity: Considering the Fisher case to forge the path ahead* (pp. 130–149). New York, NY: Routledge.

Empowering Pacific Islander Communities & Asian Americans Advancing Justice (2014). *A community of contrasts: Native Hawaiians and Pacific Islanders in the United States.* Los Angeles, CA: Authors.

Espiritu, Y. (1992). *Asian American panethnicity: Bridging institutions and identities.* Philadelphia, PA: Temple University Press.

Espiritu, Y. (2008). Asian American panethnicity: Challenges and possibilities. In Paul M. Ong (Ed.), *The State of Asian America: Trajectory of Civic and Political Engagement* (pp. 119–136). Los Angeles, CA: LEAP, Asian Pacific American Public Policy Institute.

Espiritu, Y., & Omi, M. (2000). Who are you calling Asian? Shifting identity claims, racial classification, and the Census. In P. M. Ong (Ed.), *Transforming Race Relations* (pp. 43–101). Los Angeles, CA: LEAP, Asian Pacific American Institute, and UCLA Asian American Center.

Fang, J. (2014, September 27). Majority of AAPI voters in CA support affirmative action — so, who are the ones that don't? [Blog post]. Retrieved from reappropriate.co/2014/09/majority-of-aapi-voters-in-ca-support-affirmative-action-so-who-are-the-ones-that-dont/

Fisher v. University of Texas, 579 U. S. ___ (2016) (Alito, S., dissenting).

Fuchs, C. (2016, August 26). California data disaggregation bill sparks debate in Asian-American community. *NBC News.* Retrieved from www.nbcnews.com/news/asian-america/california-data-disaggregation-bill-sparks-debate-asian-american-community-n638286

Ghosh, A. (2016, February 13). Asian Americans rally to support key data equity bills. *The Universal News Network.* Retrieved from theunn.com/2016/02/asian-americans-rally-to-support-key-data-equity-bills/

Joshi, H. (2016, May 13). Stop anti-Asian bias. *Inside Higher Education.* Retrieved from www.insidehighered.com/views/2016/05/13/elite-colleges-should-not-penalize-asian-applicants-essay

Krupnick, M. (2007, November 20). UC gets strong response to Asian 'Count Me In' campaign. *East Bay Times.* Retrieved from www.eastbaytimes.com/oaklandtribune/localnews/ci_7517823

Lee, C. (2007, December 11). Students: 'Count me in!' *UCLA Newsroom.* Retrieved from: newsroom.ucla.edu/stories/071211_ethnic-identities

Lee, S. J. (1996). *Unraveling the "model minority" stereotype: Listening to Asian American youth.* New York, NY: Teachers College Press.

Lee, S. S. (2006). Over-represented and de-minoritized: The racialization of Asian Americans in higher education. *InterActions: UCLA Journal of Education and Information Studies, 2*(2), Article 4.

Mantle, L. (2016, August 19). State bill to expand definition of 'Asian American' draws ire, praise. *AirTalk.* Los Angeles, CA: South California Public Radio KPCC. Retrieved from www.scpr.org/programs/airtalk/2016/08/19/51424/state-bill-to-expand-definition-of-asian-american/

McGavin, K. (2014). Being "nesian": Pacific Islander identity in Australia. *The Contemporary Pacific, 26*(1), 126–154.

Museus, S. D., & Kiang, P. N. (2009). Deconstructing the model minority myth and how it contributes to the invisible minority reality in higher education research. *New Directions for Institutional Research, 142,* 5–15. doi.org:10.1002/ir.292

Museus, S. D., Nguyen, T. K., Vue, R., & Yeung, F. (2013). A model of Southeast Asian American identity development: Merging theoretical perspectives. In S.

D. Museus, D. C. Maramba, & R. T. Teranishi (Eds.), *The misrepresented minority: New insights on Asian Americans and Pacific Islanders, and the implications for higher education* (pp. 47–66). Sterling, VA: Stylus.

Nakanishi, D., & Yamano, T. (Eds.). (1995). *The Asian American educational experience: A sourcebook for teachers and students.* New York, NY: Routledge.

National Commission on Asian American and Pacific Islander Research in Education (CARE) (2013). *iCount: A data quality movement for Asian Americans and Pacific Islanders in higher education.* New York, NY: Author.

National Commission on Asian American and Pacific Islander Research in Education (CARE) (2015). *The hidden academic opportunity gaps among Asian Americans and Pacific Islanders: What disaggregated data reveals in Washington State.* Los Angeles, CA: Author.

National Commission on Asian American and Pacific Islander Research in Education (CARE) (n.d.). *iCount: Equity through representation.* Retrieved from care.gseis.ucla.edu/icount-

Ngo, B., & Lee, S. J. (2007). Complicating the image of model minority success: A review of Southeast Asian American education. *Review of Educational Research*, 77(4), 415–453.

Okamoto, M. (2007, May 17). *Count me in.* [Video] Retrieved from www.youtube.com/watch?v=Qen8GWQZ3to

Omi, M. & Winant, H. (2014). *Racial formation in the United States* (3rd ed.). New York, NY: Routledge.

Pew Research Center (2012). *The rise of Asian Americans.* Washington, DC: Author.

Poon, O. A., Dizon, J. P. M., & Squire, D. (2017). Count me in!: Ethnic data disaggregation advocacy, racial mattering, and lessons for racial justice coalitions. *JCSCORE*, 3(1), 91–124.

Poon, O., Squire, D., Kodama, C., Byrd, A., Chan, J., Manzano, L., . . . & Bishundat, D. (2016). A critical review of the model minority myth in selected literature on Asian Americans and Pacific Islanders in higher education. *Review of Educational Research*, 86(2), 469–502.

Robles, R. A. (2006). *Asian Americans and the shifting politics of race: The dismantling of affirmative action at an elite public high school.* New York, NY: Routledge.

Shyong, F. (2015, October 21). The term 'Asian' may be overly broad but California is stuck with it. *Los Angeles Times.* Retrieved from www.latimes.com/local/california/la-me-asian-veto-20151021-story.html

Students for Fair Admissions. (n.d.). *About.* Retrieved from studentsforfairadmissions.org/about/

Takagi, D. Y. (1993). *The retreat from race: Asian-American admissions and racial politics.* New Brunswick, NJ: Rutgers University Press.

Teranishi, R. T., & Nguyen, T-L. K. (2012). Asian Americans and Pacific Islanders: The changing demography of the United States and implications for education policy. *Asian American Policy Review*, 22, 17–27.

U.S. Department of Education. (2016). Program Description—D2 Program. *Asian American and Pacific Islander Data Disaggregation Initiative.* Retrieved from www2.ed.gov/programs/d2/index.html

Wang, F. K. (2014, July 23). A campaign to disaggregate data and ensure all students count. *NBC News.* Retrieved from www.nbcnews.com/news/asian-america/campaign-disaggregate-data-ensure-all-students-count-n163536

Wang, F. K. (2016, April 14). California advocates push 'AHEAD' with data disaggregation bill. *NBC News*. Retrieved from www.nbcnews.com/news/asian-america/california-advocates-push-ahead-data-disaggregation-bill-n556221

Wong, P. (1972). The emergence of the Asian-American movement. *Bridge*, 2, 33–29.

Wu, F. (2002). *Yellow: Race in American beyond Black and White*. New York, NY: Basic Books.

Yam, K. (2017, June 29). Rhode Island House passes act that would expose Asian-American achievement gap. *Huffington Post*. Retrieved from www.huffingtonpost.com/entry/rhode-island-education-asian-americans_us_59526cb9e4b02734df2d7e06

Zhang, C. (2018). *WeChatting American politics: Misinformation, polarization, and immigrant Chinese media*. New York, NY: Tow Center for Digital Journalism. Retrieved from www.cjr.org/tow_center_reports/wechatting-american-politics-misinformationpolarization-and-immigrant-chinese-media.php.

CHAPTER 5

The "Invisible" Minority
Finding a Sense of Belonging After Imperialism, Colonialism, and (Im)migration for Native Hawaiian and Pacific Islanders in the United States

*'Inoke Hafoka, Kēhaulani Vaughn,
Iosefa Aina, and Cynthia M. Alcantar*

"Koe mokopuna koe 'a tutu fale 'oku ha'u ki he 'etau fonua ko Faleloa" (*The grandson of burning house has come to our land of Faleloa*). This was the greeting Hafoka received when he visited the village of Faleloa in the Ha'apai island group, a central and historically significant part of the archipelago that makes up the Kingdom of Tonga. When Hafoka returned to the United States, he asked his grandfather why the people in his home village referred to him as tutu fale (*burning house*)? Hafoka's grandfather shared with him that as a young boy he disliked going to primary school because he hated getting harshly and physically disciplined by the teachers and spending long hours in a tiny school hut. So, one morning, in the mid-1940s, he went there before anyone arrived and set the school on fire.

The story of Hafoka's grandfather is reflective of the sentiments felt by many People of the Pacific about their experiences with Eurocentric models of primary schooling that greatly impacted their culture, history, and identity—often stripping students of their rich heritage (Thaman, 2003; Valdez, Dowrick, & Maynard, 2007). With westward expansion exploding into the Pacific, people and ideas began to influence, and, at times dominate, ways of life. This included education. With the spread of capitalism and growing globalization, many Pacific Islanders were not able to practice subsistence lifestyles and were forced to find homes elsewhere, including many who came to the United States. Some remained in homelands and unwillingly became subjects to other nations. Although there are a plethora of histories and experiences among Pacific Islanders, these schooling and colonizing experiences continue to have an effect on the People of the Pacific, known in the United States context as Native Hawaiians and Pacific Islanders (NHPI), and are reflected in current policies and practices that impact this population in the United States.

Today, less than 1% (0.40%) of the entire U.S. population identifies as NHPI (Hixon, Hepler, & Kim, 2012). Although 0.40% of the 308,746,538 total U.S. population may seem like a marginal number, it amounts to over 1.2 million NHPI people in the United States ($N = 1,225,195$) and reflects a fast-growing population (Hixon et al., 2012). In fact, the NHPI population grew by 40 percent in the decade from 2000 to 2010 and is expected to grow to over 2 million by 2030 (Empowering Pacific Islander Communities & Asian Americans Advancing Justice [EPIC & AAAJ], 2014). Moreover, the NHPI population grew by an estimated 13% in just 5 years (between 2010 and 2015), which places them as the second fastest growing group behind Asian Americans (Asian Americans Advancing Justice [AAAJ], 2016).

However, although NHPIs are a fast-growing population here in the United States, they are still marginalized within the margins. The past and current experiences and needs of NHPIs are often masked by categorization and data practices in the United States (Chang, Nguyen, & Chandler, 2015; EPIC & AAAJ, 2014). The NHPI category represents an ethnically and culturally diverse population extending far beyond Oceania. Hauʻofa (1994) describes Oceania as "a sea of islands with their inhabitants" (p. 8), people who were (and are still) able to navigate, explore, and populate the many lands of Oceania. They used advanced technology and were expert seafarers, sailing from one island to the next to trade, gather resources, and expand social relationships. The vast waters of Oceania were not barriers, but a highway that connected islands with one another (Hauʻofa, 1994). Although there are some commonalities in cultural values and traditions among NHPIs, this category represents over 20 diverse cultural and ethnic groups, inhabitants of Oceania, past and present, and their descendants (EPIC & AAAJ, 2014). Despite this diversity, NHPIs are often lumped into an umbrella Asian American and Pacific Islander (AAPI) racial category, a practice that renders NHPIs—their individuality, stories, and needs—invisible.

This chapter presents the historical context of the People of the Pacific and the challenges imperialism, colonialism, and (im)migration imposed on this community in the United States. The authors illustrate how all Pacific Islanders are Indigenous peoples while some have particular political relationships with the United States. We argue that data disaggregation for the population is a first step to acknowledging Pacific Islanders as Indigenous peoples. Lastly, the authors offer implications of research for policies and practices that better support, and are more inclusive of, the NHPI community.

THE RACIAL & ETHNIC CATEGORIZATION OF NHPIS

> Oceania is vast, Oceania is expanding, Oceania is hospitable and generous, Oceania is humanity rising from the depths of brine and regions of fire deeper still, Oceania is us. We are the sea, we are the ocean, we must wake up to this ancient truth. . . . We must not allow anyone to belittle us again, and take away our freedom (Hau'ofa, 1994, p. 160).

In order to fully grasp the complexity of the racial and ethnic categorization of NHPIs, we must first present the labels or categories often ascribed to this population. As mentioned before, NHPIs are often lumped together under the Pacific Islander category within the AAPI label. However, NHPIs represent a vast diversity of ethnic groups. Table 5.1 presents the various ethnic groups (from the regions of Melanesia, Micronesia, and Polynesia) within the NHPI category that have an extensive history of colonization as far back as the late 1700s and 1800s (Thomas, Kana'iaupuni, Balutski & Freitas, 2012). Their diversity is reflected in religion, language, and cultural practices, traditions, and values.

Furthermore, migrant and immigrant communities to (and from) the Pacific Islands is further complicated as there are Pacific Islanders who are immigrants to the United States (hence the "*(im)*migration" in the chapter's title) (EPIC & AAAJ, 2014). Native Hawaiians and some Pacific Islanders have U.S. citizenship, but many have different immigration statuses, such as U.S. national for American Samoans and Swains Islanders; Compact of Free Association (or COFA meaning "freely associated states that signed an agreement with the U.S. to allow military presence in their countries in exchange for a variety of benefits including allowing residents to live and work in the U.S. without applying for citizenship"); migrant for people from the Federated States of Micronesia, the Marshall Islands, and Palau; and immigrant for citizens of other Pacific nations) (EPIC & AAAJ, 2014). For example, Tongans have no special status and may come to the United States as documented or undocumented immigrants (Davidson, 2011; EPIC & AAAJ, 2014; Hafoka, 'Ulu'ave, & Hafoka, 2014; Rojas, 2011; Small & Dixon, 2004). Thus, some Pacific Islanders are undocumented immigrants in the United States (see EPIC & AAAJ, 2014; Rojas, 2011).

There are also differences in the experiences of NHPIs who live in the U.S. Pacific Islands and those who migrate to the U.S. continent, many seeking greater economic opportunities (Davidson, 2011). In Hawai'i the high cost of living due to the military and the tourism industries using massive amounts of land and resources, coupled with low-paying service industry jobs, has caused homelessness, a high rate of incarceration, and a massive diaspora of Native Hawaiians to the U.S. continent (Trask, 1991; Trask, 1993). California, Washington, and Utah are home to some of the largest

Table 5.1. Native Hawaiian and Pacific Islander Ethnic Groups

Melanesian	Micronesian	Polynesian
Fijian	Carolinian	Cook Islander
New Caledonian	Chamarro Islander	Native Hawaiian
New Guinean	Guamanian	Kapingamarangan
Papuan	Kiribatese	Maori
Solomon Islander	Kosraean	Niuean
Yanuatuan	Nauruan	Samoan
	Marshallese	Tahitian
	Palauan	Tokelauan
	Pohnpeian	Tongan

Note: Ethnic categories retrieved and modified from www2.census.gov/programs-surveys/acs/tech_docs/code_lists/2014_ACS_Code_Lists.pdf

populations of NHPIs outside of Hawai'i (EPIC & AAAJ, 2014). These settler, immigration, and migration histories have also influenced the high rates of mixed-race status among NHPIs, which further complicates this category (Dinh, 2013; EPIC & AAAJ, 2014; Kana'iaupuni & Liebler, 2005; Krogstad, 2015; Thomas et al., 2012).

Pacific Islanders represent island communities from Melanesia ("black islands"), Micronesia ("tiny islands"), and Polynesia ("many islands"). Regardless of the colonizer or political status, all are considered Indigenous people and communities of Oceania, and should be referred to as such due to the genealogical, linguistic, and cultural connections between communities. Part of the decolonial process is to recognize that Pacific Islanders, like other Indigenous communities, should be able to self-determine membership to their own community rather than have their community be determined by a colonial definition. NHPI is a term developed by the U.S. federal government and is commonly used within governmental policy, but still encompasses communities of the Pacific regardless of colonial or non-colonial status. Thus, NHPI and Pacific Islander will be used interchangeably throughout this work.

AGGREGATE RACIAL CATEGORIZATION

In 1977, the establishment of federal standards for collecting data on race and ethnicity led to the racial categorization of AAPIs as "Asian or Pacific Islander" (API) (Office of Management and Budget [OMB], 1995). Prior to this, merging Asian Americans with Native Hawaiian and Pacific Islanders as a panethnic identity was an intentional coalition-building practice for 1960s civil rights groups (Asian & Pacific Islander Institute on Domestic Violence [APIIDV], 2011; Inouye & Estrella, 2012). Inouye and Estrella (2012) state that the panethnic identity:

> [W]as a successful strategy—banding together increased their numbers and resulted in greater power to effect change in electoral politics, in services to their communities, in advancing civil rights, and in efforts to create more equitable systems that were inclusive of their communities. Since then, for [Asian American] AA and NHPI panethnic coalitions representing oppressed communities, mobilizing under a collective identity has been critical to their effectiveness as political instruments. (p. 4).

However, the panethnic category, which aggregates Asian Americans with NHPIs, is problematic when examining needs and outcomes for these ethnic populations. In the aggregate, data on economic and educational outcomes for AAPIs perpetuates the stereotype of Asians as being highly successful, often referred to as the model minority (Teranishi, Nguyen, & Alcantar, 2015). Additionally, aggregate data have been used to present AAPIs as faring as well as, if not better than, Whites, and to compare them against other minoritized populations (Nguyen, Nguyen, Chan, & Teranishi, 2016). This practice has completely erased the experiences of NHPIs.

Invisibility Through Aggregate Data

The development of racial categories and groupings represents a series of classifications that are often ascribed with certain meanings and values. These are usually reinforced through research methodologies and practices and are integral to imperialist and colonial processes. Māori scholar Linda Tuhiwai Smith (2012) discusses the development of categorization and the importance of representation. She argues that the colonial racialization of Indigenous peoples and the ways the West has represented them produces an illusion of truth. She states, "Colonialism wasn't just about collection. It was also about the rearrangement, representation and redistribution" (p. 65). This includes peoples, animals, plants, ideas and diseases. Colonial powers (re)arranged life based on their ideas and values. For example, the way that Indigenous people have been classified, counted, or recognized varies, and these classifications have consequences. Moreover, in the aggregate, the AAPI population is doing well, but if the continual social disparities of NHPI populations are broken out, we see something different. Data on educational outcomes and statistics of Asian Americans and NHPIs demonstrates how aggregate data erases the experiences of NHPIs. Approximately 18% of NHPIs hold a bachelor's degree compared with an aggregate figure of 45% of Asian American and Pacific Islanders (EPIC & AAAJ, 2014). In

2011, the national enrollment population of AAPIs was estimated at around 1.4 million students. If this figure is not disaggregated, it can be easy to overlook the 66,000 students that represent the NHPI population—that's less than 5%. In California, one of the states with the largest Asian American and NHPI populations, the six-year college completion rates for bachelor's degrees for the fall 2007 cohort shows more than a 20-percentage point difference between Asian American (60%) and NHPI (39%) students (The Campaign for College Opportunity, 2015). In the state of Washington through the Washington Assessment of Student Learning (WASL) test, the disaggregation of Pacific Islanders from Asian Americans students in 4th, 7th, and 10th grades reveals stark gaps across testing subject areas (reading, writing, math, and science) that would otherwise be undetected in aggregate data (Takeuchi & Hune, 2008).

The disparities in college completion among NHPIs is further magnified with disaggregated data. CARE (2013) reported that among people 25 or older who had at least some college, only 14.3% of Samoans, 22.7% of Native Hawaiians, 24.8% of Tongans, and 25.0% of Guamanians held a bachelor's degree, compared to 46.8% of Koreans, 46.9% of Filipinos, and 43.9% of Japanese. Looking at this data another way, 57.9% of Tongans, 56.8% of Samoans, 53.0 % of Guamanians, and 49.3 % of Native Hawaiians, aged 25 and over with at least a high school diploma had yet to attend college, compared to 29.3% of Koreans, 27.8% of Japanese, and 23.8% of Filipinos (CARE, 2011).

Keeping these contrasting figures in mind, Kauanui (2008) calls the aggregation of AAPI educational data "deeply disingenuous [and] unethical" (para. 8). Positioning Pacific Islanders as Indigenous people also works against colonial categorizations, which naturalize Pacific Islanders solely as ethnic minorities. Thus, the aggregate AAPI category dismisses the history of colonialism, imperialism, and (im)migration that differentiates the experiences of NHPIs from Asian Americans in the United States.

Recognizing Challenges and the Urgency of Disaggregated Data

Calls for the need to disaggregate data by ethnicity for AAPIs have been well documented for the last 40 years (EPIC & AAAJ, 2014; Kitano & Sue, 1973; National Commission on Asian American and Pacific Islander Research in Education [CARE], 2008, 2010, 2011, 2013; Teranishi, Nguyen, & Alcantar, 2015). However, an amendment to the racial categorization of NHPIs came about after extensive multiyear campaigning and advocacy by the Native Hawaiian community (OMB, 1997) and still faced opposition even after disaggregation was put into practice. Demands from NHPI activist and advocacy groups to disaggregate data for AAPIs led to an amendment of the initial federal standards for collecting data on race and ethnicity by the Office of Management and Budget (OMB); in 1997 it passed OMB

The "Invisible" Minority 73

directive 15, which required federal agencies to disaggregate NHPI as a separate racial category from AAPI (McGregor & Moy, 2003; OMB, 1997).

However, the committee assigned by OMB to review the reclassification of racial categories recommended that the original AAPI classification remain. The Native Hawaiian community responded against it:

> This recommendation was opposed by the Hawaiian congressional delegation, the 7,000 individuals who signed and sent preprinted yellow postcards, the State of Hawai'i departments and legislature, Hawaiian organizations, and other individuals who commented on this recommendation. Instead, the comments from these individuals supported reclassifying Native Hawaiians in the American Indian or Alaska Native category, which they view as an "indigenous peoples" category (although this category has not been considered or portrayed in this manner in the standards). Native Hawaiians, as the descendants of the original inhabitants of what is now the State of Hawai'i, believe that as indigenous people they should be classified in the same category as American Indians and Alaska Natives. (OMB, 1997, para. 39)

They also stated their classification under the AAPI category "provided inadequate data for monitoring the social and economic conditions" of NHPIs (OMB, 1997, para. 39). This recommended change by the Native Hawaiian community in the reclassification of Native Hawaiians received resistance from the Native American and Alaska Native community, specifically the American Indian tribal governments, because they believed it would be counterproductive for data requirements for federal funding for American Indians (OMB, 1997). At the end, OMB reclassified the AAPI category as two separate categories: "Asian" and "Native Hawaiian or Other Pacific Islander" (Asian & Pacific Islander American Health Forum [APIAHF], 2013; OMB, 1997).

However, even with federal recognition in data collection practices and institutional change in data practices, when analyzed and reported, race data for NHPIs continues to be lumped together with that of Asian Americans; it is rarely disaggregated between "Asian American" and "Native Hawaiian and Pacific Islander," and even less often by ethnic subgroups within the NHPI category. Persisting invisibility of the social inequities of NHPIs creates the need for disaggregated data for NHPIs.

HISTORICAL LEGACY THAT DIFFERENTIATES THE NHPI EXPERIENCE

The foundation of the United States as a settler colonial nation is based on the continual erasure of Indigenous people and is amplified by the narrative of the country as a "nation of immigrants" (Trask, 2000). Consequently, in our current era of neoliberal multiculturalism, many settlers of color assert rights to U.S. lands and political and social inclusion based on their specific histories of exploitation and marginalization by dominant white America. Although these histories of exploitation and marginalization of settlers of color are true and should not be discounted, the advancement of political agendas based on logics of a shared oppression fall short of acknowledging differing relationships to white supremacy. The naturalization of settler colonialism (Trask, 2000) within these various histories can serve to mute ongoing Indigenous assertions of self-determination. These settler histories are also reinforced by a colonial education system. Ongoing struggles for self-determination by Indigenous people (including a culturally relevant education) become foreclosed by individuals' access to land and resources.

In recognizing that people of color have distinctive relationships to white supremacy, we can start to evaluate how people can be both oppressed and complicit in a settler colonial project. As settlers of color seek inclusion, equity, and access to territory within a colonial landscape, they seek access to the same territory that Native people are struggling to reclaim.

Critical of replicating these dynamics within the Asian American community, Fujikane (2005) discussed antinationalist sentiment and the homogenization of nationalisms within Asian American Studies that ultimately oppose Native nationalists. She stated, "As Asian American scholars and activists committed to social and political justice, we need to hold ourselves accountable for the ways in which our settler scholarship undermines the nationalist struggles of Native people" (Fujikane, 2005, p. 74). To discuss racisms and power in Hawai'i, Fujikane (2005) relied on a race relation framework modeled on civil rights framings "that were ill-equipped for analyzing a colonial situation" (p. 74). She conceded that by doing so she reduced Native Hawaiians as an ethnic minority without specific recognition of their continued colonization and the occupation of their lands by the United States. Disaggregating Pacific Islander data from Asian Americans is a necessary first step in acknowledging Pacific Islanders as Indigenous people. Understanding the importance of Indigenous education, culturally relevant outreach and retention models specifically for Pacific Islanders will assist in empowering the community in finding solutions and addressing specific needs.

Colonialism

As western imperial powers arose in the 19th century, boundaries were constructed and Oceania became known as the Pacific Islands (Howe, 1979). A new outsider narrative was created due to the lack of understanding and validating of Oceanic epistemologies. For example, the use of the term "Pacific Islander" is problematic as it denotes smallness in geographic origin and state of mind, isolation, and a dependency on others due to the boundaries and lack of material resources needed to keep up with the global market (Hau'ofa, 1994).[1] However, the histories of Pacific Islanders, as of many other Indigenous groups, do not begin from their "discovery" by western imperial powers; rather, Pacific Islanders have creation stories that tie them to specific places. These symbiotic relationships to land and sea dictate societal structures and traditional educational systems that were built around these shared values.

Colonialism drastically altered Pacific Islander society and self-determination. In particular, the United States continues to have a colonial presence in parts of the Pacific including Hawai'i, American Samoa, Guam, and many parts of Micronesia. Some of the colonial legacies include nuclear testing, a huge military presence, environmental degradation, a colonial educational system, and increased displacement of people and resources. As the United States continues to be a settler colonial nation, the public education system continues to center western values and a history that is largely disconnected from non-Anglo populations, including Pacific Islanders. Due to this educational disconnect, Pacific Islanders, like other Indigenous communities, are underrepresented within higher education in all facets (Kana'iaupuni, Malone, & Ishibashi, 2005). To address these specific educational challenges and to positively identify methods, policies, and structures that can increase Pacific Islanders within higher education, accurate data is necessary.

Furthermore, having Pacific Islanders identified not only as an ethnic minority, but also as Indigenous can open meaningful collaborations between communities in order to learn best practices that can successfully create culturally relevant education policy, models, and programs and lead toward community empowerment. One example of Indigenous responsive practices that can lead toward community empowerment is 'Aha Pūnana Leo schools in Hawai'i. 'Aha Pūnana Leo schools are a cluster of language-immersion pre-K–12 schools that are a combination of private, charter, and public schools and programs in partnership with the Department of Education and the College of Hawaiian language. They serve over 90% Native Hawaiian students, of which the majority are from low-income backgrounds (Aguilera & LeCompte, 2007). In the early primary school levels students are fully immersed in Indigenous language and schools work with elders and families to teach students the language, culture, and history (Aguilera & LeCompte, 2007). In the secondary school levels students continue to learn the Indigenous language while also having the option of English language classes (Aguilera & LeCompte, 2007). Since the schools' inception over 80% of their graduates have gone on to college, many of whom have earned college and graduate degrees (Aguilera & LeCompte, 2007). These schools are an example of what can happen when schools recognize NHPIs' Indigenous heritage and work with families and communities to empower these communities.

Pacific Islanders, like Native Americans, are Indigenous people with inherent rights to self-determination including a culturally relevant education. Native Hawaiian scholar Goodyear-Kaʻōpua (2013) poignantly says, "Indigenous scholars have shown that the power to define what counts as knowledge and to determine what our people should be able to know and do is a fundamental aspect of peoplehood, freedom, collective well-being, and autonomy" (p. 6). The legacies of colonial education have left many Indigenous communities disconnected from language, cultural values, and practices. This disconnect within an education system that is not relevant for Indigenous populations is highlighted by similar statistics of educational attainment for both Native Americans and Pacific Islanders. To address various issues affecting Indigenous communities, including colonialism and the colonial education system in particular, the United Nations states, "Indigenous peoples have the right to revitalize, use, develop and transmit to future generations their histories, languages, oral traditions, philosophies, writing systems and literatures, and to designate and retain their own names for communities, places and persons" (United Nations, 2007, p. 7). Pacific Islanders continue to be Indigenous and are engaging in cultural traditions including relationships between Oceania and other Indigenous groups. Pacific Islanders are both "rooted" and "routed" (Diaz & Kauanui, 2001). They continue to enlarge their worlds inside and outside of the Pacific. Creating culturally relevant educational systems and research will continue to strengthen the specific needs of Indigenous populations. Having accurate data will be integral in creating productive avenues to increase educational success and resilience.

(Im)migration

During the last several decades, many Pacific Islanders have migrated to the United States continent, primarily for educational and employment purposes. This largely has been due to settler colonial displacement and globalization in the Pacific. The population of Pacific Islanders in the U.S. may be small, but their presence can be as a dormant volcano—easy to dismiss, but when ready to erupt, many take notice (Huffer & Qalo, 2004). The People of the Pacific have a unique, valuable history, and culture that has the potential to enrich and intrigue the rest of the population if they are allowed a space and a voice. For example, when we are able to recognize the presence of Tongan people and their history, they become more than just keepers of cultural relics (Manuʻatu & Kēpa, 2006). They unleash a production of unique knowledge and contexts. This knowledge is vital to providing insights about educational practices with Pacific Islander students. It also provides an opportunity to connect many of the Pacific Islander communities with the educational system to enhance the wealth of cultural knowledge in academic spaces (Vakalahi, 2009).

RECOMMENDATIONS FOR DATA DISAGGREGATION FOR NHPIS

Data disaggregation for NHPIs, and specifically from the panethnic AAPI category, goes beyond identity politics (Trask, 2000); it is a visibility issue, a civil rights issue, and an issue of better serving this population. Disaggregation of the AAPI political category is a necessary first step to identify the disparities and solutions found within and between NHPIs.

To achieve this, both more qualitative and more quantitative research on NHPIs is needed: quantitative research that disaggregates by ethnic subgroups, so that we can identify social and economic trends, and also qualitative research that can express the experiences and identify the challenges and needs of this population. Some areas of research needed to gain a deeper understanding of NHPIs include studies that capture the (im)migrant experiences of NHPIs such as those residing in the Pacific Islands versus those in the U.S. continent (like Chang, Nguyen, & Chandler, 2015) and research on undocumented PIs and mixed-race/ethnic NHPIs, and examining NHPIs in different states (like EPIC & AAAJ, 2014). Furthermore, qualitative research may be essential in capturing the nuanced and intersecting experiences of NHPIs, such as the exploration of the experiences of Pacific Islander women (Kupo, 2010). Disaggregated data by NHPI ethnic subgroups can help policymakers and practitioners identify what resources and support are best suited for specific ethnic subgroups.

Furthermore, aggregating data of Pacific Islanders with Asian Americans continues to perpetuate the educational disparities and ineffective policies and strategies to address achievement gaps for NHPIs. However, in situations where disaggregating NHPI data is absolutely impossible and the data has to be aggregated due to sample sizes and significance levels, among many other possible data issues, the authors recommend considering the context and purpose for which the data is being aggregated for NHPIs. In some instances, aggregating "Native Hawaiians" and "Pacific Islanders" will make sense, as some past studies have demonstrated, and in other instances having Native Hawaiians grouped with other Indigenous populations, including Native Americans, could be effective. Centering Pacific Islanders as Indigenous people is essential to not only empower Pacific Islander students but also to create more effective educational models that support Indigenous people. Advocating for NHPIs either to be disaggregated from Asian Americans or at the very least be aggregated with other Indigenous populations including Native Americans could create meaningful educational policies and strategies and more culturally relevant education, research, and policy.

Additionally, research conducted about and with NHPI populations must consult with the community and ask what research the community needs. Include NHPI community members in the research process or help support these communities to conduct their own research. If we create conditions for community members to be an active part of the research process, we can engage in research that practices decolonial methodologies. This will enable Pacific Islander communities to actively be in control of the research that is done in our communities. Furthermore, this process will also empower the community to decide the research priorities and thus become active participants in the research process. Holistically, this will allow the community to address its needs through solutions that are culturally appropriate and allow us to demystify research and use it fully as a tool that can empower the community.

It is also important for research to shed light on the strengths of this population so that we can develop more asset-based, culturally relevant and responsive approaches to serving this population. For example, Alo (2014), rather than examining what causes Native Hawaiian students to drop out of college, examined the motivational and sociocultural factors that promote the retention of these students. Another case in point is Valdez, Dowrick, and Maynard's (2007) study that took into account cultural values and practices of one ethnic group to develop culturally responsive practices in a middle school in Hawai'i. As these studies demonstrate, asset-based, applied, and policy-oriented culturally relevant and responsive research takes into account NHPIs (im)migration histories, experiences with colonialism, language, religion, and cultural traditions and practices. To understand NHPI educational experiences, it essential to consider this population as Indigenous people to inform educational policy and programs that are intentional in Indigenous student success.

Aside from collecting disaggregated data for NHPIs and utilizing this data to inform research, policy, and practice, equally important for transformational change is the continuation of advocacy, coalition-building, and raising awareness about the experiences and needs of NHPIs. One way to do this is by supporting Indigenous studies at colleges and universities that include Pacific Islanders. Student support centers focused on NHPIs or Indigenous students are also key to educating other students, teachers, staff, and administrators to create outreach and resiliency strategies and models that work for Indigenous communities. The further disaggregation and potential aggregation of data with other Indigenous populations is necessary and can be the first step in acknowledging the need for different strategies within higher education, especially to address the needs that will lead to educational success for Pacific Islanders and other Indigenous communities.

CONCLUSION

We would like to push beyond the limitations understood about the assumed cultural and educational hegemony associated with the hut Hafoka's grandfather burnt down as a boy. Although the school of Hafoka's grandfather brought knowledge that was valuable in a changing world, it invalidated the generational knowledge and way of being in his community. In Tongan, the word 'apiako is used for *school;* however, translated directly in English, it has a slightly different meaning: *home of study* or *home of learning* (Thaman, 1995). It brings new meaning: that this place should embody characteristics of a home. We assert that 'apiako should be a place where relevant, valuable knowledge is sought both within and without the hut, or the established western systems of learning. We want to see, teach, and create curricula that are culturally relevant to the students and communities they impact and that consider the multidimensionality of our society, culture, and histories.

Correspondingly, Native Indigenous scholars discuss the potential and importance that Indigenous education will have not only for Indigenous people, but for society in general. Gregory Cajete (1994) states:

> At a more inclusive level, exploration of Indigenous education liberates the Indian learner and educator to participate in a creative and transformative dialogue that is inherently based on equality and mutual reciprocity. This is a way of learning, communicating, and working in relationship that mirrors those found in Nature. It also destigmatizes the Indian learner from being disadvantaged and the educator from being the provider of aid. It allows both the learner and the educator to co-create a learning experience and mutually undertake a pilgrimage to a new level of self-knowledge. The educator enters the cultural universe of the learner and no longer remains an outside authority. By co-creating a learning experience, everyone involved generates a critical consciousness and enters into a process of empowering one another (p. 230).

Although Cajete is describing the transformative potential of "Indian" education, his research applies to the transformative potential of Pacific Islander and Indigenous education in general. Creating culturally relevant education that centers Indigenous knowledge(s) and epistemes can be supportive of empowering Indigenous communities, and also will aid in creating positive changes to society overall.

We consider this chapter the start of a fruitful conversation of data disaggregation needs, policies, and practices for NHPIs, rather than the end-all, be-all. Being able to examine and present disaggregated data for NHPIs not only has the potential to inform targeted culturally responsive policies and practices to support this population, but may also impact the way in which the community and our society as a whole conceptualizes the NHPI identity as one of strength rather than deficit. Ultimately, our intent with this chapter, and the book more generally, is to call attention to the diverse histories, characteristics, and experiences within the NHPI population so that we can better serve and support this population. The diversity and continual marginalization of NHPIs call for better informed data categorization practices, so that we can have more accurate data that informs policies and practices that consider the varied experiences with colonialism, imperialism, and (im)migration for this population. Data practices must also change with time to align with the fluid and rapidly changing demography of our country if we are to address some of the most pressing contemporary civil rights issues. As a society we must question data practices, research, and the (in)visibility of communities and consider the ways in which invisibility and culturally insensitive policies and practices do harm.

NOTE

1. Furthermore, it dismisses and marginalizes cultural beliefs and practices of the People of the Pacific. This outsider perspective is even more problematic because it is and has been internalized by many inhabitants of Oceania, those living in the diaspora, and their descendants.

REFERENCES

Aguilera, D., & LeCompte, M. D. (2007). Resiliency in native languages: The tale of three indigenous communities' experiences with language immersion. *Journal of American Indian Education, 46*(3), 11–36.

Alo, K. M. B. C. (2014). *Motivational and sociocultural factors for Native Hawaiian students attaining a post-secondary degree.* (Master's thesis). Hawai'i Pacific University, Honolulu, HI. Retrieved from ProQuest Dissertations and Theses. (1558176)

Asian and Pacific Islander American Health Forum. (2013). *Case studies to improve Asian American, Native Hawaiian, and Pacific Islander HIV/AIDS data collection, reporting, and dissemination.* San Francisco, CA: Author. Retrieved from www.apiahf.org/wp-content/uploads/2013/05/2013-05-20_AANHPIHIVCase-Study_OCB-1.pdf

Asian Americans Advancing Justice (AAAJ). (2016). *Asian Americans and NHPI are the two fastest growing racial groups, according to new census population estimates* [Press release]. Los Angeles, CA. Authors. Retrieved from www.advancingjustice-la.org/sites/default/files/20160628%20Census%20Report%20PR.pdf

Asian and Pacific Islander Institute on Domestic Violence. (2011). *Asian & Pacific Islander identities, definitions, & groupings.* San Francisco, CA: Author. Retrieved from s3.amazonaws.com/gbv-wp-uploads/wp-content/uploads/2017/07/20183008/API-identities-definitions-groupings-2011.pdf

Cajete, G. (1994). *Look to the mountain: An ecology of Indigenous education.* Skyland, CO: Kivaki Press.

Campaign for College Opportunity (2015). *The state of higher education in California: Asian American Native Hawaiian Pacific Islander report.* University of California, Los Angeles, CA: Author. Retrieved from files.eric.ed.gov/fulltext/ED571127.pdf

Chang, M. J., Nguyen, M. H., & Chandler, K. L. (2015). Can data disaggregation resolve blind spots in policy making? Examining a case for Native Hawaiians. *AAPI Nexus, 13*(1 & 2), 297–320.

Davidson, L. (2011, September 12). One in every four Tongans in the U.S. calls Utah home. *The Salt Lake Tribune.* Retrieved from archive.sltrib.com/story.php?ref=/sltrib/politics/52551592-90/california-family-hawaii-population.html.csp

Diaz, V., & Kauanui, J. K. (2001). Native Pacific Studies on the edge. *The Contemporary Pacific: A Journal of Island Affairs, 13*(2), 318.

Dinh, Q. (2013). *Moving beyond the "Asian" check box.* Washington, DC: Southeast Asia Resource Action Center. Retrieved from www.searac.org/wp-content/uploads/2018/04/Moving-Beyond-the-22Asian22-Checkbox.pdf

Empowering Pacific Islander Communities & Asian Americans Advancing Justice (2014). *A community of contrasts: Native Hawaiians and Pacific Islanders in the United States.* Los Angeles, CA: Authors. Retrieved from www.empoweredpi.org/uploads/1/1/4/1/114188135/a_community_of_contrasts_nhpi_us_2014-1.pdf

Fujikane, C. (2005). Foregrounding Native nationalisms: A critique of antinationalist sentiment in Asian American studies. In K. A. Ono (Ed.), *Asian American studies after critical mass* (pp. 73–97). Oxford, UK: Blackwell.

Goodyear-Kaʻōpua, N. (2013). *The seeds we planted: Portraits of a Native Hawaiian charter school.* Minneapolis, MN: University of Minnesota Press.

Hafoka, M. P., ʻUluʻave, M. F., & Hafoka, ʻI (2014). Double bind: The duality of Tongan American identity. In H. F. Ofahengaue Vakalahi & M. T. Goninet (Eds.), *Transnational Pacific Islander Americans and social work: Dancing to the beat of a different drum* (pp. 127–138). Washington, DC: NASW Press.

Hauʻofa, E. (1994). Our sea of islands. *The Contemporary Pacific, 6*(1), 148–161.

Hixon, L., Hepler, B. B., & Kim, M. O. (2012). *Native Hawaiian and Other Pacific Islander population: 2010.* 2010 Census Brief Series. Washington, DC: U.S. Census. Retrieved from www.census.gov/prod/cen2010/briefs/c2010br-12.pdf

Howe, K. R. (1979). Pacific Islands history in the 1980s: New directions or monograph myopia? *Pacific Studies, 3*(1), 81–90.

Huffer, E., & Qalo, R. (2004). Have we been thinking upside down?: The contemporary emergence of Pacific theoretical thought. *The Contemporary Pacific, 16*(1), 87–116.

Inouye, T. E., & Estrella, R. (2012). *Building panethnic coalitions in Asian American, Native Hawaiian and Pacific Islander communities: Opportunities and challenges.* Social Policy Research Associates. Retrieved from www.spra.com/wordpress2/wp-content/uploads/2014/07/HTA-Building-Panethnic-Coalitions-Paper.pdf

Kanaʻiaupuni, S. M., & Liebler, C. A. (2005). Pondering Poi Dog: Place and racial identification of multiracial Native Hawaiians. *Ethnic and Racial Studies, 28*(4), 687–721.

Kanaʻiaupuni, S. M., Malone, N., & Ishibashi, K. (2005). *Ka Huakaʻi: 2005 Native Hawaiian educational assessment.* Honolulu, HI: Kamehameha Schools, Pauahi Publications. Retrieved from www.ulukau.org/elib/collect/nhea/index/assoc/D0.dir/book.pdf

Kauanui, J. K. (2008, September 8). Where are all the Native Hawaiians and Pacific Islanders in higher education? *Diverse Issues in Higher Education: The Academy Speaks.* Retrieved from diverseeducation.wordpress.com/author/kauanui/

Kitano, H. H. L., & Sue, S. (1973). The model minorities. *Journal of Social Issues, 29(2)*, 1–9.

Krogstad, J. M. (2015, June 17). *Hawaii is home to the nation's largest share of multiracial Americans.* Washington, DC: Pew Research Center. Retrieved from www.pewresearch.org/fact-tank/2015/06/17/hawaii-is-home-to-the-nations-largest-share-of-multiracial-americans/

Kupo, V. L. (2010). *What is Hawaiian?: Explorations and understandings of Native Hawaiian college women's identities.* (Doctoral dissertation). Bowling Green State University, Bowling Green, OH. Retrieved from scholarworks.bgsu.edu/he_diss/34/.

Manu'atu, L., & Kēpa, M. (2006). TalanoaMālie: Social and educational empowerment for Tongans by Tongans in the "Pasifika" education proposal. In I. Abu-Saad & D. Champagne (Eds.), *Indigenous education and empowerment: International perspectives* (pp. 169–177). Lanham, MD: AltaMira Press.

McGregor, D. & Moy, E. (2003). Native Hawaiians and Pacific Islander Americans. *Asian-Nation:The landscape of Asian America.* Retrieved from www.asian-nation.org/hawaiian-pacific.shtml

National Commission on Asian American and Pacific Islander Research in Education (CARE). (2008). *Facts, not fiction: Setting the record straight.* University of California, Los Angeles, CA: Author. Retrieved from care.gseis.ucla.edu/wp-content/uploads/2015/08/2008_CARE_Report.pdf

National Commission on Asian American and Pacific Islander Research in Education (CARE). (2010). *Federal higher education policy priorities and the Asian American and Pacific Islander community.* University of Los Angeles, Los Angeles, CA: Author. Retrieved from care.gseis.ucla.edu/wp-content/uploads/2015/08/2010_CARE_Report.pdf

National Commission on Asian American and Pacific Islander Research in Education (CARE). (2011). *The relevance of Asian Americans and Pacific Islanders in the college completion agenda.* University of California, Los Angeles, CA: Author. Retrieved from care.gseis.ucla.edu/wp-content/uploads/2015/08/2011_CARE_Report.pdf

National Commission on Asian American and Pacific Islander Research in Education (CARE). (2013). *iCount: A data quality movement for Asian Americans and Pacific Islanders in higher education.* University of California, Los Angeles, CA: Author. Retrieved from /care.gseis.ucla.edu/wp-content/uploads/2015/08/2013_iCount_Report.pdf

Nguyen, B. M. D., Nguyen, M. H., Chan, J., & Teranishi, R. T. (2016). *The racialized experiences of Asian American and Pacific Islander students: An examination of campus racial climate at the University of California, Los Angeles.* University of California, Los Angeles: National Commission on Asian American and Pacific Islander Research in Education. Retrieved from care.igeucla.org/wp-content/uploads/2016/05/2016_CARE_Report.pdf

Office of Management and Budget (OMB). (1995, August 28). *Standards for the classification of federal data on race and ethnicity.* Washington, DC: White House Office of Management and Budget. Retrieved from www.whitehouse.gov/wp-content/uploads/2017/11/fedreg_race-ethnicity.pdf

Office of Management and Budget (OMB). (1997, October 30). *Revisions to the standards for the classification of federal data on race and ethnicity.* Washington,

DC: White House Office of Management and Budget. Retrieved from www.whitehouse.gov/wp-content/uploads/2017/11/Revisions-to-the-Standards-for-the-Classification-of-Federal-Data-on-Race-and-Ethnicity-October 30-1997.pdf

Rojas, L. B. (2011, October 17). An undocumented Pacific Islander shared her story and others'. [Blog post] *Southern California Public Radio, Multi-America: How immigrants are redefining "American" in Southern California.* Retrieved from www.scpr.org/blogs/multiamerican/2011/10/17/7861/an-undocumented-pacific-islander-shares-her-story-/

Small, C. A., & Dixon, D. L. (2004, February 1). *Tonga: Migration and the homeland.* Washington, DC: Migration Policy Institute. Retrieved from www.migrationpolicy.org/article/tonga-migration-and-homeland

Smith, L. T. (2012). *Decolonizing methodologies: Research and Indigenous people.* London, UK: Zed.

Takeuchi, D., & Hune, S. (2008). *Growing presence, emerging voices: Pacific Islanders and academic achievement in Washington.* A report submitted to The Washington State Commission on Asian Pacific American Affairs. Seattle, WA: University of Washington.

Teranishi, R. T., Nguyen, B. M. D., & Alcantar, C. M. (2015). The data quality movement for the Asian American and Pacific Islander community: An unresolved civil rights issue. In P. A. Noguera, & R. Ahram (Eds.), *Race, Equity, and Education: Sixty Years from Brown* (pp. 139–154). New York, NY: Springer.

Thaman, K. H. (1995). Concepts of learning, knowledge and wisdom in Tonga, and their relevance to modern education. *Prospects, 25*(4), 723–733.

Thaman, K. H. (2003). Decolonizing Pacific studies: Indigenous perspectives, knowledge, and wisdom in higher education. *The Contemporary Pacific, 15*(1), 1–17.

Thomas, S. L., Kanaʻiaupuni, S. M., Balutski, B. J. N., & Freitas, A. K. (2012). Access and success for students from Indigenous populations. In J. C. Smart & M. B. Paulsen (Eds.), *Higher Education: Handbook of Theory and Research Vol. 27* (pp. 335–367). New York, NY: Springer.

Trask, H.-K. (1991). Coalition-building between natives and non-natives. *Stanford Law Review,* 1197–1213.

Trask, H.-K. (1993). Lovely hula hands: Corporate tourism and the prostitution of Hawaiian culture. *From a native daughter: Colonialism and sovereignty in Hawaiʻi,* 179–197.

Trask, H.-K. (2000). Settlers of color and "Immigrant" hegemony: "Locals" in Hawaiʻi. *Amerasia Journal, 26*(2), 1–24.

United Nations (2007). *United Nations Declaration on the Rights of Indigenous Peoples.* Retrieved from www.un.org/esa/socdev/unpfii/documents/DRIPS_en.pdf

Vakalahi, H. F. O. (2009). Pacific Islander American students: Caught between a rock and a hard place? *Children and Youth Services Review, 31,* 1258–1263.

Valdez, M. F., Dowrick, P. W., & Maynard, A. E. (2007). Cultural misperceptions and goals for Samoan children's education in Hawaiʻi: Voices from school, home, and community. *The Urban Review, 39*(1), 6–92.

CHAPTER 6

Draw Your Own Box?
Further Complicating Racial Data for Multiracial/Two or More Races College Students

Marc P. Johnston-Guerrero and Karly Sarita Ford

Multiracial people make up 7% of the U.S. population and are predicted to be 20% of the population by 2050 (Pew Research Center, 2015), with much of the growth among younger Americans (Humes, Jones, & Ramirez, 2011), many of whom are college-bound (Johnston-Guerrero & Renn, 2016). Despite this significant proportion and rapid growth, people who self-identify with two or more races are often recoded/reclassified into monoracial groups, leaving their presence literally erased from many data reports. A clear example of this reclassification that leads to erasure is illustrated by guidelines issued by the Department of Education of the State of Tennessee (Figure 6.1). The guidance states how students who self-identified with two or more races should be reclassified. While students are asked to "check all that apply" at the time of data collection, their self-identifications are transformed into monoracial categories at the time of data coding and reporting. In addition, although the student may identify more closely with one race over another, they have no say in how they are reclassified, as the state of Tennessee uses its "hierarchy" of race assignment, which holds White as racially pure (i.e., students who select White and any other race are reclassified as the minoritized race). According to the educational reports generated at the district and state levels, there are no mixed-race students in K–12 in the state of Tennessee.

Because researchers often operate within a paradigm of universal monoraciality—that is, a preference for and prioritization of monoracial categorization—multiracial identities continue to be afterthoughts within the racial landscape in U.S. society, particularly when examining racial disparities in access to and outcomes of higher education. In other cases, multiraciality is considered, but only tangentially or in ways that do not honor

Figure 6.1. Tennessee Department of Education Hierarchy for Determining Reported Race/Ethnicity

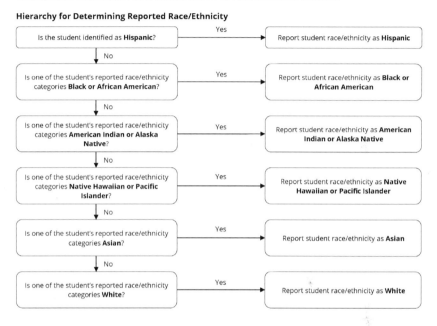

Source: Tennessee Department of Education, *2018 Accountability Protocol*, p. 9. (www.tn.gov/content/dam/tn/education/data/Accountability_Protocol_2018.pdf)

self-identification or align with a growing sense of multiracial community. In this chapter, we tackle some of these issues, beginning with the historical underpinnings of current constructions of *race* and *mixed race*. Then we discuss how race data collection practices hinder and complicate our understandings of mixed-race students at the K–12 and higher education levels. We provide theoretical and practical recommendations, particularly for dealing with racial data and capturing the complex identities of multiracial people. In closing the chapter, we highlight some questions that provoke and motivate considerations for future research about mixed identity: Do multiracial people constitute a racial group? And how can data collection, which often depends on discrete categories, grapple with racial fluidity? Our goal is to highlight heterogeneity as well as illuminate current and historical data limitations in capturing and representing the complex identities of multiracial people.

THEORIZING MULTIRACIALITY

The understanding of multiracial identity and experiences has progressed over time, from notions of the "marginal man" (Park, 1928; Stonequist, 1937) and "tragic mulatta" (Raimon, 2004), to various stage models of multiracial identity development (e.g., Poston 1990) and ecological analyses of multiracial identities (Renn & Lunceford, 2004; Root, 1999). A common theme within the progression has been movement away from depending on laws of "hypodescent" or the "one-drop rule" (Davis, 1991) for racial identification, prompted by an increasing value placed on the right to self-identify or choose one's race (Root, 1996, Wijeyesinghe, 2001). In a recent continuation of theory development around multiracial identity, Rockquemore, Brunsma, and Delgado (2009) argued that researchers must discontinue using "race" as an all-encompassing construct and start to differentiate between racial *category* (a person's chosen racial category in a given situation), racial *identity* (a person's internalized understanding of their racial identity), and racial *identification* (how others perceive or identify a person racially). The distinction between a personally held sense of racial identity and publicly reported identification (either based on selected or externally ascribed categories) is important for understanding the potential discrepancies between how students might self-identify and the ways in which researchers and institutions represent them (e.g., through aggregation).

Constructing Contemporary Notions of Multiraciality

Contemporary discourse on multiraciality tends to begin with either the 1967 *Loving v. Virginia* Supreme Court decision, which fully legalized interracial marriage across the nation (Pascoe, 2009), or the 2000 U.S. Census, which was the first to allow respondents to "Mark One or More" racial categories (Williams, 2006). These events are certainly important for understanding the current social contexts that have allowed for individuals to more freely identify as biracial, multiracial, or any number of terms capturing mixedness.[1] However, using 1967 or 2000 as a starting place is problematic because it promotes ahistorical ideas that mixed-race people are an entirely new phenomenon separated from the legacy of the one-drop rule (Elam, 2011; Harris, 2016). This perceived newness is magnified by the generational increase among young Americans indicating two or more racial categories in the U.S. Census (Humes, Jones, & Ramirez, 2011; Pew Research Center, 2015)—many of whom are college-bound (Johnston-Guerrero & Renn, 2016). Yet, when focusing solely on this sense of newness, multiracial people can easily be used to further claims about the declining significance of race (e.g., D'Souza, 1995) and views that multiraciality may be in collusion with white supremacy (Elam, 2011). We have heard too many arguments against race-conscious practices (e.g., admissions, student services) that used multiracial young people as evidence for why such practices don't work. By further contextualizing and complicating notions of mixedness, such arguments are more easily seen as flawed.

We start our contextualization of multiraciality in the 1800s, when racial mixing was first acknowledged by the U.S. Census (in the categories of Octoroon, Quadroon and Mulatto) and scientific racism became solidified with the emergence of eugenics. Mixed-race enumeration first appeared in the 1850 Census with the mulatto category (Morning, 2005). Such enumeration can be thought of as a way to document and protect White racial purity, a common goal of the racist eugenics movement (Duster, 2003; Gould, 1996; Montagu, 1964; Roberts, 2011). White racial purity and racism converged within the eugenics movement to influence quota-based immigration laws (e.g., the National Origins Act of 1924; Black, 2003) and antimiscegenation laws preventing racial mixing (e.g., the Virginia Racial Integrity Act of 1924; Lombardo, 2008). At the heart of these eugenic wrongdoings was an essentialist belief in races as biologically distinct (Roberts, 2011).

This idea of biological distinctions between races arose from the first modern "scientific" classifications of human beings, usually credited to Carolus Linnaeus, the Swedish naturalist who originated the taxonomic classification system in the 18th century (Corcos, 1997; Morning, 2011). During this time, Linnaeus and other taxonomists, like German medicine professor Johann Blumenbach, classified humans into four to five larger groups, which roughly equate to the so-called ethnoracial pentagon (i.e., black/African, white/European, red/Indian, yellow/Asian, brown/Hispanic; Hollinger, 1995) still used today (Smedley, 2007; Zuberi, 2001). In her extensive review of the origins of the idea of race, Smedley (2007) argued that these 18th century classifications have had lasting impact since they set up beliefs regarding the permanence and rigidity of group differences, which were linked to physical characteristics and purported behavioral traits. These classifications easily became hierarchical, and the fact that they were created by renowned scientists legitimized the classifications of difference as part of the "natural" order (Smedley, 2007). These ideas were then easily transformed into a more modern concept of race that grew from Europeans' attempts to classify and organize the populations they encountered in the expansion of their empires (Montagu, 1964; Smedley, 2007), ultimately solidifying the racial purity of whiteness and placing Whites at the top of the U.S. racial hierarchy through laws and slavery (Roediger, 2008). Recall the example we opened this chapter with, the racial hierarchy flowchart from the Tennessee Department of Education. It is a galling demonstration that these notions of racial hierarchy and purity continue to exist and influence the way that race data are categorized today.

Multiracial or Two or More Races?

Another contemporary issue facing race scholars is how to make sense of the increasing use of "Two or More Races" a single aggregated category. While *multiracial* is an identity that people proactively identify with, Two or More Races is a constructed, aggregate category made up of people who self-identified with more than one racial group. To be clear, these are not people who necessarily proactively identify as multiracial, but they do identify with more than one monoracial group. Identifying as multiracial, in contrast, implies some identification with a mixed-race identity in addition to identification with more than one race. This distinction may be more clear given the theorizing by Rockquemore et al. (2009) discussed earlier. Their differentiations between racial category (a person's chosen racial category in a given situation), racial identity (a person's internalized understanding of their racial identity), and racial identification (how others perceive or identify a person racially), remind scholars of the possibilities that a personally held sense of racial identity (e.g., multiracial) may be different from externally applied racial identification (e.g., "two or more races").

During the 1990s, leaders and advocacy groups representing multiracial communities effectively lobbied to be able to capture multiracial individuals within the U.S. Census. Although a relatively small subset within that movement, led by Susan Graham of Project RACE, wanted the creation of a "multiracial" box on the U.S. Census, the ability to "Mark One or More" won out, given the eventual support from traditional (mono)racial civil rights groups. This compromise allowed groups to still be able to capture their populations—those who identified with the group "alone or in combination"—without deflating numbers, which was a fear among many established civil rights groups (Williams, 2006). It also then allowed multiracial groups to gain a better sense of who identified with more than one race—9 million Americans in 2010, up from 6.8 million in 2000 (Jones & Bullock, 2012). However, it is still unclear how many of the individuals marking "two or more races" actually identify as multiracial.

Researchers and evaluators are dealing with understanding racial trends using data before and after implementation of the United States Office of Management & Budget's (OMB) Directive 15. This instruction changed the federal racial identification categories in order to accommodate the changing U.S. racial demographic landscape with particular attention to multiracial individuals. In accordance with Directive 15, federal guidelines for race reporting to the U.S. Department of Education now included the addition of the multiple check box option, prompting institutions of higher education to track trends in racial disparities before and after compliance was mandated by 2011 (Johnston-Guerrero & Renn, 2016).

The Department of Education required institutions to aggregate any student identified with more than one racial group into a "Two or more races" category when reporting to the Integrated Postsecondary Education Data System (IPEDS). This countered civil rights groups' purpose for lobbying for the U.S. Census to not include a "multiracial" box in the first place (and the compromise on "mark one or more"). We know this category of "two or more races" is flawed. Not only does it not tell us much about who is within such a diverse, aggregated group, it also does not tell us who identifies as multiracial. To be clear, people who identify as multiracial may be in the "two or more races" category, but not everyone in "two or more races" would identify as multiracial. For example, someone with Asian and White parentage may select both races, which would put them in the "two or more races" category. However, they do not self-identify as "multiracial": that is not one of the choices provided in data collection. Rather, they may more closely identify as biracial, Hapa, Asian, White or any number of identities (Renn & Lunceford, 2004). Interestingly, when researchers download raw IPEDS data, the "Two or More Races" variable in the dataset actually has the variable name "multi"—illustrating inconsistency in understanding and use of terminology at the federal level.

However, "Two or more races" is by far the most popular term used by universities to describe students who self-identify with more than one race category. Among the doctoral granting universities (Carnegie Classification R1, R2 and R3s) that describe mixed-race students on their websites, "Two or more races" is the label currently used in the vast majority of cases (Patterson, Ford, & Cate, 2019). The next most common term is Multiracial (or some variant such as Multiple Races, Bi-racial, Multi, or Multi-Ethnic), which appears much less frequently. The terminology that higher education institutions use and how they represent their data is not neutral or without consequences. Multiracial students may feel a sense of erasure if they do not see themselves represented by their institutions (Harris, 2017).

FURTHER COMPLICATING RACIAL DATA COLLECTION AND REPRESENTATION

Racial Data Collection

Racial demographic data collection efforts from current and prospective college students has not been uniform (Padilla & Kelley, 2005: Renn & Lunceford, 2004). While these shifts in racial data collection likely impact counts of all racial groups, there is reason to believe that counts of multiracial students are especially sensitive to ways that questions are posed (Harper, 2016; Johnston et al., 2014). The most obvious would be examples of race data collection that did not allow for respondents to select more than one race before 2010. In effect, there were no multiracial students in federal reports of higher education enrollment. IPEDs data before and after

2010 are frequently used together to display trends in higher education enrollment by race; however, changes in race data collection make the data pre- and post-2010 difficult to interpret. The racial data collection and reporting may impact all students, but particularly multiracial students whose very existence is acknowledged or denied depending on how the data are collected or represented.

Other examples of places where there is variation with less severe consequences may include standardized tests of aptitude (e.g., SAT), admissions applications, and pre- and postsurveys of engagement and involvement. For instance, the Cooperative Institutional Research Program (CIRP) Freshman Survey, a questionnaire that students at colleges and universities across the country complete during the first weeks they are on campus, asks, "Are You: (Select *all* that apply)" followed by twelve racial and ethnic group categories including an "other" option (Higher Education Research Institute, n.d.). Another prominent example comes from the 2015–16 Common Application, which follows Directive 15 closely by using a two-question format where the first question asks, "Are you Hispanic or Latino?" (with a yes or no response option) followed by a second question asking, "Regardless of your answer to the prior question, please indicate how you identify yourself. (Select one or more)" (The Common Application, n.d.). The five race options and the ability to select multiple races aligns with federal guidelines. Additionally, each of these data collection instruments are further complicated by the fact that they have changed the way they ask this question over time. The Common App offered a totally different wording of the item stem and answer choices of the years before 2010. In the 2008 Common Application, an applicant was asked to fill in a race only "if you wish to be identified with a particular ethnic group" (see Figure 6.2). The new reporting rules required institutions to use a two-part question format in which the first part collects ethnicity, and the second part collects race. For the first time, no "other" option was allowed. In addition, the language in the question stem was more assertive. Rather than asking students if they *wished* to be identified with an ethnic group, the question simply directed students to "indicate how you identify yourself." (Figure 6.3).

Racial Data Representation

The ways that multiraciality gets constructed, researched, and put into policy can inform people's racial realities, including their understanding of who they are and how they fit within society. Individuals who want to identify themselves with a group (be it a monoracially constructed group or mixed group), but do not see themselves represented within public discourse or academic scholarship on that group, may feel the identity is not theirs to claim. For example, Ford, Patterson, and Johnston-Guerrero (2020) found that even though all universities in the United States have populations of

Figure 6.2. Excerpt from the Common App 2008

If you wish to be identified with a particular ethnic group, please check all that apply:
○ African American, African, Black
○ Native American, Alaska Native (date enrolled _____
   Tribal affiliation _____)
○ Asian American (country _____)
○ Asian, incl. Indian Subcontinent (country _____)
○ Hispanic, Latino (country _____)
○ Mexican American, Chicano
○ Puerto Rican
○ Native Hawaiian, Pacific Islander
○ White or Caucasian
○ Other (specify _____)

Figure 6.3. Excerpt from the Common App 2010

1. Are you Hispanic/Latino?

○ Yes, Hispanic or Latino (including Spain) ○ No

2. Regardless of your answer to the prior question, please indicate how you identify yourself. (Check all that apply.)

○ American Indian or Alaska Native (including all Original Peoples of the Americas)
   Are you Enrolled? ○ Yes ○ No If yes, please enter Tribal Enrollment Number_____

○ Asian (including Indian subcontinent and Philippines)

○ Black or African American (including Africa and Caribbean)

○ Native Hawaiian or Other Pacific Islander (Original Peoples)

○ White (including Middle Eastern)

multiracial students (ranging from 2% to 12%), when they represent their student body composition on their websites, most only refer to monoracial groups. This practice effectively erases multiracial student populations and perpetuates the idea that everyone has a monoracial identity. In addition, many universities reclassified students who selected two or more races to monoracial groups. Some double- or triple-counted these students so that their student body totals exceeded 100% (Ford et al., 2020).

Outside of institutional-level data collection and representation, individual researchers have agency when constructing multiracial identities. Qualitative research on multiraciality in higher education is limited by who "counted" as multiracial in terms of inclusion criteria. For instance, Kristen Renn's (2000, 2008, 2009) extensive work on mixed-race college students has been path-breaking, but her inclusion criteria also limited which voices in the diverse multiracial communities could be heard. Renn only included those mixed-race students who "had parents from more than one federally designated racial or ethnic category" (Renn & Lunceford, 2004, p. 56). This common definition of who is multiracial within the extant scholarship suggests that only "first-generation mixed race" students count as mixed. However, we know from more recent research that individuals with long histories of racial mixing in their heritage are claiming their mixedness (Pew Research Center, 2015).

OTHER CONSIDERATIONS FOR HETEROGENEITY WITHIN MULTIRACIALITY

Self-Identification, Observer Identification by Physical Appearance, and Colorism

While self-identification is now the accepted norm in race data collection, as it values the individual's lived experiences, this is a relatively recent development (Renn, 2012; Renn & Lunceford, 2004). Observer identification, that is, having a survey taker look at a respondent and determine their racial classification, was once the norm in race data collection in the United States. American census takers went door to door making determinations of individuals' races until the 1970 Census. In 90% of U.S. public schools, teachers and school personnel selected all student racial identifications well into the 1990s (NCES, 1996). Some datasets, like Add Health, include both self-identified and observer-identified indicators of student race. Where the identifications are the same and where they differ reveal important information about how the students' self-identities match or diverge from how they are perceived by others. Some scholars argue that how students are perceived by others is much more important than how they self-identify because this has consequences for their social interactions with peers and authority figures, which has implications for their daily social realities and access to opportunities (Hunter, 2007). This notion is perhaps strongest for students who are mixed with Black and another race. For example, for most students who proactively self-identified with two or more races, institutions under the Texas Higher Education Coordinating Board (e.g., Lamar University) report them as "multiracial" in their descriptive data. However, if one of the races selected by students was Black, they were not considered "multiracial," they were recoded as monoracially Black. Ford et al. (2020) documented how Lamar University reported a category of student diversity labeled "Multiracial excluding Black." Ho, Sidanius, Levin, and Banaji (2011) suggest that this practice of recoding by using rules of hypodescent reflects societal beliefs that multiracial people are identified with their most minoritized group. Specifically, it reproduces colorism in society by assuming that students who have any Black heritage likely identify as Black.

Should Multiracial Be Its Own Group?

Is multiracial a racial group, or just a group that is a catchall outside of monoracial categories? This debate partly comes from the multiracial community itself, given the complicated and potentially contradictory positioning of their identities in relation to monoracial groups. DaCosta (2007) articulated this dynamic clearly:

> In their negotiations with each other (and within themselves) over the meaning of being multiracial and what they do and do not share with other mixed race people, the notion of a multiracial collective identity takes shape. Yet in this process two seemingly contradictory impulses are at work. At the same time as they elaborate a sense of shared groupness, multiracials are deconstructing the basis upon which racial membership has been erected. (p. 147)

Asserting a multiracial identity may be a way to deconstruct traditional notions of race and the often nonporous borders around monoracial groups. Leading scholar of multiraciality Paul Spickard (2015) shared similar questions and sentiments:

> In 1995, in a paper at a mixed-race conference in Hawai'i, I posed this grammatically awkward question: "Is there a groupness in mixedness?" That is, given that people of mixed ancestry tend to have a complex of similar experiences, do they constitute a meaningful social group, or are these simply individual experiences that are similar? In particular, do mixed people constitute an ethnic or racial group of their own, independent from the groups with which they may share partial ancestry? . . . Two decades later, the question remains. (pp. 352–353)

Should this category be considered "a racial group" even though it represents so many individuals and identities?

What to Do About Racial Fluidity?

Existing research has consistently demonstrated that mixed-race college students may change their racial identification based on the timing, context, or format of questions (Harper, 2016; Kellogg & Liddell, 2012; Renn & Lunceford, 2004). As the Pew Research Center (2015) outlined:

> An added layer of complexity is that racial identity can be fluid and may change over the course of one's life, or even from one situation to another. About three-in-ten adults with a multiracial background say that they have changed the way they describe their race over the years—with some saying they once thought of themselves as only one race and now think of themselves as more than one race, and others saying just the opposite. (p. 7)

Further, defining populations based solely on federal racial designations provides further limitations on capturing everyone who considers themselves multiracial. For example, someone with a Filipino father and Pakistani mother may experience their life as a multiracial person, but would be considered monoracially Asian American based on federal classification. Multiracial Arab Americans or others from the North Africa and Middle Eastern (MENA) region would not necessarily be captured as multiracial given the limitations of U.S. data collecting and reporting definitions (Arabs are defined as White in OMB directive 15). This is all problematic because mixedness encompasses much more diversity than first-generation mixing between racial groups constructed and legitimized by the government, and is well-informed by the historical constructions of race. These constructions matter for how we count multiracial students. As Martin and Lynch (2009) argue: "How a count is produced depends very much on who is doing the counting, what the count is for, and the occupational and physical location of the counting event. When treated as a contextual performance, the situated work of counting is subject to practical, organizational, and political contingencies" (p. 245).

RECOMMENDATIONS

We offer a few recommendations and ideas to consider for researchers and data practitioners who collect and report ethnoracial data. First, always acknowledge the existence of people who are not monoracial when collecting and reporting ethnoracial data. Multiracial people of all ages report that encountering surveys that force them to identify with a monoracial group as being stressful, identity-denying, microaggression-filled experiences (Harris, 2017). Multiracial people are one of the fastest growing groups and may soon account for 20% of the U.S. population, but if surveys fail to account for them we lose rich data on the complexity of lived racial realities. Allowing respondents to "select one or more" ethnoracial categories during data collection is an important first step.

Second, do not assume that all missing data are students who identify with two or more races. Currently, the State of California Department of Education (CDE) provides the following guidance to schools and districts: If students do not racially self-identify, CDE "will report such respondents in the 'Two or more races' category in federal reports" (CDE, n.d.). While this is the official policy statement, featured on the CDE.CA.Gov website for schools and districts to see, it is not clear whether or not this is the official practice of California, as it would conflate statewide missing data with students who actively identify with more than one ethnoracial group. Because data quality certainly varies between schools and districts, it would be difficult to disentangle which California locales have large populations of multiracial students and which simply have large amounts of missing data due to poor data collection strategies. We recommend against this practice of using "Two or More Races" as a default category for missing data.

In addition, good researchers know the value of reporting about variables in categories that are as close as possible to the categories in which the survey data were collected. This practice preserves data validity (i.e., are you measuring what you think you are measuring?). If you are collecting "self-reported" race and ethnicity, then you must use what students self-report. We advise against the practice of reassigning students who self-reported multiple races to monoracial groups. If you do this, do not label your data "self-reported race and ethnicity," because it is not. It is now "researcher reassigned race and ethnicity," so you may need to revise your labeling.

CONCLUSION

Meghan Markle, Duchess of Sussex, and arguably the most high-profile person to identify as mixed-race (her mother is Black, her father is White) famously shared an experience she had as a schoolgirl struggling to fill in a form that asked her to choose a single race.

> There I was (my curly hair, my freckled face, my pale skin, my mixed race) looking down at these boxes, not wanting to mess up, but not knowing what to do. You could only choose one, but that would be to choose one parent over the other—and one half of myself over the other. My teacher told me to check the box for Caucasian. "Because that's how you look, Meghan.". . .When I went home that night, I told my dad what had happened. He said the words that have always stayed with me: "If that happens again, you draw your own box." (Markle, 2016)

This vignette is significant because it features two of the powerful players in education (the *teacher* and the *institution,* manifested in the form of the survey) that shape how students see themselves. Both are overtly directing Markle to select a monoracial identification. Markle hesitates because she is confronted with a racial choice schema that does not reflect her self-identity and lived reality. For Markle, "draw your own box" has become a rallying call as she has lived into her mixed-race identity—she draws her own box as she moves through the world.

Yet the people with the power to "draw the boxes" are rarely the students themselves. Education researchers and practitioners make meaning of the world and describe the world back to us using survey data collection, reporting, and representation. As we have argued here, these processes are historically and contextually contingent, especially when the data are ethnoracial identifications. For multiracial students, self-identity gets transformed to fit one or more of the ethnic/racial categories provided during data collection. This response, in turn, becomes a variable that can be aggregated, recategorized, or erased when the data are reported or represented. This process is problematic for all racial identities; however, because the system has at its foundation an assumption of monoraciality, it is particularly problematic for students who identify outside of the monoracial paradigm.

NOTE

1. Although terminology like biracial, multiracial, and mixed race tend to be used interchangeably, they may have specific meanings to individuals who have preferences in how they are named. In this chapter, we also use them interchangeably, while recognizing the distinction between these terms as identifiers and the "two or more races" aggregated reporting category.

REFERENCES

Black, E. (2003). *War against the weak: Eugenics and America's campaign to create a master race.* New York, NY: Four Walls Eight Windows.

California Department of Education (n.d.). "FAQs—Race and Ethnicity Collection and Reporting." Retrieved from www.cde.ca.gov/ds/dc/es/refaq.asp

The Common Application. (n.d.). Demographics section. Retrieved from apply.commonapp.org/

Corcos, A. (1997). *The myth of human races.* East Lansing, MI: Michigan State University Press.

DaCosta, K. M. (2007). *Making multiracials: State, family, and market in the redrawing of the color line.* Stanford, CA: Stanford University Press.

Davis, F. J. (1991). *Who is Black? One nation's definition.* University Park, PA: Pennsylvania State University Press.

D'Souza, D. (1995). *The end of racism: Principles for a multiracial society.* New York, NY: Free Press.

Duster, T. (2003). *Backdoor to eugenics* (2nd Ed.). New York, NY: Routledge.
Elam, M. (2011). *The souls of mixed folk: Race, politics, and aesthetics in the new millennium*. Stanford, CA: Stanford University Press.
Ford, A., Patterson, K. S., & Johnston-Guerrero, M. P. (2020). Monoracial normativity in university websites: Systematic erasure and selective reclassification of multiracial students. *Journal of Diversity in Higher Education*. doi.org/10.1037/dhe0000154
Gould, S. J. (1996). *The mismeasure of man*. New York, NY: W. W. Norton & Company.
Harper, C. E. (2016). Pre-college and college predictors of longitudinal changes in multiracial college students' self-reported race. *Race Ethnicity and Education*, 19(5), 927–949.
Harris, J. C. (2016). Toward a critical multiracial theory in education. *International Journal of Qualitative Studies in Education*, 29(6), 795–813.
Harris, J. C. (2017). Multiracial college students' experiences with multiracial microaggressions. *Race Ethnicity and Education*, 20(4), 429–445.
Higher Education Research Institute (HERI). (n.d.). *Cooperative Institutional Research Program (CIRP) Freshman Survey*. Retrieved from heri.ucla.edu/cirp-freshman-survey/
Ho, A. K., Sidanius, J., Levin, D. T., & Banaji, M. R. (2011). Evidence for hypodescent and racial hierarchy in the categorization and perception of biracial individuals. *Journal of Personality and Social Psychology*, 100(3), 492–506.
Hollinger, D.A. (1995). Postethnic America: Beyond multiculturalism. New York, NY: Basic Books.
Humes, K. R., Jones, N. A., & Ramirez, R. R. (2011). *Overview of race and Hispanic origin: 2010*. Washington, DC: U.S. Department of Commerce, Economics and Statistics Administration, U.S. Census Bureau.
Hunter, M. (2007). The persistent problem of colorism: Skin tone, status, and inequality. *Sociology Compass*, 1(1), 237–254.
Johnston, M. P., Ozaki, C. C., Pizzolato, J. E., & Chaudhari, P. (2014). Which box(es) do I check? Investigating college students' meanings behind racial identification. *Journal of Student Affairs Research and Practice*, 51(1), 56–68.
Johnston-Guerrero, M. P., & Renn, K. A. (2016). Multiracial Americans in college. In K. O. Korgen (Ed.), *Race policy and multiracial Americans* (pp. 139–154). Bristol, UK: Policy Press.
Jones, N. A., & Bullock, J. (2012). *The two or more races population: 2010*. 2010 Census Brief Series. Washington, DC: U.S. Census Bureau.
Kellogg, A. H., & Liddell, D. L. (2012). "Not half but double": Exploring critical incidents in the racial identity of multiracial college students. *Journal of College Student Development*, 53(4), 524–541.
Lombardo, P. A. (2008). *Three generations, no imbeciles: Eugenics, the Supreme Court, and Buck v. Bell*. Baltimore, MD: The Johns Hopkins University Press.
Markle, M. (2016). I'm More Than An 'Other.' *Elle Magazine*. Retrieved from www.elle.com/uk/life-and-culture/news/a26855/more-than-an-other/
Martin, A., & Lynch, M. (2009). Counting things and people: The practices and politics of counting. *Social Problems*, 56(2), 243–266.
Montagu, A. (1964). *Man's most dangerous myth: The fallacy of race* (4th ed.). Cleveland, OH: World Publishing Co.

Morning, A. (2005). Multiracial classification on the United States census: Myth, reality, and future impact. *Revue européenne des migrations internationales, 21*(2), 111–134.

Morning, A. J. (2011). *The nature of race: How scientists think and teach about human difference*. Berkeley, CA: The University of California Press.

National Center for Education Statistics. (1996). *Racial and ethnic classifications used by public schools*. Retrieved from nces.ed.gov/pubs/96092.pdf

Padilla, A., & Kelley, M. (2005). *One box isn't enough: An analysis of how U.S. colleges and universities classify mixed heritage students*. Seattle, WA: MAVIN Foundation.

Park, R. E. (1928). Human migration and the marginal man. *American Journal of Sociology, 33,* 881–893.

Pascoe, P. (2009). *What comes naturally: Miscegenation law and the making of race in America*. New York, NY: Oxford University Press.

Patterson, A., Ford, K. S., & Cate, L. (2019). Digital formations of racial understandings: how university websites are contributing to the 'Two or More Races' conversation. *Race, Ethnicity, and Education*, 1–20.

Pew Research Center (2015). *Multiracial in America: Proud, diverse and growing in numbers*. Washington, DC: Pew Research Center.

Poston, W. S. C. (1990). The biracial identity development model: A needed addition. *Journal of Counseling and Development, 69,* 152–155.

Raimon, E. A. (2004). *The "tragic mulatta" revisited: Race and nationalism in nineteenth-century antislavery fiction*. New Brunswick, NJ: Rutgers University Press.

Renn, K. A. (2000). Patterns of situational identity among biracial and multiracial college students. *Review of Higher Education, 23,* 399–420.

Renn, K. A. (2008). Research on bi- and multiracial identity development: Overview and synthesis. *New Directions for Student Services, 2008*(123), 13–21.

Renn, K. A. (2009). Education policy, politics, and mixed heritage students in the United States. *Journal of Social Issues, 65*(1), 165–183.

Renn, K. A. (2012). *Mixed race college students: The ecology of race, identity, and community*. Albany, NY: State University of New York Press.

Renn, K. A., & Lunceford, C. J. (2004). Because the numbers matter: Transforming postsecondary education data on student race and ethnicity to meet the challenges of a changing nation. *Educational Policy, 18*(5), 752–783.

Rockquemore, K. A., Brunsma, D. L., & Delgado, D. J. (2009). Racing to theory or retheorizing race? Understanding the struggle to build a multiracial identity theory. *Journal of Social Issues, 65*(1), 13–34.

Root, M. P. P. (1996). A bill of rights for racially mixed people. In M. P. P. Root (Ed.), *The multiracial experience: Racial borders as the new frontier* (pp. 3–14). Thousand Oaks, CA: Sage.

Root, M. P. P. (1999). The biracial baby boom: Understanding the ecological constructions of racial identity in the 21st century. In R. H. Sheets & E. R. Hollins (Eds.), *Racial and ethnic identity in school practices: Aspects of human development* (pp. 67–90). Mahwah, NJ: Erlbaum.

Roberts, D. (2011). *Fatal invention: How science, politics, and big business re-create race in the twenty-first century*. New York, NY: The New Press.

Roediger, D. R. (2008). *How race survived U.S. history: From settlement and slavery to the Obama phenomenon.* London, UK, and New York, NY: Verso.

Smedley, A. (2007). *Race in North America: Origin and evolution of a worldview* (3rd Ed.). Boulder, CO: Westview Press.

Spickard, P. (2015). *Race in mind: Critical essays.* Notre Dame, IN: University of Notre Dame Press.

Stonequist, E. V. (1937). *The marginal man: A student in personality and culture conflict.* New York, NY: Russell & Russell.

Wijeyesinghe, C. L. (2001). Racial identity in multiracial people: An alternative paradigm. In C. L. Wijeyesinghe & B. W. Jackson, III (Eds.), *New perspectives on racial identity development: A theoretical and practical anthology* (pp. 129–152). New York, NY: New York University Press.

Williams, K. M. (2006). *Mark one or more: Civil rights in multiracial America.* Ann Arbor, MI: The University of Michigan Press.

Zuberi, T. (2001). *Thicker than blood: How racial statistics lie.* Minneapolis, MN: The University of Minnesota Press.

PART II

UNMASKING EDUCATIONAL INEQUALITY THROUGH DISAGGREGATED DATA

CHAPTER 7

Similar, But Not the Same

Considering the Intersections of Race, Ethnicity, and Immigrant Status in the Lives of Black Students

Kimberly A. Griffin and Chrystal A. George Mwangi

There was much to celebrate as Black Harvard University alumni gathered for their reunion in the summer of 2004. There had been significant growth in the diversity of the undergraduate population, and Black students had reached approximately 8% of the student body. However, professors Lani Guinier and Henry Louis Gates, Jr., pointed out an interesting fact: Most of these students were children of immigrants from Africa or the Caribbean, or had immigrated themselves. This observation reflects a larger trend, particularly at elite universities. Approximately 13% of all college-age Blacks in the United States are African or Caribbean immigrants (first generation) or are the children of immigrants (second generation) (Kent, 2007). This population is often collectively referred to as Black immigrants, and data suggest they are more likely to enroll in college generally, and selective institutions in particular. Black immigrants have been described in the media and recent publications as a potential new "model minority" (e.g., Chua & Rubenfeld, 2014; Page, 2007), citing data that show that African immigrants have higher levels of educational attainment than White Americans, on average (Erisman & Looney, 2007; Kent, 2007). Further, over the past 3 years, news articles have highlighted multiple examples of first- and second-generation Black immigrants being accepted into all eight Ivy League institutions (Jacobs, 2015; John, 2014; Sorto, 2016).

These trends have led education leaders, policymakers, and scholars to engage in conversations about what the increased representation of Black students from immigrant backgrounds means. Some social justice advocates and educators question whether recruiting students from Africa and the Caribbean meets the corrective social justice goals associated with affirmative action. Others find recruiting and retaining foreign-born Blacks to be an important goal, bringing increased racial and ethnic diversity to campuses

(George Mwangi, 2014; Onyenekwu & George Mwangi, 2017; Rimer & Arenson, 2004). Underlying this discourse are larger questions that have gone unanswered: What does it mean to be "Black" in the United States? How do ethnicity and immigration status relate to racial identity and access to opportunity? Does being Black and raised in Africa or the Caribbean mean something different than being a Black American, not only culturally, but in terms of experiences with and exposure to racism and oppression? Finally, how do we interpret and explain the access and success observed among Black immigrants compared to those with longer histories in the United States?

Race is often centered in conversations about the identities and outcomes of Black students without considering additional identities that expose people to marginalization or provide access to resources and privilege (Crenshaw, 1991). Racial categorization may mean little to Black immigrants, and may not be their primary mode of self-definition (Dache-Gerbino & Mislán, 2015; Fries-Britt et al., 2014a; George Mwangi, 2014). Foreign-born Blacks and their children may connect in more meaningful ways to their ethnic group or nation of origin than to their race, relying on cultural markers like language, dress, food, traditions, and values for identification and connection. The legacy of systemic racism and slavery, as well as misunderstandings about the centrality of race in one's identity development, may lead higher education leaders and policymakers to focus exclusively on racial identity, but this emphasis misses the importance of ethnic identity in the lives of many Black students.

In this chapter, we examine demographic data on Black immigrants in the United States, as well as scholarship on the patterns of access, experiences in higher education, and educational outcomes of Black students from various ethnic backgrounds. We close by offering suggestions for higher education practitioners and researchers, reminding our field of the importance of acknowledging diversity within the Black community, and consider how better to account for nationality/ethnicity, immigrant/generational status, and citizenship in education practice and research.

TRENDS AND PATTERNS IN THE BLACK IMMIGRANT POPULATION

According to a 2018 Pew Research Center report, approximately 4.2 million Black immigrants were living in the United States in 2016, representing almost 10% of the Black population. This number has increased fourfold since 1980. Much of the growth in the Black community over the past four decades is due to immigration (Anderson, 2015; Kent, 2007; Waters, Kasnitz, & Asad, 2014), with nearly 20% of Black community growth in the 2000s due to the Black immigrant population (Kent, 2007).

Immigrants are the fastest growing group within the U.S. Black population (Kent, 2007). The Immigration and Nationality Act of 1965, Refugee

Act of 1980, and Immigration Act of 1990 facilitated the increased representation of Black immigrants by targeting skilled laborers, allowing immigrants from high conflict areas to seek asylum, and targeting nations underrepresented in the U.S. immigration landscape, creating opportunities for Black immigrants generally, and immigrants from Africa in particular (Anderson, 2015; Kent, 2007). In addition, the birthrate among immigrants contributes to population growth. Black immigrant women report higher birth rates than Black women born in the United States (Anderson, 2015), and almost 12% of Black children (0–10 years old) in the United States have at least one Black immigrant parent, a percentage that has nearly doubled since 1990 (Hernandez, 2012). Twenty percent of youth growing up in the United States have parents who emigrated from other countries, and it is projected that by 2040, one in every three children in the United States will grow up in an immigrant family (Suarez-Orozco, Suarez-Orozco, & Todorova, 2008).

WITHIN-GROUP DIVERSITY AND REPRESENTATION

The U.S. Black immigrant population is ethnically diverse, with individuals from Europe, Africa, the Caribbean, and Central and South America, representing Spanish-speaking, Anglophone, and Francophone nations. Approximately 9% of Black immigrants are from Latin or Central America, including groups from Guyana, Mexico, Cuba, Panama, and Belize (Anderson, 2015). Early waves of Black immigrants in the 18th century were largely from the Caribbean (Kent, 2007; Waters, Kasinitz, & Asad, 2014), and approximately half of all Black immigrants continue to be from this region (see Table 7.1). In 2016, Jamaicans (18%) and Haitians (15%) represented the two largest groups of Black immigrants (Anderson & Lopez, 2018).

While their numbers have been smaller historically (Waters, Kasinitz, & Asad, 2014), the African immigrant population has grown substantially, and immigration from Africa is responsible for much of the most recent growth in the Black immigrant population (Hernandez, 2012). This growth was spurred by the Immigration Act of 1990, which targeted immigration from underrepresented nations, and the Refugee Act of 1980, which made it easier for Somalians and Ethiopians to seek asylum in the United States (Anderson, 2015). There was a 137% increase in the number of African immigrants in the United States between 2000 and 2013, with approximately 1.8 million Africans residing in the United States in 2013 as compared to 80,000 in 1970 (Anderson, 2015).

Immigrants from Africa now represent more than a third (36%) of foreign-born Blacks (Anderson, 2015), and between 2010 and 2018, the size of the Sub-Saharan African population grew faster than the the overall rate for foreign-born individuals in the United States (52% vs 12%)

Table 7.1. Top Five African and Caribbean Nations Represented in Black Foreign-Born Population in the United States (2013)

Nation of Origin	Percent of Black Immigrant Population	Population (in thousands)
AFRICA		
Nigeria	6%	226
Ethiopia	5%	191
Ghana	4%	147
Kenya	3%	107
Liberia	2%	83
CARIBBEAN		
Jamaica	18%	682
Haiti	15%	586
Trinidad & Tobago	5%	192
Dominican Republic	4%	161
Barbados	1%	51

Source: Anderson, 2015

(Echeverria-Estrada & Batalova, 2019). The vast majority of African immigrants in the United States are from sub-Saharan nations, with Nigeria, Ethiopia, Ghana, Kenya, and Somalia being the most highly represented (Anderson, 2015; Anderson & Lopez, 2018; see Table 7.1).

Many Black immigrants settle in metropolitan areas, and the largest concentrations reside on the East Coast. While there are similarities in the states with the highest representation of Caribbean and African immigrants (e.g., New York, California, Texas, New Jersey, and Florida), Caribbean immigrants tend to be more geographically concentrated and African immigrants are more widely dispersed. Almost two-thirds of all Caribbean immigrants live in New York City or Miami, and New York, Florida, and New Jersey are the most popular states. African immigrants are most concentrated in New York and Washington, DC; however, there are also sizable populations in Minneapolis, Los Angeles, Dallas, and Houston (Kent, 2007).

SOCIOECONOMIC INDICATORS AND EDUCATIONAL ATTAINMENT

Although they may be categorized as members of a larger Black racial category or as immigrants, there are many characteristics that make Black immigrants unique and distinct from both groups (Okonofua, 2013). According to reports analyzing data from the 2005 and 2013 American Community

Survey (Anderson, 2015; Kent, 2007), Black immigrants are more likely to be married and to have higher median household incomes and lower rates of poverty than Black Americans. They also are more likely to be proficient at English and to be U.S. citizens, and less likely to be undocumented or have unauthorized status than the immigrant population overall.

There are also unique patterns in educational attainment and post-secondary enrollment at the intersection of race, ethnicity, and immigrant status. More than a quarter of Black immigrants over age 25 have a post-secondary degree, as compared to 19% of U.S.-born Blacks (Anderson, 2015). Close to 40% of African immigrants possess a college degree, which is higher than college degree attainment of the overall U.S. population of immigrants (28%), nonimmigrant Blacks (19%), and U.S. population overall (30%; Anderson, 2015; Hernandez, 2012). The degree attainment rates for Caribbean- (20%) and Central American- (17%) born Blacks are fairly close to those of U.S.-born Blacks (19%) (Anderson, 2015). Still, it is important to note that the experiences of Black immigrants in the United States are complex. Research indicates that they do not earn incomes or have occupational status commensurate with their education levels and are more likely to be underemployed than other foreign groups (Bureau of Labor Statistics, 2017; Kent, 2007).

COLLEGE TRAJECTORIES OF BLACK IMMIGRANT STUDENTS

While higher education scholarship on Black immigrant collegians is scant in comparison to Black Americans or other immigrant populations, there is an emerging body of work that highlights how ethnicity, culture, and immigration status influence students' educational journeys. In this section, we review three dimensions of the extant literature: college access, experiences, and outcomes of Black immigrants.[1]

College Access

Much of the research acknowledging Black immigrants' college experiences examines patterns of college enrollment, access, and choice. While there have been general increases in the number of Black students in college, researchers identify steady increases in the enrollment of Black immigrants (Bennett & Lutz, 2009; Kent, 2007). First- and second-generation Black immigrants have higher levels of college attendance compared to their third-plus generation Black peers, and one study suggests the odds of first-generation Black immigrants attending college are 27.8% higher than U.S.-born Whites (Keller & Tillman, 2008).

Black immigrants are also more likely to attend highly selective institutions than both Black American and White students (Bennett & Lutz, 2009;

Byrd, Brunn-Bevel & Sexton, 2014). In 2007, Massey, Mooney, Torres, and Charles published one of the most heavily cited higher education empirical studies on Black immigrants. The researchers used data from the National Longitudinal Survey of Freshman (NLSF) to examine Black immigrant and Black American students attending selective colleges and universities in the United States. Although first- and second-generation Black immigrants comprise only 13% of the 18- to 19-year-old Black population, they comprised 27% of Black students at selective colleges and 41% of Black students at Ivy League institutions in their dataset (Massey et al., 2007).

While these data suggest Black immigrants have great success in college enrollment, there is limited understanding of how they navigate the college choice process and whether they consider or are influenced by factors related to their racial and ethnic identities. Immigrants to the United States are often positively selected: They tend to have more education, and potentially more access to educational resources, than those who remain in their home country (Model, 2008). Scholars argue that socioeconomic status, parental emphasis on education, and academic preparation make Black immigrants more likely to attend college. For example, Haynie (2002) found that major factors contributing to Black immigrants' high rate of enrollment at Harvard included: high levels of parental educational attainment among African students; participation in college preparatory programs among Caribbean students; and African and Caribbean students' global kinship networks. Similarly, Black immigrant collegians, and particularly African students, were more likely than their native Black peers to come from two-parent households and to have fathers who graduated from college and hold advanced degrees (Haynie, 2002; Massey et al., 2007). Black immigrants were also more likely to have gone to private schools and to have lived in racially integrated neighborhoods (Massey et al., 2007). Yet, Massey et al. (2007) and Bennett and Lutz (2009) also acknowledge that the college-going gap between immigrant and American Black students was significantly reduced when social and economic factors are controlled for. Thus, it seems that Black immigrants may be more likely to have the socioeconomic resources valued in the college admissions process, rather than being individualistically more prepared for college.

Family and cultural expectations may also impact Black immigrants' college-going. Researchers have described a collectivist or familistic worldview as a motivating force; students saw attending college as part of a family investment or accomplishment (George Mwangi, 2018; George Mwangi, Daoud, English, & Griffin, 2017; Griffin, del Pilar, McIntosh, & Griffin, 2012). Black immigrants describe the value of education, the discipline required to achieve academically, and college aspirations as cultural norms embedded in their ethnic and/or immigrant identities (Griffin et al., 2012). High parental/family expectations about academic achievement and college-going can inform a habitus or worldview that emphasizes the importance of attaining a college education as part of their cultural legacy (Griffin et al., 2012).

Immigration history and the importance of taking advantage of opportunities in the United States were discussed across studies as sources of motivation to attend college among Black immigrant students and families (George Mwangi & English, 2017; Griffin et al., 2012; Haynie, 2002). Griffin and colleagues (2012) introduced displaced capital as a factor in the college-going process of Black immigrants. Displaced capital refers to when Black immigrants' affluence in the home country is not transferable to the United States; yet the memory of their former social/economic status acts as a motivator and expectation toward upward mobility through higher education (Griffin et al., 2012). Thus, while it may not always translate to financial resources, displaced capital can act as a protective factor to some of the challenges associated with low socioeconomic status in the United States and in the college-going process.

While research largely frames Black immigrants as more likely to gain access to college and as having more resources to promote college-going, few studies attend to ethnic differences in college access or choice. However, Erisman and Looney (2007) disaggregated college enrollment data and found stark differences in rates of college access for Black students from immigrant backgrounds by citizenship status, nation of origin, and time of migration. African immigrants have higher college attendance rates than Caribbean immigrants, and first-generation Black immigrants are significantly more likely to attend college than their nonimmigrant White peers (Erisman & Looney, 2007); however, there are few differences in rates of college attendance between subsequent generations and their peers (Keller & Tillman, 2008).

College Experiences

Although scholars have written about how college access and choice experiences vary between Black immigrants and those with longer histories in the United States, less is known about the differences and similarities between Black students' college experiences based on ethnicity and immigrant status. The limited extant work offers insights into the distinctiveness of Black immigrant students' transition into college, identity development, and level of engagement in the campus community. An overarching theme addressed across much of this scholarship positions Black immigrants as racialized beings in the United States, and considers how their campus experiences reflect and are situated within this (for some, new) status as a racial minority.

Studies describe challenges Black international and first-generation immigrant students have with the cultural adjustment to predominantly White institutions (PWIs) (Constantine, Anderson, LaVerne, Caldwell, & Utsey, 2005; Fries-Britt, George Mwangi & Peralta, 2014b; George

Mwangi, Changamire & Mosselson, 2019; Lee & Rice, 2007). For newer immigrants and international students from nations where the majority of the population is Black, becoming a college student in the United States means adjusting to a new status as a racial minority (George Mwangi, 2016; George Mwangi & Fries-Britt, 2015). Social constructions of race in Africa and the Caribbean are not the same as in the United States, and some can be perplexed by their new racial status. These students often report experiences with racial discrimination from U.S. peers and faculty and social isolation (Awokoya, 2012; Constantine et al., 2005; Fries-Britt et al., 2014b; Griffin, George Mwangi, & Patterson, 2017; Lee & Rice, 2007). These experiences are also complicated by their immigrant status, which can evoke xenophobia and nativism (Awokoya, 2012; Constantine et al., 2005; George Mwangi, 2016; George Mwangi et al., 2019; George Mwangi & Fries-Britt, 2015; Lee & Rice, 2007).

Another related theme of the literature on Black immigrant collegians examines students' identity development. Black immigrants may be perceived as African American due to a shared racial background; however, research suggests that Black immigrants, particularly first generation immigrants, may find racial identity to be less salient than their ethnic identity/nationality (Dache-Gerbino & Mislán, 2015; Fries-Britt, George Mwangi, & Peralta, 2014a; George Mwangi, 2014; Griffin, Cunningham, & George Mwangi, 2016). A study on the racialized experiences of foreign-born Black students revealed that their perceptions and experiences deviate from traditional scholarship on Black student identity development, leading to the creation of an emergent framework, Learning Race in the U.S. Context (LRUSC; Fries-Britt et al., 2014a). Participants did not initially feel connected to issues of race and racism in the United States, but over time and with a number of campus racial encounters, began to consider their own racial status and identity (Fries-Britt et al., 2014a). Attempting to distance oneself from race and racism was often an initial strategy for students to remain focused on their goal of attaining a college degree (Fries-Britt et al., 2014a; George Mwangi & Fries-Britt, 2015). Black immigrants may be the target of negative perceptions about their academic abilities due to race, while more often receiving positive affirmation about their academic ability based on their ethnicity (Daoud, George Mwangi, Griffin, & English, 2018; George Mwangi, Fries-Britt, Peralta, & Daoud, 2016; Griffin et al., 2017). Focusing on ethnicity or immigrant identity may act as a form of protection from racism, which is important given that exposure to racism can result in decreased academic confidence, stereotype threat, pressures to prove academic merit, and poorer academic performance (George Mwangi, 2014). Yet racial encounters eventually led students to respond (Fries-Britt et al., 2014a). Some withdrew, some voiced a deeper commitment to action that leads to social change against racism, and others used racial encounters as a source of academic motivation.

The third major theme of the literature focuses on students' perceptions of racism and the campus climate for diversity and inclusion. While research suggests native-born Black students view campus in more racialized terms, immigrants describe campus diversity in terms of ethnicity and culture, and not just race (George Mwangi & Fries-Britt, 2015; Griffin et al., 2016). Second- (U.S.-born child of two immigrant parents) and 2.5-generation (U.S.-born child of one immigrant and one U.S.-born parent) Black immigrants are more likely to experience and perceive campus climate in ways similar to their native Black peers, calling attention to a lack of racial diversity on campus and experiences with marginalization. Conversely, first-generation immigrants describe their campuses as more diverse and note fewer encounters with racial discrimination (Griffin et al., 2016).

A few studies document the distinctive ways in which Black immigrant students respond to marginalization. Although Afro-Caribbean and African students had higher college GPAs compared to Black native peers in Byrd and colleagues' study (2014), they demonstrated higher levels of performance burden and experienced self-consciousness about negative stereotypes regarding their racial group's academic abilities, worrying they would confirm these perceptions. Similarly, Griffin and colleagues (2016) found that Black immigrants most often encountered stereotypes in the classroom, and responded by engaging in a proving process to demonstrate their intellectual aptitude. George Mwangi et al. (2016) also revealed that foreign-born Black students believed their U.S. peers perceived them as less academically prepared or talented due to stereotypes regarding their nationality, accent, and skin color. Despite these challenges, students believed they could leverage their academic preparedness to prove their expertise and gain their peers' respect (George Mwangi et al., 2016). These academic experiences resemble literature on the experiences of high achieving Black American students who resist stereotypes, suggesting Black students are less academically capable and believe they must prove their academic abilities to White peers and faculty (Fries-Britt, Younger, & Hall, 2010). The experiences of Black immigrants extend this concept of a "proving process," by highlighting its unique manifestation at the intersection of nativity and ethnicity in addition to race.

While they are exposed to similar stereotypes about academic ability, Black immigrants may be less academically marginalized on their campuses than Black American peers. Williamson (2010) found African and Caribbean students were more academically engaged in their campus communities than Black American students, and African students reported more often interacting with and forming relationships with faculty outside of the classroom. Similarly, faculty held international Black males enrolled in a Historically Black College and University (HBCU) to a higher academic standard and had higher expectations for them than for domestic Black males (Burrell, Fleming, Fredericks, & Moore, 2015). Thus, while Black immigrants face academic challenges, they may have more positive academic engagement experiences as compared to Black Americans.

Regarding social engagement, Black immigrants often discuss having both international/immigrant and domestic student friendships (Byrd et al., 2014; George Mwangi & Fries-Britt, 2015; Griffin et al., 2016; Griffin & McIntosh, 2015). Black immigrants seek opportunities to interact with those who share their own background and identity; however, many simultaneously describe intentional strategies to engage with peers from multiple racial and ethnic groups. In a study by Griffin and McIntosh (2015), Black immigrants described how they sought and found affirmation for both their racial and ethnic identities through campus organizations. Students saw differences between groups with racially and ethnically focused missions; however, they rarely limited themselves to one or the other. Black immigrant students did not report pressure to hide their multiple identities; instead, they gained different benefits from the different groups.

While students might embrace both their racial and ethnic identities, they may not receive complete acceptance from their racial or ethnic group peers. For example, Griffin and McIntosh (2015) found that some Black immigrant students born in the United States (second or 2.5 generation), did not feel completely welcome and comfortable in student organizations with ethnically focused missions. Despite their interest and attempts at participation, some second-generation students perceived these groups as unwelcoming and were questioned by first-generation immigrants about their ties to their ethnic heritage or were accused of being "not ethnic enough." Thus, identity and identity development play a role in Black immigrants' campus engagement, particularly in how they are perceived by others.

College Outcomes

While there appears to be a "Black immigrant advantage" in college access, their college grades and academic achievements demonstrate the same racial gaps with White peers that are present with Black Americans (Massey et al., 2007), and there is little published research on immigrants' college outcomes. Rong and Brown (2001) found that Caribbean and African students had lower graduation rates than their White peers. In a more recent study, Erisman and Looney (2007) confirmed that Black immigrants' 5-year college completion numbers are lower than those of their White and Asian immigrant peers and that most who had completed received associate's degrees or certificates, not bachelor's degrees. Some scholars have found that Afro-Caribbean and African students have higher college GPAs and rates of persistence than native Black students (Byrd et al., 2014; Tauriac & Liem, 2012). Yet after controlling for high school grades and socioeconomic status, immigration status no longer predicts persistence.

RECOMMENDATIONS

As the size of the Black immigrant population increases both in the United States and on college campuses and more students in the Black community embrace ethnic and racial identities, higher education must adjust to meet these students' distinct needs and offer support. Generations of research have informed our understanding, as a field, of the many issues Black students may be navigating as they gain access to and persist in college. New waves of scholarship are just beginning to inform education researchers, leaders, and policymakers about distinctions in Black students' backgrounds and experiences based on ethnicity, nationality, and immigrant status. We offer recommendations to guide future research, practice, and policy with the goal of better understanding and meeting the needs of the diverse Black student population in years to come.

Researchers must continue to engage in work that elucidates and disaggregates immigrants' educational experiences to move beyond a one-dimensional, model minority depiction of Black immigrants. Data should be disaggregated by factors such as country of origin, mode of entry into the United States (e.g., family reunification, international student visa, refugee/asylee), and socioeconomic status both pre- and postimmigration to glean a more nuanced understanding of Black immigrants' experiences in the United States and how they engage in the U.S. education system. At the individual level, disaggregating data by factors such as gender, age, generation status, sexuality, religion, and racial/ethnic self-identity could also provide richer understandings of the educational experiences of this population. In addition, we recommend scholars more specifically focus on refugee, asylee, and undocumented Black immigrant populations. As compared to other Black immigrants, these groups may have different experiences due to trauma experienced in their home countries, distinctive encounters with immigration barriers and policies, and less access to capital.

Another way to demonstrate the diversity within the Black population is to move beyond research that compares the experiences and outcomes of Black immigrants and U.S.-born Black students attending highly selective institutions. Many Black immigrant students are adult learners and/or are pursuing associate's degrees and certificates (Erisman & Looney, 2007). However, there is no research to date that has used community colleges as a site for research related to Black immigrants. In order to understand Black immigrants' educational pathways holistically, it is important to understand their experiences at diverse institutional types.

Finally, while research is beginning to address distinctions in students' experiences by immigrant generational status, less attention has been given to ethnic identity or how nation of origin may play a role in Black students' development or experiences. African immigrants appear to have different access and pathways to higher education as compared to their Caribbean peers; however, this has rarely been the focus of study. Further, little work has stepped outside of the immigrant discourse, exploring how Black students generally think about, manage, and evolve in their ethnic identities. For example, there are increasingly frequent conversations about the identity development and community engagement of Afro-Latinos (e.g., Dache-Gerbino & Mislán, 2015); yet few scholars have examined the college access, experiences, and outcomes of this population. Deeper exploration of distinctions in ethnic identity would add texture to students' narratives, providing insight into differences and similarities in students' values, traditions, opportunities for community connection, and access to educational resources.

As we encourage continued work in this area, it also is important to acknowledge that engaging in research on the educational experiences of Black immigrants is challenging for at least two reasons. First, research on the academic successes of Black immigrants can be used to wrongly suggest that the United States is now a postracial society and that institutionalized racism does not exist. Therefore, scholars must take care not to frame their work in ways that position Black immigrants as superior to Black Americans or that negate the marginalization experienced by Black people in the U.S. education system (Onyenekwu & George Mwangi, 2017). Second, efforts to identify Black students from different ethnic backgrounds on a given campus, or in higher education generally, are challenged by the limited ways in which demographic information is captured on survey instruments. Surveys usually limit Black students to indicating their racial identity with no acknowledgment of their ethnicity, unless they also identify as Latinx. There is no box to check that indicates that "African American" means African immigrant, or a way to share one's Jamaican or Haitian background. In evaluating multiple national surveys (e.g., the National Study of Student Engagement, the Cooperative Institutional Research Program) and institutional level assessments, there is no consistent way for Black students to acknowledge their ethnic identities. However, as the U.S. Census moves to capture the ethnicity of Black people beginning in 2020 (U.S. Census Bureau, 2018), we recommend that higher education also shift in this direction to make empirical research related to Black immigrants' experiences more feasible.

As we aim to better support Black students, those working on college campuses must move away from placing the onus on Black immigrants, international students, and students with strong connections to their ethnic identities to navigate their less inclusive campus environments. Rather, faculty, student affairs professionals, and institutional leaders must move toward understanding how campus environments can be reshaped to better support these students in their transition and experiences in order to reach the highest levels of success (Lee & Rice, 2007). Emerging research on the diversity within the Black community serves as a reminder to student affairs professionals, faculty, and institutional leaders that all Black students are not the same. It is also important to remind these stakeholders that extant research also makes clear that not all foreign-born Black students are the same. The research suggests that students have varying experiences, needs, and resources based on how their immigrant status, ethnic identity, socioeconomic background, and family resources intersect and manifest in their lives. Thus, we urge individuals working with Black students to inquire more deeply about their backgrounds, learning more about students' identities, values, and cultural connections as they develop interventions or recommend campus resources.

NOTE

1. Unless otherwise noted, the term "Black immigrant" refers to students born abroad or who are the children of immigrants. Black native-born and Black Americans refer to students born in the United States to two U.S.-born parents. Much of the scholarship does not disaggregate research findings beyond immigrant and native-born status; however, when further data disaggregation does occur in the literature (e.g., by geographic region or generation status) we present those findings. Additionally, some scholarship refers to international students, rather than immigrant students. International students are collegians on temporary student visas, while immigrant students are considered individuals planning to permanently reside in the United States. Because immigration status can impact students' experiences, when this distinction of terms is used in the literature, we also reflect it in this review.

REFERENCES

Anderson, M. (2015). *A rising share of the U.S. Black population is foreign born; 9 percent are immigrants; and while most are from the Caribbean, Africans drive recent growth*. Washington, DC: Pew Research Center.

Anderson, M., & Lopez, G. (2018). *Key facts about black immigrants in the U.S.* Washington, DC: Pew Research Center.

Awokoya, J. (2012). Identity constructions and negotiations among 1.5- and second-generation Nigerians: The impact of family, school, and peer contexts. *Harvard Educational Review, 82*(2), 255–281.

Bennett, P. R., & Lutz, A. (2009). How African American is the net Black advantage? Differences in college attendance among immigrant Blacks, native Blacks, and Whites. *Sociology of Education, 82*, 70–100.

Bureau of Labor Statistics (2017). *Foreign-born workers: Labor force characteristics summary (USDL-17-0618)*. Washington, DC: U.S. Department of Labor.

Burrell, J. O., Fleming, L., Fredericks, A. C., & Moore, I. (2015). Domestic and international student matters: The college experiences of Black males majoring in engineering at an HBCU. *The Journal of Negro Education, 84*(1), 40–55.

Byrd, W. C., Brunn-Bevel, R. J., & Sexton, P. R. (2014). 'We don't all look alike': The academic performance of black student populations at elite colleges. *Du Bois Review*, *11*(2), 353–385.

Chua, A., & Rubenfeld, J. (2014). *The triple package: How three unlikely traits explain the rise and fall of cultural groups in America*. New York, NY: Penguin Press.

Constantine, M. G., Anderson, G. M., LaVerne, A. B., Caldwell, L. D., & Utsey, S. O. (2005). Examining the cultural adjustment experiences of African international college students: A qualitative analysis. *Journal of Counseling Psychology*, *52*(1), 57–66.

Crenshaw, K. (1991). Mapping the margins: Intersectionality, identity politics, and violence against women of color. *Stanford Law Review*, *43*(6), 1241–1299.

Dache-Gerbino, A., & Mislán, C. (2015, May). *Passin' for Latin@ and the Politics of Black-imiento*. Paper presented at the annual meeting, Critical Race Studies in Education Association (CRSEA), Nashville, TN.

Daoud, N., George Mwangi, C. A., Griffin, K. A., & English, S. (2018). Beyond stereotypes: Examining the role of social identities in the motivation patterns of Black immigrant and Black native students. *American Journal of Education*, *124*(3), 285–312.

Echeverria-Estrada, C., & Batalova, J. (2019). Sub-Saharan African Immigrants in the United States. Washington, DC: Migration Policy Institute. Retrieved from www.migrationpolicy.org/article/sub-saharan-african-immigrants-united-states.

Erisman, B. W., & Looney, S. (2007). *Opening the door to the American dream: Increasing higher education access and success for immigrants*. Washington, DC: Institute for Higher Education Policy.

Fries-Britt, S., George Mwangi, C. A., & Peralta, A. M. (2014a). Learning race in the U.S. context: Perceptions of race among foreign-born students of color. *Journal of Diversity in Higher Education*, *7*(1), 1–13.

Fries-Britt, S., George Mwangi, C. A., & Peralta, A. M. (2014b). The acculturation experiences of foreign-born students of color in physics. *Journal of Student Affairs Research and Practice*, *51*(4), 459–471.

Fries-Britt, S. L., Younger, T. K., & Hall, W. D. (2010). Lessons from high-achieving students of color in physics. *New Directions for Institutional Research*, *2010*(148), 75–83.

George Mwangi, C. A. (2014). Complicating Blackness: Black immigrants and racial positioning in U.S. higher education. *Journal of Critical Thought and Praxis*, *3*(2), 1–27.

George Mwangi, C. A. (2016). Exploring sense of belonging among Black international students at an HBCU. *Journal of International Students*, *6*(4), 1015–1037.

George Mwangi, C. A. (2018). A family affair: Examining the college-going strategies of sub-Saharan African immigrants in the U.S. through funds of knowledge. In J. Kiyama & C. Rios-Aguilar (Eds.), *Funds of knowledge in higher education: Honoring students' cultural experiences and resources as strength* (pp. 10–124). New York, NY: Routledge.

George Mwangi, C. A., Changamire, N., & Mosselson, J. (2019). An intersectional understanding of African international graduate students' experiences in U.S. higher education. *Journal of Diversity in Higher Education*, *12*(1), 52–64.

George Mwangi, C. A., Daoud, N., English, S., & Griffin, K. A. (2017). Me and my family: Ethnic differences and familial influences on academic motivations of Black collegians. *Journal of Negro Education, 86*(4), 479–493.

George Mwangi, C. A., & English, S. (2017). Being Black (and) immigrant students: When race, ethnicity, and nativity collide. *International Journal of Multicultural Education, 19*(2), 100–130.

George Mwangi, C. A., & Fries-Britt, S. (2015) Black within Black: The perceptions of Black immigrant collegians and their U.S. college experience. *About Campus, 20*(2), 16–23.

George Mwangi, C. A., Fries-Britt, S., Peralta, A. M., & Daoud, N. (2016). Examining intra-racial dynamics and engagement between native-born and foreign-born Black collegians in STEM. *Journal of Black Studies, 47*(7), 773–794.

Griffin, K., Cunningham, E., & George Mwangi, C. A. (2016). Defining diversity: Ethnic differences in Black students' perceptions of racial climate. *Journal of Diversity in Higher Education, 9*(1), 34–49.

Griffin, K., del Pilar, W., McIntosh, K., & Griffin, A. (2012). "Oh, of course I'm going to go to college": Understanding how habitus shapes the college choice process of Black immigrant students. *Journal of Diversity in Higher Education, 5*(2), 96–111.

Griffin, K. A., George Mwangi, C. A., & Patterson, S. M. (2017). The experiences of Black immigrant women transitioning into college: Moving in and moving through. In L. Patton & N. Croom (Eds.), *Critical perspectives on Black women and college success* (pp. 101–112). New York, NY: Routledge.

Griffin, K. A., & McIntosh, K. L. (2015). Finding a fit: Understanding black immigrant students' engagement in campus activities. *Journal of College Student Development, 56*(3), 243–260.

Haynie, A. C. (2002). Not just Black policy considerations: The influence of ethnicity on pathways to academic success amongst Black undergraduates at Harvard University. *Journal of Public International and International Affairs, 13*, 40–62.

Hernandez, D. J. (2012). *Changing demography and circumstances for young Black children in African and Caribbean families*. Washington DC: Migration Policy Institute.

Jacobs, P. (2015, April 9). An elite group of students accepted to all 8 Ivy League schools have one thing in common. *Business Insider*. Retrieved from www.businessinsider.com/students-accepted-to-all-8-ivy-league-schools-have-one-specific-thing-in-common-2015-4

John, A. (2014, April 1). Why the all-Ivy League story stirs up tensions between African immigrants and Black Americans. *The Wire: News from The Atlantic*. Retrieved from www.thewire.com/politics/2014/04/why-the-all-ivy-league-story-stirs-up-tensions-between-african-immigrants-and-black-americans/359978/

Keller, U., & Tillman, K. H. (2008). Post-secondary educational attainment of immigrant and native youth. *Social Forces, 87*(1), 121–152.

Kent, M. M. (2007). Immigration and America's Black population. *Population Bulletin, 62*(4), 3–16.

Lee, J., & Rice, C. (2007). Welcome to America? International student perceptions of discrimination. *Higher Education, 53*, 381–409.

Massey, D. S., Mooney, M., Torres, K. C., & Charles, C. Z. (2007). Black immigrants and Black natives attending selective colleges and universities in the United States. *American Journal of Education, 113*(2), 243–271.

Model, S. (2008). *West Indian immigrants: A Black success story?* New York: Russell Sage Foundation.

Okonofua, B. A. (2013). "I am Blacker than you": Theorizing conflict between African immigrants and African Americans in the United States. *SAGE Open, 3*(3), 1–14.

Onyenekwu, I., & George Mwangi, C. A. (2017, November 27). "Who counts as a Black student" is not a new debate. *Inside Higher Ed*. Retrieved from www.insidehighered.com/admissions/views/2017/11/27/debate-about-who-counts-black-student-not-new-essay

Page, C. (2007, March 19). Invisible 'model minority.' *Washington Times*. Retrieved from www.washingtontimes.com/news/2007/mar/19/20070319-092045-6645r/

Rimer, S., & Arenson, K. W. (2004, June 24). Top colleges take more Blacks, but which ones? *The New York Times*. Retrieved from www.nytimes.com/2004/06/24/us/top-colleges-take-more-blacks-but-which-ones.html

Rong, K. L., & Brown, F. (2001). The effects of immigrant generation and ethnicity on educational attainment among young African and Caribbean Blacks in the United States. *Harvard Educational Review, 71*(3), 536–565.

Sorto, G. (2016, April 6). Teen gets accepted by all eight Ivy League schools. *CNN*. Retrieved from www.cnn.com/2016/04/05/us/ivy-league-student-2016-irpt/

Suarez-Orozco, C., Suarez-Orozco, M., & Todorova, I. (2008). *Learning a new land: Immigrant students in American society*. Cambridge, MA: The Belknap Press.

Tauriac, J. J., & Liem, J. H. (2012). Exploring the divergent academic outcomes of immigrant-origin Black undergraduates. *Journal of Diversity in Higher Education, 5*(4), 244–258.

U.S. Census Bureau (2018, January). *2020 Census program memorandum series* (2018.02). Washington, DC: U.S. Department of Commerce.

Waters, M. C., Kasinitz, P., & Asad, A. (2014). Immigrants and African Americans. *Annual Review of Sociology, 40*, 369–390.

Williamson, S. Y. (2010). Within-group ethnic differences of black male STEM majors and factors affecting their persistence in college. *Journal of International & Global Studies, 1*, 45–73.

CHAPTER 8

Beyond Reservations
Exploring Diverse Backgrounds and Tribal Citizenship Among Native College Students

Heather J. Shotton

Lack of understanding of the Native student population remains an ongoing issue in higher education. The limited understanding of Native people in general, and Native college students in particular, coupled with longstanding issues of invisibility (Shotton, Lowe, & Waterman, 2013) have perpetuated the myth of homogeneity among the Native student population. When Native college students are discussed, there is often a misconception that they represent a single homogenous racial group. Furthermore, they are often assumed to represent a singular experience, that being the stereotypical image of a deeply traditional Native person who comes from a reservation. The reality is that Native students come from diverse backgrounds and represent varied experiences. While there are some common experiences in higher education for Native students, there is not a singular Native higher education experience (Minthorn & Shotton, 2015; Shotton et al., 2013).

Key to understanding Native students in higher education is the recognition of the diversity that exists among tribes, as well as the political status of tribal nations in the United States. "Most higher education professionals appear to be unaware of the unique histories—which have present-day realities attached to them—of Indigenous peoples in the United States" (Brayboy, Fann, Castagno, & Solyom, 2012, p. 6). There are 574 federally recognized tribes in the United States (Federal Register, 2018; U.S. Department of Interior, 2018), each with its own distinct history, culture, language, and identity. Native people live in areas throughout the United States that extend beyond reservations. There is no singular Native experience or reality; the daily and historical experiences of Native people are diverse and vary by tribe (Brayboy et al., 2012; Minthorn & Shotton, 2015; Shotton et al., 2013).

A critical piece of this understanding lies in the responsibility of institutions of higher education to advance their own knowledge of Indigenous communities. Brayboy et al. (2012) explain:

Institutions of higher education do not operate in vacuums free of context and all that surround them: they are intimately tied to the larger contexts of communities, states, and nations. Understanding American Indian and Alaska Native participation in postsecondary education, then, requires some knowledge of Indigenous communities and tribal nations broadly speaking. (p. 3)

In order to do this, institutions must seek at least a basic knowledge of tribes and the diversity that exists among the broader Native population, Tribal Nations, and the students who represent those tribal nations. Honoring the unique political status of Native college students through collection of accurate tribal data would help institutions better serve Native students, further develop university and tribal relationships, and provide much needed data for tribal nations.

BEYOND RESERVATION BORDERS

In 2010, American Indians and Alaska Natives accounted for 1.7% (approximately 5.2 million) of the total U.S. population; this includes those who reported American Indian/Alaska Native alone or in combination with another race on the decennial census (Norris, Vines, & Hoeffel, 2012). When discussing Native populations, it is important to understand where Native people actually live. One major misconception about Native people is that all Natives, or at least the majority, reside on tribal reservations. Often the conversation on Native residential patterns is framed within the binary of reservation and urban areas, when the issue is much more complex. Native people reside on reservations and in reservation border towns, rural communities, and urban areas (Shotton, Lowe, & Waterman, 2013).

Native land issues are tied to our histories with the U.S. federal government and policies of removal, allotment, and relocation. American Indian/Alaska Native specified areas include not only federal reservations, but state reservations and off-reservation trust land, as well as Alaska Native, state, and tribal statistical areas. According to the most recent U.S. Census, only 21% of American Indians and Alaska Natives live inside an American Indian area or Alaska Native village statistical area (Norris et al., 2012). In fact, the majority (78%) of American Indian/Alaska Natives reside outside of American Indian and Alaska Native areas; this includes a large proportion of Natives who reside in urban areas (Norris et al., 2012). To illustrate this, the figure provided below shows federal and state American Indian reservations in the continental United States (Figure 8.1). However, high concentrations of American Indian/Alaska Native populations reside outside of designated tribal reservation areas in largely urban areas. Cities with the largest American Indian/Alaska Native populations include New York, Los

Figure 8.1. American Indian Federal and State Reservations

American Indian Reservations

MAP KEY
- Federal American Indian Reservations
- State American Indian Reservations

Source: U.S. Census Bureau, 2016

Angeles, Phoenix, Oklahoma City, Anchorage, Tulsa, Albuquerque, Chicago, Houston, and San Antonio (Norris et al., 2012).

Understanding the broader Native population, particularly residential patterns, helps us to better understand our students and their diverse backgrounds, their precollege educational experiences, and the cultural and social environments in which they grow up. For example, approximately 92% of American Indian/Alaska Native students attend public schools while only about 8% attend schools (often located on reservations) that are operated or funded by the Bureau of Indian Education (BIE) and tribes (DeVoe, Darling-Churchill, & Snyder, 2008; U.S. Executive Office of the President, 2014). Schools operated by the BIE are often poorly funded, located in geographically isolated areas, and faced with issues related to poor facilities. That is not to say that schools in urban areas do not face their own issues related to funding and facilities, but the issues related to reservation and BIE schools are unique and thus the experiences of Native students who attend those schools are likely different. Furthermore, Native students who grow up on reservations are likely to have different experiences than those who grow up in urban areas. Native students from urban areas are more likely to be exposed to various tribes and tribal cultures. This is in contrast to Native students from reservation areas, where the culture, practices, and traditions are likely to be more reflective of a single tribal culture and students are surrounded by a majority Native population. To be clear, I in no way intend to imply that Native students from urban areas are any less Native than those from reservations, just that their experiences and daily lives are different.

UNDERSTANDING TRIBAL NATIONS

The recognition of tribal nations as political entities (Brayboy et al., 2012), and Native students as citizens of tribal nations, is critical to understanding the unique status and experiences of Native college students. Native students' experience is tied to their connection with sovereign Tribal Nations—peoples who inhabited North America long before the United States was established or conceived (Brayboy et al., 2012).

Sovereignty is rooted in the understanding that tribes had their own forms of governance prior to contact with European colonizers. The first colonizers recognized tribes as legitimate entities and made treaties with them, which established the legal and political relationship between tribes and European colonists (Deloria & Lytle, 1983). When the United States was formed, the government adopted the practice of treaty-making with tribes (Deloria & Lytle, 1983), thus establishing the nation-to-nation relationship between Tribal Nations and the United States.

At the heart of tribal sovereignty is the right to self-governance (National Congress of American Indians [NCAI], 2016). As sovereign nations, tribes have their own distinct systems of government. The powers of tribal governments include determining citizenship, establishing civil and criminal laws, taxation, and licensing, as well as the provision and regulation of tribal activities including land management, education, health care, law enforcement, and basic infrastructure (Kalt, 2007; NCAI, 2016). Two key functions of tribal governments as they relate to higher education are determining tribal citizenship and providing primary and secondary education.

Federally Recognized vs. State Recognized

Some Tribal Nations are federally recognized; others are state-recognized. Federal tribes are located throughout the United States, with approximately 229 in Alaska and the remaining 345 tribes in 33 other states across the nation (NCAI, 2016). Additionally, there are state-recognized tribes in 16 states (Administration for Native Americans [ANA], 2014). The issue of federal recognition and state recognition can be complex and contentious. While it is beyond the scope of this chapter to fully explore this issue, it is important to understand the difference between federally recognized and state-recognized tribes when discussing Native populations.

Federally recognized tribes are American Indian or Alaska Native tribes or entities that are recognized by the federal government as having a government-to-government relationship with the United States (U.S. Department of the Interior, 2016). At the crux of federal recognition is the acknowledgment of sovereign rights established by the distinct government-to-government relationship of federally recognized tribes with the United States government (Brayboy et al., 2012; NCAI, 2016). As a result of that distinction, tribal citizens possess dual citizenship in that they are both citizens of their tribal nations and citizens of the United States (Deloria & Lytle, 1983; NCAI, 2016).

State-recognized tribes are those American Indian tribes or groups that are recognized by their respective state governments, but not officially recognized by the federal government (ANA, 2014). State-recognized tribes do not operate on a government-to-government basis with the federal government and are not afforded the benefits and resources available to federally recognized tribes. The discussion of state-recognized tribes is not intended to imply that a tribe is only "real" if recognized by the federal government (Brayboy et al., 2012), it is merely an attempt to point out the complex nature and multiple layers of the political status of tribes in the United States.

Tribal Differences

There is often an erroneous assumption by mainstream society that Native culture is monolithic, and forget that tribes have status as separate and independent nations with their own cultures, languages, governments, and histories. It is important to recognize intertribal differences and tribes' special political status in order to honor and support Native American communities.

Each tribe possesses its own distinct culture, history, language, and identity. There are more than 200 different Native languages spoken today and each tribe has its own unique linguistic tradition (Faircloth, Alcantar, & Stage, 2015). Differences exist among the ceremonial cycles and practices, government structures, and kinship systems of tribes; fully explicating these differences is difficult "without interacting and talking with members of these groups" (Faircloth et al., 2015, p. 15). What is important to understand is that "there is a range and diversity in both the day-to-day experiences and the history of tribal peoples across the United States" (Brayboy et al., 2012, p. 5). Even the word *tribe* does not accurately describe all groups of Indigenous people. Moreover, terms such as tribe, nation, band, pueblo, community, and Native village have been imposed by outside colonial entities and are not reflective of the names that Indigenous groups traditionally have for themselves.

Tribal Citizenship vs. Ancestry

There is a distinct difference between tribal *citizenship* and tribal *ancestry*. That is, someone may have Native ancestry or be a descendent of a tribe, but not be enrolled or acknowledged as a citizen of that particular tribe. Neither ancestry nor citizenship alone should be equated with degree of cultural ties or degree of Indigeneity. A Native person may be an enrolled or recognized citizen of a Tribal Nation and have little or no cultural ties to that tribe, and likewise, someone who has ancestry, but is not a recognized citizen, may possess strong connections to their tribal community and be deeply immersed in their tribal culture. Indigenous identity is not determined by tribal citizenship alone; other factors such as knowledge of tribal culture, history, language, kinship, and strength of Indigenous identification are also important (U.S. Department of the Interior, 2016).

The discussion of tribal citizenship here is rooted in the recognition of tribal citizenship as a function of tribal sovereignty and intended to acknowledge the political status of tribes and tribal citizens. One of the basic and most important functions of Tribal Nations is determining citizenship. As Kalt (2007) explains, one of the most fundamental aspects for Native Nations is defining the "self" in self-government and answering the question of who a people are.

The parameters and criteria for tribal citizenship are complex and vary from tribe to tribe. Common criteria include blood quantum, descendancy from a tribal ancestor on the original tribal roll, or some combination of blood quantum and other criteria (e.g., residency or enrollment of a parent; Kalt, 2007). Generally speaking, Native people may only possess citizenship in one tribe, as many tribes prohibit simultaneous citizenship in other tribes (Kalt, 2007). The growing number of individuals who descend from multiple tribes further complicates the issue of tribal citizenship and blood quantum.

The mobility of Native people today (Kalt, 2007) coupled with historical federal policies and interactions between tribes throughout the years have resulted in a growing number of Native people who have descendancy from multiple tribes. According to the 2010 census, some 131,674 American Indians and Alaska Natives reported descendancy from two or more tribes (Norris et al., 2012). This means that many of our Native students today may be citizens of one tribe, but may very well have ancestry and identify with multiple tribes. Understanding all of these elements and how they relate to tribal sovereignty and the unique status of Native people helps to shape our understanding of the complexity of identity for Native students, as well as variations that exist within this broader population. Furthermore, it helps to dispel the myth of homogeneity among Native students.

PROFILE OF NATIVE COLLEGE STUDENTS

Native college students constitute approximately 1% of the total undergraduate population (NCES 2015a). Enrollment trends for Native college students indicate that they are more likely to enroll in public 2-year institutions and continue to be underrepresented in more prestigious private and 4-year institutions (Lowe, 2005; NCES, 2015b). In fall 2014, approximately 37% of Native college students were enrolled in public 4-year institutions, and 40% were enrolled in public 2-year institutions. The total enrollment of American Indian and Alaska Native students in Tribal Colleges and Universities (TCU) was 14,393, which accounted for approximately 9% of the total American Indian and Alaska Native student population in postsecondary education (NCES, 2015a, 2015b).

In terms of precollege education, the majority of Native students, approximately 92%, attend public schools operated by state and local education agencies (U.S. Executive Office of the President, 2014). These public schools are located in both rural and urban settings. Only roughly 8% of Native students are enrolled in BIE schools, which are located on 63 reservations in 23 different states (U.S. Executive Office of the President, 2014). While much of the discussion of the precollege educational experiences of Native students focuses on lack of academic preparation and the struggles of BIE schools, it is important to recognize that Native students arrive on our campuses with diverse educational backgrounds and experiences, the majority of them outside of reservation areas.

As with any student population, it is important to acknowledge the diversity that exists among Native students. Unfortunately, Native students, when discussed at all, are often treated as a homogenous racial group. The data is very rarely disaggregated so that we can understand the differences that exist among tribal groupings. In fact, much of the data on Native college students does not even account for tribal affiliation. Furthermore, Native students are often lumped in with other underrepresented populations and discussed in terms of their "minority" status, ignoring them and rendering their status as tribal citizens invisible (Minthorn & Shotton, 2015).

RACIAL SELF-IDENTIFICATION AND DATA ISSUES

The data that is currently collected by higher education institutions oversimplifies Native identity and does not reflect Native students' status as tribal citizens. When collecting student demographic data on race and ethnicity, most institutions rely on self-identification. That is, students choose the racial group or groups with which they identify. However, when it comes to Native students, most institutions do not go beyond asking for racial identification, nor do they ask two simple questions: (1) Are you an enrolled citizen of your Tribal Nation? (2) What is your tribal affiliation/citizenship? Most higher education institutions do not require or even provide a mechanism for Native students to report tribal citizenship. Some institutions do ask questions regarding tribal citizenship, but often this is tied only to student scholarships. Most institutions simply do not ask.

Why is the question of tribal citizenship relevant? As previously explained, Native people are not merely a racial group; we have the distinction of being both a racial group and a political group. Supreme Court decisions (*Morton v. Mancari* and *Fisher v. District Court*) have asserted that the relationship that tribes maintain with the federal government is political in nature (Deloria & Lytle, 1983), affirming the political status of Native people. However, this does not negate our status as a racial group. Brayboy (2006) explains this best in his discussion of the liminality of Native people:

> American Indians are both legal/political and racialized beings; however, we are rarely treated as such, leaving Indigenous peoples in a state of inbetweenness wherein we define ourselves as both, with an emphasis on the legal/political, but we are framed as racialized groups by many members of society. The racialized status of American Indians appears to be the main emphasis of most members of U.S. society; this status ignores the legal/political one, and is directly tied to notions of colonialism, because larger society is unaware of the multiple statuses of Indigenous peoples (pp. 432–433).

Invisibility is a longstanding problem with Native populations in higher education. Historically, Natives have been excluded from the data and rendered invisible (Shotton et al., 2013). Faircloth et al. (2015) explain that issues of small sample size for Native students in national datasets often result in excluding Native students, grouping Native students as "Other," or not reporting findings because of issues with statistical significance or low effect size. For example, before 2003 the U.S. Department of Education and the U.S. Office of Management and Budget did not report on American Indian/Alaska Native students in key annual reports (Faircloth et al., 2015).

Another way of perpetuating invisibility is the treatment of Native people as only a racial group, rather than acknowledging the political status of tribes as sovereign nations and Native students as citizens of Tribal Nations. Treating Native students solely as a racial group ignores the political status of tribes and Native students. It is important for institutions to collect data that acknowledges the unique status of tribes and accurately represents the diversity that exists among Native college students. Native students in higher education "cannot be understood independently from the unique political status of tribes" (Brayboy et al., 2012, p. 11). Data that reflects only the racial status of Native students ignores a central part of Native student identity. Institutional data that includes information on tribal citizenship will benefit institutions of higher education, Tribal Nations, and Native students.

HONORING TRIBAL CITIZENSHIP

Institutional data that includes information on tribal citizenship will improve the overall accuracy of institutional data, which benefits institutions of higher education, Tribal Nations, and Native students. Current data aggregates tribal affiliations, generalizing and oversimplifying Native student experiences (Tachine, 2015). Native students are assumed to come to educational institutions from reservations and to have grown up deeply immersed in their tribal culture. We know that this is not the case for all students and that our students come from varied backgrounds and home communities, and fall on a spectrum in terms of their tribal and cultural identity. Data that accounts for tribal citizenship and tribal affiliation moves beyond stereotypical notions of Native students and acknowledges tribal differences and the varied backgrounds and experiences of Native students. Collecting this data would help institutions better serve Native students, further develop university and tribal relationships, and provide critical data for Tribal Nations. It would allow better analysis of retention and graduation rates for Native students. More importantly, it is a critical step in acknowledging and honoring the unique status of Native people.

Tribal citizenship and affiliation data could be used to develop more targeted and effective recruitment and retention strategies. It would help colleges identify the Tribal Nations represented on any given campus and assist them in fostering relationships with those nations. One recommendation that has been echoed by Native higher education scholars has been the need for universities to partner with tribes to better serve Native students (Shotton et al., 2013; Minthorn & Shotton, 2015; Minthorn, Wanger, & Shotton, 2013). Institutional data that identifies tribal representation would assist institutions in more effectively reaching out to and developing relationships with Tribal Nations to serve their tribal citizens. It may also facilitate institutional and tribal partnerships to identify specific student needs and develop tribally focused academic programs (e.g., living-learning communities), Native student programming, and more effective retention strategies.

The inclusion of tribal citizenship and affiliation data could be important for tribes. Many tribes do not have consistent or reliable data, or a mechanism for collecting data on tribal citizens in higher education. Often, the data that tribes have only captures those citizens who may be receiving assistance from the tribe to attend college (e.g., those receiving tribal scholarships) and not all tribal citizens attending an institution of higher education. When tribes work with colleges and universities to seek ways to better serve their citizens, they often have difficulty identifying all of their citizens on a campus, because institutional and tribal data are incomplete. The result is that a number of students who might benefit from such partnerships likely missed. Accurate and comprehensive data on tribal citizens in higher education would alleviate this issue and provide valuable information to tribes for programming, development and improvement of services, assessment of tribal resources, and overall nation building.

CONCLUSION

Issues of invisibility that have perpetuated the lack of understanding of Native people, and Native college students in particular, are undergirded by the misconception of Native people as homogenous. Despite the assertion from Native scholars that Native students come from diverse backgrounds and that there is not a singular Native higher education experience (Brayboy et al., 2012; Minthorn & Shotton, 2015; Shotton et al., 2013), broader discussions of Native college students continue to center on the assumption of homogeneity and ignorance of their status as citizens of Tribal Nations.

Understanding the complexity of Indigenous identity, recognizing the diversity that exists among Native college students, and honoring their status as tribal citizens who occupy a liminal (Brayboy, 2006) space is key to understanding and serving this population. Moreover, it forces institutions to move beyond inaccurate assumptions of homogeneity that have not served Native students well. A necessary step in this effort is collecting data that accurately reflects the Native student population, the diversity within this population, and their status as citizens of Tribal Nations.

REFERENCES

Administration for Native Americans (ANA). (2014). *American Indians and Alaska Natives—What are state recognized tribes?* Retrieved from www.acf.hhs.gov/programs/ana/resource/american-indians-and-alaska-natives-what-are-state-recognized-tribes

Brayboy, B. M. J. (2006). Toward a tribal critical race theory in education. *The Urban Review, 37*(5), 425–446.

Brayboy, B. M. J., Fann, A. J., Castagno, A. E., & Solyom, J. A. (2012). *Postsecondary education for American Indian and Alaska Natives: Higher education for nation building and self-determination*: ASHE Higher Education Report 37: 5. San Francisco, CA: Jossey-Bass.

Deloria Jr., V., & Lytle, C. M. (1983). *American Indians, American justice*. Austin, TX: University of Texas Press.

DeVoe, J. F., Darling-Churchill, K. E., & Snyder, T. D. (2008). *Status and trends in the education of American Indians and Alaska Natives: 2008*. (NCES 2008-08). Washington, DC: U.S. Department of Education.

Faircloth, S. C., Alcantar, C. M., and Stage, F. K. (2015). Use of large-scale data sets to study educational pathways of American Indian and Alaska Native students. *New Directions for Institutional Research, 2014*(163), 5–24. doi.org: 10.1002/ir.20083.

Federal Register, (2018). 81 FR 26826. Retrieved from www.federalregister.gov/documents/2018/07/23/2018-15679/indian-entities-recognized-and-eligible-to-receive-services-from-the-united-states-bureau-of-indian

Kalt, J. P. (2007). The role of constitutions in Native nation building: Laying a firm foundation. In M. Jorgensen (Ed.), *Rebuilding Native nations: Strategies for governance and development* (pp. 78–114). Tucson, AZ: University of Arizona Press.

Lowe, S. C. (2005). This is who I am: Experiences of Native American students. *New Directions for Student Services, 2005*, (109), 33–40.

Minthorn, R. S. & Shotton, H. J. (2015). Native American students in higher education. In P. A. Sasso & J. L. DeVitis (Eds.), *Today's college students: A reader* (pp. 31–43) New York, NY: Peter Lang Publishing.

Minthorn, R. S., Wanger, S., & Shotton, H. J. (2013). Developing Native student leadership skills: The success of the Oklahoma Native American Students in Higher Education (ONASHE) conference. *American Indian Culture and Research Journal, 37*(3), 59–74.

National Center for Education Statistics (NCES). (2015a). *Fall enrollment and degrees conferred in degree-granting tribally controlled postsecondary institutions, by state and institution: Selected years, fall 2000 through fall 2013, and 2011-12 and 2012-13*. Washington, DC: U.S. Department of Education.

National Center for Education Statistics (NCES). (2015b). *Total fall enrollment in degree-granting postsecondary institutions, by level of enrollment, sex, attendance status, and race/ethnicity of student: Selected years, 1976 through 2014*. Washington, DC: U.S. Department of Education.

National Congress of American Indians (NCAI). (2016). *Tribal nations and the United States: An introduction*. Retrieved from www.ncai.org/about-tribes

Norris, T., Vines, P. L., & Hoeffel, E. M. (2012). *American Indian and Alaska Native population: 2010*. Washington, DC: U.S. Census Bureau.

Shotton, H. J., Lowe. S. C., & Waterman, S. J. (Eds.). (2013). *Beyond the asterisk: Understanding Native students in higher education*. Sterling, VA: Stylus Publishing.

Tachine, A.R. (2015). *Monsters and weapons: Navajo students' stories on their journeys toward college* (Doctoral dissertation). Retrieved from hdl.handle.net/10150/556873

U.S. Census Bureau. (2010). *Census redistricting data (Public 94-171) summary file.* Retrieved from www.census.gov/prod/cen2010/doc/pl94-171.pdf

U.S. Census Bureau. (2016). *American Indian reservations.* Retrieved from http://www.census.gov/dmd/www/pdf/512indre.pdf

U.S. Department of the Interior, Bureau of Indian Affairs. (2018). *Frequently asked questions.* Retrieved from www.bia.gov/FAQs

U.S. Executive Office of the President. (2014). *Native youth report.* Retrieved from obamawhitehouse.archives.gov/sites/default/files/docs/20141129nativeyouthreport_final.pdf

CHAPTER 9

The Mismeasure of Native American Students
Using Data Disaggregation to Promote Identity Safety

Laura M. Brady, Zoe Higheagle Strong, and Stephanie A. Fryberg

From primary school to higher education, national data suggest, Native American students struggle academically (Musu-Gillette et al., 2017; Walter & Andersen, 2013). Compared to White students, Native Americans begin school behind in reading and mathematics (Snyder & Dillow, 2012). By high school, Native students have higher than average rates of dropout, suspension, juvenile delinquency, and school absence (DeVoe & Darling-Churchill, 2008; Faircloth & Tippeconnic III, 2010; U.S. Commission on Civil Rights, 2003). These statistics, while important for identifying group-level disparities, obscure the fact that there is wide variation among Native American groups, individuals, and contexts, and that a large number of Native American students *are* academically successful. Instead, aggregated data emphasize students' "deficits" and ignore social, political, historical, and other contextual determinants of racial achievement gaps (see Fryberg, Covarrubias, & Burack, 2018).

In this chapter, we draw attention to the potential for racially aggregated educational data to create an inaccurate, monolithic, and stigmatizing narrative of Native American students as "strugglers." We contend that this narrative undermines *identity safety* (i.e., the belief that one belongs and can be successful in a given domain, such as education ([Markus, Steele, & Steele, 2002; Steele, 1997; Steele & Aronson, 1995]) and academic performance for Native American students. In the remainder of this chapter, we discuss how identity safety influences academic performance and how relying on aggregated data regarding Native American students is likely to undermine identity safety. We then use three national datasets to illustrate how educational data can be disaggregated to better understand variability in Native students' outcomes and promote identity safety. We conclude by discussing implications for researchers, policymakers, and educators who wish to better understand and assist diverse Native American students.

IDENTITY SAFETY AND THREAT IN EDUCATIONAL CONTEXTS

In educational contexts, messages about who belongs and can be successful shape students' experiences of *identity safety*. Identity-safe contexts celebrate, value, and legitimize diverse people and ways of being such that individuals do not fear being devalued or treated negatively based on their identities or experiences (Markus et al., 2002). Identity-safe contexts are free of *identity threats*—environmental cues that undermine identity safety (Davies, Spencer, & Steele, 2005; Steele, 1997; Steele, Spencer, & Aronson, 2002). These cues include underrepresentation of one's social groups (e.g., racial, gender, national origin, or sexuality; Purdie-Vaughns, Steele, Davies, Ditlmann, & Crosby, 2008; Sekaquaptewa & Thompson, 2003), assimilationist ideologies (e.g., colorblind ideologies; Markus et al., 2002; Purdie-Vaughns et al., 2008), exclusionary beliefs (e.g., portraying one perspective as more important or "right" than others), and the grouping of individuals according to potentially stigmatizing social identities (e.g., race, gender, social class) (Murphy & Taylor, 2012; Steele et al., 2002). All of these cues undermine identity safety by communicating that individuals' groups—and thus individuals themselves—may be viewed negatively in a given context.

In academic settings, identity threats most often arises from negative stereotypes about students' racial/ethnic, gender, and socioeconomic groups. Decades of research suggest that threats undermines students' academic performance, even among high-achieving students (Croizet & Claire, 1998; Sherman et al., 2013; Spencer, Logel, & Davies, 2016; Spencer, Steele, & Quinn, 1999; Steele, 1997; Steele et al., 2002). For example, Steele and Aronson (1995) demonstrated that when reminded of negative stereotypes of their racial group, African American students underperformed on an academic task relative to White students. However, when racial identity threat was removed, African American and White students performed equally well. While identity threat undermines performance on specific short-term academic tasks (e.g., assignments or tests), chronic exposure to identity threat also leads students to withdraw or disengage from academics, creating long-term negative effects for stigmatized students (Davies, Spencer, Quinn, & Gerhardstein, 2002; Osborne & Walker, 2006; Schmader, Major, & Gramzow, 2001).

DATA AGGREGATION UNDERMINES IDENTITY SAFETY

While research suggests that Native American students experience identity threat as a function of their racial group membership, we suggest here that the ways in which educational data represent these students also exacerbate identity threat. Specifically, the use of aggregated data leads to conclusions about Native American students that (1) reify negative stereotypes, (2) homogenize experiences and outcomes, and (3) render invisible positive representations in educational contexts. In the next sections, we discuss each of these arguments in more detail and provide examples utilizing three national data sets.

First, aggregated data often depict Native Americans as a monolithically underperforming group (Walter & Andersen, 2013) and thus appear to confirm the longstanding stereotype that Native American students are academic strugglers. This stereotype can create identity threat for Native students, causing them to worry that their teachers and peers hold negative expectations regarding their academic potential and that their performance may confirm these expectations. These concerns consume cognitive resources (e.g., Logel, Iserman, Davies, Quinn, & Spencer, 2009) and prevent Native students from performing to their potential.

Second, aggregated data obscure the distinct accomplishments and challenges of Native Americans with diverse experiences and backgrounds. A wide range of variability exists among Native Americans, both within and between tribes (e.g., Hoopes, Petersen, Vinson, & Lopez, 2012; Johnson, Call, & Blewett, 2010). However, aggregated data homogenize Native American experiences, suggesting that all Native students are the same, regardless of tribal affiliations, ways of life, and cultural traditions. If educational contexts fail to acknowledge Native students' diverse identities and experiences, these students may believe that their teachers and schools do not value important aspects of their identity. Instead, Native students may thus come to expect that in educational contexts, they will be seen only as members of an underperforming group, not as individuals with particular experiences, talents, and goals (Markus et al., 2002). This homogenization may create identity threat for Native American students.

Third, aggregated data render Native American academic successes invisible, which can undermine Native students' academic aspirations. All people consciously and unconsciously search situations for self-relevant information from which they draw inferences about what is possible for them to achieve (Fryberg, Markus, Oyserman, & Stone, 2008; Fryberg & Townsend, 2008; Oyserman & Fryberg, 2006). The available representations in a given context afford certain possibilities and constrain others (Oyserman & Markus, 1993). By obscuring examples of high-achieving Native American students, aggregated data constrain representations of

Native American students to examples of struggle and failure. Indeed, research demonstrates that a lack of positive representations of high-achieving Native American students undermines Native American students' sense of belonging in school—a key component of identity safety (Covarrubias & Fryberg, 2015). In this way, aggregated data have the potential to undermine identity safety and perpetuate achievement gaps that separate Native American students from their peers (Kena et al., 2016; U.S. Department of Education, as cited in *Chronicle of Higher Education*, 2006).

Academic contexts are riddled with negative and inaccurate information about Native American peoples. This information has serious consequences for how educators and policymakers view Native American students, how Native American students view themselves, and how Native American students perform in academic contexts. As long as Native American educational outcomes are understood primarily through aggregated data—which is often the case—Native American students are likely to experience identity threat and thus underperform. Disaggregated data, however, can promote identity safety by 1) breaking down negative stereotypes of Native Americans, 2) de-homogenizing social representations of Native Americans, and 3) making visible Native Americans who are academically successful. This identity safety is critical to improving Native Americans' educational experiences.

DISAGGREGATED DATA ILLUSTRATES VARIABILITY IN NATIVE AMERICAN STUDENTS' OUTCOMES

To provide a variety of examples of educational data that can be disaggregated to promote identity safety for Native American students, we selected three datasets that allowed us to differentiate academic outcomes according to social class, school location, and tribal affiliation. First, we analyzed data from the 2011 National Assessment of Educational Progress (NAEP) public use dataset, which constitutes the largest nationally representative sample of students' math and reading performance scores. Second, we used the 2011 National Indian Education Study (NIES), which was conducted through the NAEP data collection process but included additional information about educational experiences specific to Native American culture and concerns (e.g., questions regarding Native American students' perceptions of themselves as well as their families, communities, schools, and classrooms. We selected data from 2011 because this is the most recent year for which both NAEP and NIES data are available. These datasets provide a fairly holistic view of academic performance and educational experiences, but neither reports Native American students' tribal affiliation. To examine variability in educational outcomes by tribal affiliation, we turned to a third dataset, the U.S. Census Bureau's 2014 American Community Survey (ACS), which includes both information on educational attainment and Native Americans' tribal affiliation.

With each dataset, we illustrate how aggregated data reflect the common deficit narrative of Native Americans' educational outcomes. Then we present examples of variables (social class, school location, and tribal affiliation) that can be used to disaggregate the same data to better capture variability in Native American students' academic experiences and outcomes. Finally, we use one of these variables (social class) to disaggregate identity safety–related academic outcomes (i.e., students' self-perceptions and academic plans).

Example 1: Social Class Predicts Academic Performance

When using aggregated racial categories, NAEP data reflect the common narrative of Native Americans' underperformance: 4th grade Native American students, on average, perform worse than White, Asian, and multiracial students in math and reading (see Figure 9.1), and similar patterns emerge in data regarding 8th grade reading and math performance. Yet these aggregated data do little to explain why a racial achievement gap occurs or to acknowledge the extent to which Native American students' individual experiences deviate from the aggregated group statistic. Without acknowledging factors that contribute to educational disparities or representing variability in Native American students' outcomes, these data are likely to create identity threat, as they suggest that Native American students themselves are the problem.

Disaggregating NAEP data by social class, however, demonstrates that there is variability in Native American students' performance. Specifically, we disaggregated reading and math performance by race (self-reported) and eligibility for the National School Lunch Program (NSLP), a proxy for social class. Students who are eligible for NSLP come from low socioeconomic status (SES) families (i.e., families with income near the poverty level), while those who are ineligible come from higher-SES families (National Center for Education Statistics, 2015). As Figure 9.2 demonstrates, NSLP eligibility predicted reading and math performance not only for Native American students, but for all students. Across all racial/ethnic categories, students from higher-SES backgrounds (i.e., those ineligible for NSLP) performed significantly better than students from lower-SES backgrounds (i.e., those eligible for NSLP). In fact, disaggregating by social class demonstrates not only that there is variability in Native American students' performance, but also that a subset of Native Americans perform as well as their counterparts from other racial/ethnic backgrounds. In addition to performing as well or better than low-SES students from all other racial groups in both reading and math, high-SES Native American 4th grade students also earned scores better than or equal to high-SES students who identified as:

Figure 9.1. 2011 NAEP Aggregated 4th Grade Reading and Math Scores

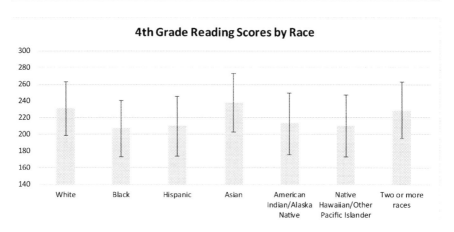

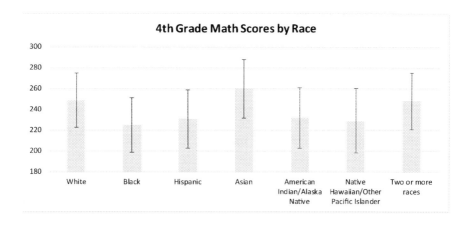

- Black:
  - 4th Grade Math difference = 8 points, $p < .001$
  - 4th Grade Reading difference = 4 points, $p < .05$,
- Hispanic:
  - 4th Grade Math difference = 2 points, $p > .05$
  - 4th Grade Reading difference = 2 points, $p > .05$, and
- Native Hawaiian/Pacific Islander:
  - 4th Grade Math difference = 8, $p < .01$
  - 4th Grade Reading difference = 5 points, $p < .05$

The Mismeasure of Native American Students

Figure 9.2. 2011 NAEP 4th and 8th Grade Math and Reading Performance Disaggregated by NSLP Eligibility

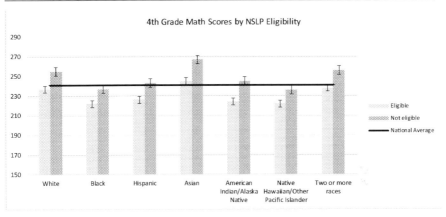

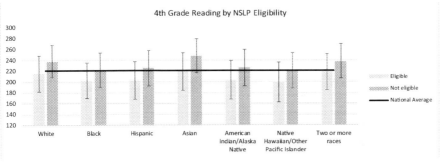

Note: Error bars represent standard deviations.

Math and reading performance at the 8th grade level showed similar patterns.

At the same time as these disaggregated data illustrate variability among Native American students and contradict the notion that all Native students are underperformers, they also depict the achievement gaps that separate White and Asian students from all other racial groups. Alhough high-SES Native American students performed as well or better than many other racial minority students, all of these groups fared worse than high-SES White and Asian students. These findings point both to the distinct disadvantages that even high-SES students face when they belong to racial groups that are typically marginalized in educational settings and to the fact that many factors contribute to different groups' academic outcomes. By exploring demographic, social, historical, and political influences (e.g., school demographics, policies and practices; teacher characteristics; governmental funding) in addition to race and social class, researchers can use disaggregated

Figure 9.2. 2011 NAEP 4th and 8th Grade Math and Reading Performance Disaggregated by NSLP Eligibility, Continued

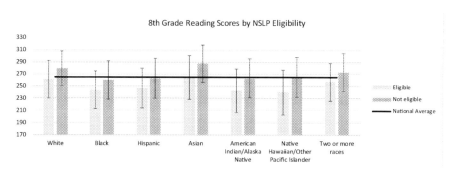

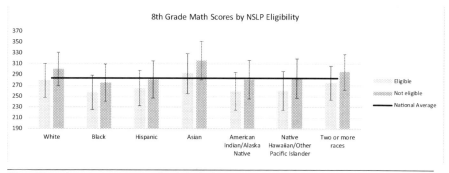

Note: Error bars represent standard deviations.

data as a starting point to better understand Native students and change the disparities they face. This approach to interpreting educational data shifts the emphasis from students themselves to the many factors outside of students' control that shape educational outcomes.

Example 2: School Location Predicts Academic Performance

Another factor that differentiates Native American students' educational outcomes is school location. Research on Native Americans has documented cultural and economic differences between urban and rural communities (e.g., National Urban Indian Family Council, 2008; Probst, Moore, Glover, & Samuels, 2004). Research on education in general also suggests that students' opportunities and outcomes depend in part upon where their schools are located. Suburban schools, for example, tend to have lower rates of poverty, better funding, and higher-quality educational opportunities than rural and urban schools (see (Bouck, 2004).

Using data from the 2011 NAEP Survey, we disaggregated 8th grade math and reading scores by school location (4 categories: city, suburb, town, rural; see Appendix) and found evidence of variability in Native American students' performance across locations (see Figure 9.3). While there were no statistically significant differences in performance among Native American students who attended schools in cities, towns, and rural communities, Native American students who attended schools in suburbs performed better in 8th grade reading than Native American students who attended schools in rural areas (difference = 10 points, $p < .05$). While this finding offers initial evidence that school location influences Native American students' educational outcomes, it is also possible that there are other performance differences that are masked by this measure. For instance, one-third of Native Americans live on reservations or trust lands (Snyder, Tan, & Hoffman, 2006), many of which cut across rural communities and towns. These students may attend schools in both rural and town areas but share common experiences as residents of reservations. Future efforts to disaggregate academic data by geographic location should consider not only where students attend school but also where students live to offer a more accurate representation of Native Americans' experiences.

Example 3: Tribal Affiliation Predicts Educational Attainment

While Examples 1 and 2 speak to the variability in educational outcomes between Native American students from different social class backgrounds and types of communities, outcomes also vary across Native American tribes. Using data from the 2014 American Community Survey, we examined rates of educational attainment among members of the 10 largest Native American tribes and found substantial between-tribe variation. Within these 10 tribes alone, the percentage of members 25 years and older holding at least a bachelor's degree ranged from 11% to 26.2% (U.S. Census Bureau, 2015). In the same year, 30.1% of the total U.S. population 25 years and older had earned a bachelor's degree or higher (U.S. Census Bureau, 2015).

These data suggest that Native Americans on average lag behind other racial groups in terms of educational attainment, but they also demonstrate that some subgroups of Native Americans are closer to the general population in terms of educational attainment than others. As in Examples 1 and 2, aggregated data could perpetuate a deficit perspective of Native American educational outcomes. However, disaggregating the same data according to tribal affiliation could help researchers, educators, and policymakers better understand the factors that promote educational attainment among Native American subgroups. They can use the existing variability among Native American tribes to learn how social, cultural, political, economic, and other factors shape these groups' differential educational outcomes and identify

Figure 9.3. 2011 NAEP 8th Grade Math and Reading Scores Disaggregated by School Location

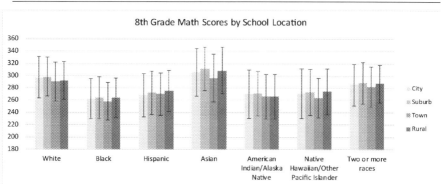

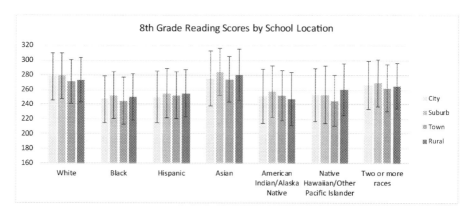

Note: Error bars represent standard deviations.

potential avenues for improving outcomes among groups that lag further behind.

Together, Examples 1–3 demonstrate that 1) even when Native Americans on average fare worse than other groups, real and predictable variability exists among Native American people, and 2) disaggregating data to uncover this variability offers useful information about how Native American students' diverse experiences shape their academic outcomes. Knowing that variability exists has implications both for how educators, researchers, and policymakers understand Native students and how Native students view themselves. In the remaining examples, we shift from exploring variability in performance-related outcomes to exploring variability in identity safety– related outcomes. As a precursor to academic success, identity safety is crucial to improving students' outcomes. While we argue that disaggregated data has the potential to foster identity safety among Native American students in general, disaggregating data can also shed light on the extent to which different Native students experience identity safety in different contexts. In Examples 4 and 5, we operationalize identity safety using Native American students' academic self-perceptions and plans to pursue higher education. We disaggregate these identity safety outcomes according to social class.

Example 4: Social Class Predicts Self-Perceptions

Because social class predicted Native American students' academic performance (Example 1), we expected it would also predict how these students viewed themselves in relation to school. Using data from the 2011 NIES Survey, we disaggregated students' self-reported performance in math and reading (i.e., How do you rate yourself in reading [math]? = Poor, Average, Good, or Very Good) according to race and social class (i.e., NSLP eligibility). As shown in Figure 9.4, compared to higher-SES Native American students, lower-SES Native American students were:

- more likely to rate themselves as performing poorly
    - Math difference = 5 points, $p < .001$
    - Reading difference = 3 points, $p < .001$; and
- less likely to rate themselves as performing very well
    - Math difference = -6 points, $p = .008$
    - Reading difference = -9 points, $p < .001$)

These findings indicate that as early as 8th grade, lower-SES Native American students have lower academic self-perceptions than higher-SES Native American students.

While these self-perceptions may reflect a reality in which higher-SES students on average perform better than lower-SES students (see Figure 9.2), this discrepancy in self-perceptions has the potential to reify and even exacerbate existing performance disparities. How students view their academic abilities influences their performance (Wigfield & Eccles, 2000) and persistence, especially when confronted with challenges (Yeager & Dweck, 2012). Negative academic self-perceptions can feed into a cycle of underperformance, and disaggregated data suggest that these self-perceptions may be particularly problematic among lower-SES Native American students. At the same time, disaggregated data can point to strengths among subgroups of Native Americans. In terms of math self-perceptions, for example, higher-SES Native Americans were as likely as higher-income Whites to rate themselves as doing "Very Good" in math (difference = -7 points, $p = .24$). Understanding how higher-SES Native students develop positive academic self-perceptions may be informative for efforts to improve self-perceptions among lower-SES Native students.

Figure 9.4. 2011 NIES 8th Grade Self-Reported Performance in Math and Reading Disaggregated by NSLP Eligibility

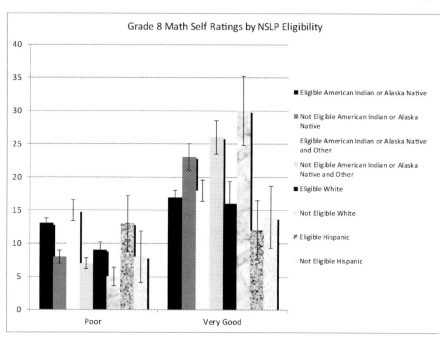

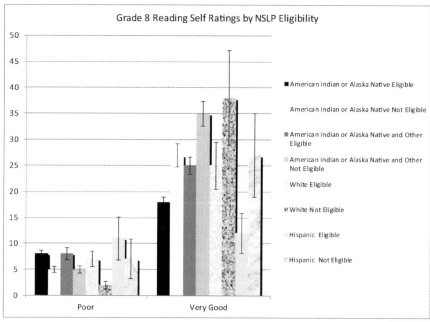

Figure 9.5. 2011 NIES 8th Grade Plans to Attend College Disaggregated by NSLP Eligibility

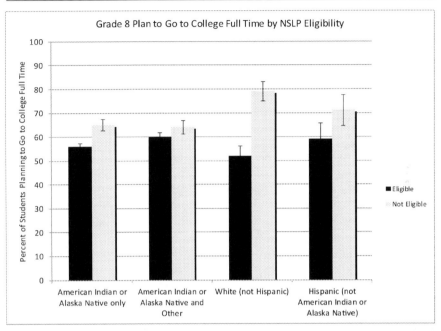

Example 5: Social Class Predicts Educational Aspirations

As a final example, we used 2011 NIES Survey data to examine how social class influences Native American students' college plans. As shown in Figure 9.5, disaggregating data according to social class suggests that there is variation in Native American students' plans to attend college. Higher-SES Native American students were more likely to report that they planned to attend college full time following high school compared to lower-SES Native American students (difference = 9%, p = .002). This suggests that as early as 8th grade, Native American students from lower-SES backgrounds have already begun to set lower academic goals than students from more privileged SES backgrounds. Many factors likely contribute to this disparity, but one explanation is that because income is often tied to education, higher-SES students may have more readily available representations of college-educated Native Americans (e.g., among family members and friends) compared to lower-SES students. As a result, higher-SES students may be more likely to believe that college is a possibility for themselves. Indeed, higher-SES Native American students were even more likely to plan to attend college following high school than were lower-SES White students (difference = 13%, p = .01).

THE IMPLICATIONS OF AGGREGATION
FOR NATIVE AMERICAN STUDENTS

Examples 1–3 illustrate that, contrary to the common portrayal of Native Americans as a monolithically underperforming group, Native American students' performance depends upon their life experiences (e.g., social class, school location, and tribal membership). Disaggregated data suggest that there are indeed subgroups of Native American students whose performance is indistinguishable from their peers from other racial/ethnic backgrounds. Higher-SES students, those who resided in suburbs, and members of certain tribes had better academic outcomes than other subsets of Native Americans. While these findings could exacerbate negative stereotypes of some Native Americans (e.g., lower-SES Native Americans), the very existence of this variability contradicts the deficit model of Native American performance derived from aggregated data. Disaggregating data has the potential to identify subgroups of Native Americans who face greater educational challenges and obstacles. A more fine-grained examination of disaggregated data may point stakeholders toward resilience factors and aid in developing appropriate, effective interventions for Native American students.

Furthermore, by highlighting variability in Native Americans' educational outcomes and thereby de-homogenizing Native American experiences, data disaggregation may challenge the negative stereotypes about Native Americans' abilities that permeate educational contexts. Aggregated data perpetuate the stereotype that Native American students struggle, and these data communicate to Native American students that people like them cannot do well in school. Disaggregated data contradict this stereotype by illuminating positive representations, demonstrating that Native American students are capable of achieving at the level of other students. In other words, data disaggregation may promote *identity safety* among Native American students.

Because identity safety is a precursor to academic success, it is also critical to identify which Native American students experience identity safety and which contextual factors within educational settings promote identity safety. Examples 4 and 5 begin to answer these questions, suggesting that variability exists in Native American students' self-perceptions and college aspirations (i.e., proxies for identity safety). Higher-SES Native American students had more positive academic self-views and higher educational aspirations than lower-SES Native American students. Furthermore, higher-SES Native American students held academic self-views and educational aspirations that were comparable to those of students from more privileged racial/ethnic backgrounds.

While the variability exposed by disaggregated data in Examples 1–3 could be used to promote identity safety among Native American students, the variability exposed by disaggregated data in Examples 4 and 5 might better be used to demonstrate how a *lack* of identity safety can undermine Native American students' academic outcomes and to identify subgroups of Native American students who might be particularly vulnerable. All Native American students contend with negative stereotypes and a lack of positive social representations in educational contexts (Fryberg & Townsend, 2008), but lower-SES Native American students also contend with negative stereotypes and a lack of social representations of people from their social class backgrounds. These students may experience identity threats arising from both their racial/ethnic backgrounds and their social class backgrounds. Racial and social class identity threats may work in tandem to undermine students' performance and beliefs about their own ability, thus placing these students at a greater disadvantage compared to higher-SES Native American students.

These findings should not be used to identify lower-SES Native American students as "problem students"; instead, disaggregated data highlight the need to build interventions that promote identity safety among Native American students with different life experiences. For example, some efforts to improve disadvantaged students' performance focus on providing positive social representations (e.g., Stephens, Hamedani, & Destin, 2014), which facilitate identity safety by showing students that people like them can succeed in school (Fryberg et al., 2008). The disaggregated data in Examples 4 and 5 suggest that efforts to provide positive social representations of Native American students in higher education should work to ensure that Native Americans from different social class backgrounds, especially lower-SES backgrounds, are represented.

CONSIDERATIONS FOR EDUCATORS AND POLICYMAKERS

Too often, educational data tell the wrong story, showing only aggregated data that perpetuate stereotypes of Native Americans as struggling, uneducated, or incapable (Walter & Andersen, 2013). Narrowing achievement gaps for Native Americans (Musu-Gillette et al., 2017) requires educators and policymakers to move beyond "evidence-based" conclusions drawn from data that obscure the diversity of Native American experiences and outcomes. Instead, they must disaggregate data to illustrate and understand variation in Native American—and other—students' academic outcomes. This variability not only challenges the negative stereotypes and assumptions that undermine Native American students' performance but also sheds light on the causes of educational disparities, the populations most in need of help, the nature and scope of interventions needed to remedy disparities, and the factors that enhance performance among Native American students. Portraying and working to understand variability in Native Americans' academic outcomes can foster identity safety for Native American students by signaling to both students and educators that Native Americans can be academically successful.

DISAGGREGATING DATA: WHAT VARIABLES ARE IMPORTANT?

In this chapter, we disaggregated data according to social class, school location, and tribal affiliation. These variables convey a wealth of information about Native American students' experiences and point to factors that promote success among Native American students. Below, we discuss the significance of each of these variables and offer suggestions for further disaggregating Native American educational data.

Social Class

Although social class is widely recognized to predict academic performance across racial/ethnic groups (see Walpole, 2003), it is often overlooked when reporting on Native American education. Our findings suggest that social class is an important factor to consider in understanding Native Americans' academic outcomes, and it is likely an important factor to consider in understanding their outcomes in many other domains. We used NSLP eligibility as a proxy for social class, but future analyses should include other indicators, such as parents' level of education or occupation. For instance, while Example 5 showed that NSLP eligibility predicted Native American students' plans to attend college full-time, Higheagle Strong, Carbonneau, and Austin (2018) found that parent education but not NSLP status predicted Native American students' plans to attend college either part-time or full-time (collapsed into a single variable). This suggests that there may be nuances in how different measures of social class predict outcomes for Native American students. Future research disaggregating Native American outcomes should examine diverse measures of social class and explore the effects of social class in combination with other important demographic variables.

School Location

We also disaggregated the data by school location and found that Native American students who attended schools in rural communities scored significantly lower in reading than those who attended schools in suburbs. School quality and funding in the United States depend in part upon school location (Heuer & Stullich, 2011; U.S. Census Bureau, 2016), and these differential educational experiences affect all students' outcomes. For Native American students in particular, geographical disparities are crucial to consider, as approximately one-third of Native Americans live on reservations, in Alaska villages, or on federal trust lands (Snyder et al., 2006) and thus attend schools where Native American students tend to underperform.

Native American educators and families are well aware of the differential needs of Native peoples living in rural versus urban areas, and researchers can learn from the conversations these communities have already initiated. Urban Native Americans, for example, are concerned that they lack political power, connection to Native American culture, and access to human capital. On the other hand, Native Americans living among tribal communities have more access to tribal and family support and cultural resources but face fewer job opportunities and increased poverty (National Urban Indian Family Council, 2008). Understanding and addressing these differences is crucial for designing interventions that successfully address the academic needs and barriers different Native American populations face.

Tribal Affiliation

Our results also show between-tribe differences: Among 10 of the largest tribes in the United States, the percentage of tribal members holding bachelor's degrees ranged from 11 to 26.2%, compared to 30.1% of the total U.S. population. Understanding differences between tribes is important when developing educational policies and interventions, to ensure tribal specificity and target those most in need of help. Disaggregating by tribal affiliation also highlights the strengths of different tribes and allows researchers to learn from the practices that contribute to different tribes' positive outcomes. Notably, when using tribal affiliation to understand Native Americans' outcomes, it is important to also consider the large number of people who report Native American identification but have no tribal affiliation (Liebler & Zacher, 2013). Outcomes for these individuals may differ from those who report tribal affiliations.

Other Variables

We have offered an initial investigation of how data disaggregation along the lines of social class, school location, and tribal affiliation can offer a better understanding of variability in Native Americans' educational outcomes. However, further research is needed to understand which variables—and combinations of variables—are useful in understanding a wider variety of outcomes. In disaggregating Native American educational data, researchers often struggle with a lack of information. Very few large-scale datasets oversample Native American populations to ensure sufficient representation across the variables discussed above or other potentially important variables. Although funding and resources are often barriers to data collection, given the ongoing struggles of many Native American populations, it is essential that researchers strive to improve data collection practices to afford greater opportunities for understanding the factors that shape Native Americans' outcomes. Based on our own research, we suspect that variables including gender, school and teacher demographics, teacher knowledge of Native American culture, segregation, and adverse childhood experiences are all likely to shape Native Americans' educational outcomes. As researchers work to better understand and address the challenges facing diverse Native American communities, collecting information about a variety of life experience variables will improve the accuracy of their conclusions.

CONCLUSION

Native Americans' educational experiences are fraught with social, cultural, and historical difficulties (Castagno & Brayboy, 2008; Higheagle Strong & Jegatheesan, 2015), and their educational outcomes are too often discussed using data that ignore the variability among these populations. Overreliance on aggregated data breeds misunderstanding and reifies negative stereotypes, which ultimately perpetuate a cycle of underperformance among Native American students. Data disaggregation allows for a deeper understanding of Native American educational experiences specific to social class, geographic location, tribal community, and many other important factors. This understanding can liberate Native American students from the biases that undermine their academic performance, self-views, and educational aspirations.

APPENDIX: DEFINITION OF SCHOOL LOCATION CATEGORIES

City	Large City: Territory inside an urbanized area and inside a principal city with population of 250,000 or more.
	Midsize City: Territory inside an urbanized area and inside a principal city with population less than 250,000 and greater than or equal to 100,000.
	Small City: Territory inside an urbanized area and inside a principal city with population less than 100,000.
Suburb	Large Suburb: Territory outside a principal city and inside an urbanized area with population of 250,000 or more.
	Midsize Suburb: Territory outside a principal city and inside an urbanized area with population less than 250,000 and greater than or equal to 100,000.
	Small Suburb: Territory outside a principal city and inside an urbanized area with population less than 100,000.
Town	Fringe Town: Territory inside an urban cluster that is less than or equal to 10 miles from an urbanized area.
	Distant Town: Territory inside an urban cluster that is more than 10 miles and less than or equal to 35 miles from an urbanized area.
	Remote Town: Territory inside an urban cluster that is more than 35 miles from an urbanized area.
Rural	Fringe Rural: Census-defined rural territory that is less than or equal to 5 miles from an urbanized area, as well as rural territory that is less than or equal to 2.5 miles from an urban cluster.
	Rural, Distant: Census-defined rural territory that is more than 5 miles but less than or equal to 25 miles from an urbanized area, as well as rural territory that is more than 2.5 miles but less than or equal to 10 miles from an urban cluster.
	Rural, Remote: Census-defined rural territory that is more than 25 miles from an urbanized area and is also more than 10 miles from an urban cluster.

Source: National Center for Education Statistics: nces.ed.gov/programs/edge/docs/LOCALE_CLASSIFICATIONS.pdf

REFERENCES

Bouck, E. C. (2004). How size and setting impact education in rural schools. *The Rural Educator*, 25(3), 38–42.

Castagno, A. E., & Brayboy, B. M. J. (2008). Culturally responsive schooling for Indigenous youth: A review of the literature. *Review of Educational Research*, 78(4), 941–993. doi.org/10.3102/0034654308323036

Chronicle of Higher Education. (2006). *Almanac*. Washington, DC.

Covarrubias, R., & Fryberg, S. A. (2015). The impact of self-relevant representations on school belonging for Native American students. *Cultural Diversity and Ethnic Minority Psychology*, 21(1), 10–18. doi.org/10.1037/a0037819

Croizet, J.-C., & Claire, T. (1998). Extending the concept of stereotype threat to social class: The intellectual underperformance of students from low socioeconomic backgrounds. *Personality and Social Psychology Bulletin*, 24(6), 588–594. doi.org/10.1177/0146167298246003

Davies, P. G., Spencer, S. J., Quinn, D. M., & Gerhardstein, R. (2002). Consuming images: How television commercials that elicit stereotype threat can restrain women academically and professionally. *Personality and Social Psychology Bulletin*, 28(12), 1615–1628. doi.org/10.1177/014616702237644

Davies, P. G., Spencer, S. J., & Steele, C. M. (2005). Clearing the air: Identity safety moderates the effects of stereotype threat on women's leadership aspirations. *Journal of Personality and Social Psychology*, 88(2), 276–287. doi.org/10.1037/0022-3514.88.2.276

DeVoe, J. F., & Darling-Churchill, K. E. (2008). *Status and trends in the education of American Indians and Alaska Natives: 2008 (NCES 2008-084)*. Washington, DC.: National Center for Education Statistics, Institute of Education Sciences, U.S. Department of Education. Retrieved from nces.ed.gov/pubs2008/native-trends/

Faircloth, S. C., & Tippeconnic III, J. W. (2010). *The dropout/graduation crisis among American Indian and Alaska Native Students: Failure to respond places the future of Native peoples at risk*. Los Angeles, CA: Civil Rights Project/Proyecto Derechos Civiles at UCLA. Retrieved from www.civilrightsproject.ucla.edu/research/k-12-education/school-dropouts/the-dropout-graduation-crisis-among-american-indian-and-alaska-native-students-failure-to-respond-places-the-future-of-native-peoples-at-risk?searchterm=dropout%2Fgraduation.

Fryberg, S. A., Covarrubias, R., & Burack, J. A. (2018). The ongoing psychological colonization of North American Indigenous People. In P. L. Hammack (Ed.), *The Oxford handbook of social psychology and social justice* (pp. 113–138). New York, NY: Oxford University Press. doi.org/10.1093/oxfordhb/9780199938735.013.35

Fryberg, S. A., Markus, H. R., Oyserman, D., & Stone, J. M. (2008). Of warrior chiefs and Indian princesses: The psychological consequences of American Indian mascots. *Basic and Applied Social Psychology*, 30, 208–218. doi.org/10.1080/01973530802375003

Fryberg, S. A., & Townsend, S. S. M. (2008). The psychology of invisibility. In G. Adams, M. Biernat, N. Branscombe, C. Crandall, & L. Wrightsman (Eds.), *Commemorating Brown: The social psychology of racism and discrimination* (pp. 173–193). Washington, DC: American Psychological Association. doi.org/10.1037/11681-010

Heuer, R., & Stullich, S. (2011). *Comparability of state and local expenditures among schools within districts : A report from the study of school-level expenditures*. Washington, DC: U.S. Department of Education, Office of Planning, Evaluation, and Policy Development, Policy and Program Studies Service.

Higheagle Strong, Z., Carbonneau, K. J., & Austin, B. (2018). "I Plan to Attend College": Gender, parent education and academic support differences in American Indian and Alaska Native educational aspirations. *Journal of American Indian Education, 57*(2), 35-57. doi.org/10.5749/jamerindieduc.57.2.0035.

Higheagle Strong, Z., & Jegatheesan, B. (2015). School culture matters: Enabling and empowering Native American students in public schools. In P. McCardle & V. Berninger (Eds.), *Narrowing the achievement gap for Native American students: Paying the educational debt* (1st ed., pp. 178–192). New York, NY: Routledge.

Hoopes, M. J., Petersen, P., Vinson, E., & Lopez, K. (2012). Regional differences and tribal use of American Indian/Alaska Native cancer data in the Pacific Northwest. *Journal of Cancer Education, 27*(Supplement 1), S73–S79. doi.org/10.1007/s13187-012-0325-4

Johnson, P. J., Call, K. T., & Blewett, L. A. (2010). The importance of geographic data aggregation in assessing disparities in American Indian prenatal care. *American Journal of Public Health, 100*(1), 122–128. doi.org/10.2105/AJPH.2008.148908

Kena, G., Hussar, W., McFarland, J., DeBrey, C., Musu-Gillette, L., Wang, X., . . . Dunlop Velez, E. (2016). *The Condition of Education 2016 (NCES 2016-144)*. U.S. Department of Education, National Center for Education Statistics, Washington, DC. Retrieved from nces.ed.gov/pubs2016/2016144.pdf

Liebler, C. A., & Zacher, M. (2013). American Indians without tribes in the twenty-first century. *Ethnic and Racial Studies, 36*(11), 1910–1934. doi.org/10.1080/01419870.2012.692800

Logel, C., Iserman, E. C., Davies, P. G., Quinn, D. M., & Spencer, S. J. (2009). The perils of double consciousness: The role of thought suppression in stereotype threat. *Journal of Experimental Social Psychology, 45*, 299–312. doi.org/10.1016/j.jesp.2008.07.016

Markus, H. R., Steele, C. M., & Steele, D. M. (2002). Colorblindness as a barrier to inclusion: Assimilation and nonimmigrant minorities. In R. A. Shweder, M. Minow, & H. R. Markus (Eds.), *Engaging cultural differences: The multicultural challenge in liberal democracies* (pp. 453–472). New York, NY: Russell Sage Foundation.

Murphy, M. C., & Taylor, V. J. (2012). The role of situational cues in signaling and maintaining stereotype threat. In M. Inzlicht & T. Schmader (Eds.), *Stereotype threat: Theory, process, and application* (pp. 17–33). New York, NY: Oxford University Press. doi.org/10.1093/acprof:oso/9780199732449.003.0002

Musu-Gillette, L., de Brey, C., McFarland, J., Hussar, W., Sonnenberg, W., & Wilkinson-Flicker, S. (2017). *Status and trends in the education of racial and ethnic groups 2017*. Washington, DC. Retrieved from nces.ed.gov/pubs2017/2017051.pdf

National Center for Education Statistics. (2015). The NAEP Glossary of Terms. Retrieved from nces.ed.gov/nationsreportcard/glossary.aspx#nslp

National Urban Indian Family Council. (2008). *Urban Indian America: The status of American Indian and Alaska Native children and families today*. Baltimore,

MD: Annie E. Casey Foundation. Retrieved from www.aecf.org/resources/urban-indian-america/

Osborne, J. W., & Walker, C. (2006). Stereotype threat, identification with academics, and withdrawal from school: Why the most successful students of colour might be most likely to withdraw. *Educational Psychology*, 26(4), 563–577. doi.org/10.1080/01443410500342518

Oyserman, D., & Fryberg, S. A. (2006). The possible selves of diverse adolescents: Content and function across gender, race, and national origin. In C. Dunkel & J. Kerpelman (Eds.), *Possible selves: Theory, research, and application* (pp. 17–39). Huntington, NY: Nova.

Oyserman, D., & Markus, H. (1993). The sociocultural self. In J. Suls (Ed.), *Psychological perspectives on the self* (pp. 187–220). Hillsdale, NJ: Erlbaum.

Probst, J. C., Moore, C. G., Glover, S. H., & Samuels, M. E. (2004). Person and place: The compounding effects of race/ethnicity and rurality on health. *American Journal of Public Health*, 94(10), 1695–1703. doi.org/10.2105/AJPH.94.10.1695

Purdie-Vaughns, V., Steele, C. M., Davies, P. G., Ditlmann, R., & Crosby, J. R. (2008). Social identity contingencies : How diversity cues signal threat or safety for African Americans in mainstream institutions. *Journal of Personality and Social Psychology*, 94(4), 615–630. doi.org/10.1037/0022-3514.94.4.615

Schmader, T., Major, B., & Gramzow, R. H. (2001). Coping with ethnic stereotypes in the academic domain: Perceived injustice and psychological disengagement. *Journal of Social Issues*, 57(1), 93–111. doi.org/10.1111/0022-4537.00203

Sekaquaptewa, D., & Thompson, M. (2003). Solo status, stereotype threat, and performance expectancies: Their effects on women's performance. *Journal of Experimental Social Psychology*, 39(1), 68–74. doi.org/10.1016/S0022-1031(02)00508-5

Sherman, D. K., Hartson, K. A., Binning, K. R., Purdie-Vaughns, V., Garcia, J., Taborsky-Barba, S., . . . Cohen, G. L. (2013). Deflecting the trajectory and changing the narrative: How self-affirmation affects academic performance and motivation under identity threat. *Journal of Personality and Social Psychology*, 104(4), 591–618. doi.org/10.1037/a0031495

Snyder, T. D., & Dillow, S. A. (2012). *Digest of education statistics 2011* (NCES 2012-001). Washington, DC.: National Center for Education Statistics, Institute of Education Sciences, U.S. Department of Education.

Snyder, T. D., Tan, A. G., & Hoffman, C. M. (2006). *Digest of Education Statistics 2005* (NCES 2006-030). Washington, DC: National Center for Education Statistics, U.S. Department of Education.

Spencer, S. J., Logel, C., & Davies, P. G. (2016). Stereotype threat. *Annual Review of Psychology*, 67, 415–437. doi.org/10.1146/annurev-psych-073115-103235

Spencer, S. J., Steele, C. M., & Quinn, D. M. (1999). Stereotype threat and women's math performance. *Journal of Experimental Social Psychology*, 35(1), 4–28. doi.org/10.1006/jesp.1998.1373

Steele, C. M. (1997). A threat in the air: How stereotypes shape intellectual identity and performance. *American Psychologist*, 52(6), 613–629. doi.org/10.1037/0003-066X.52.6.613

Steele, C. M., & Aronson, J. (1995). Stereotype threat and the intellectual test performance of African Americans. *Journal of Personality and Social Psychology*, 69(5), 797–811. doi.org/10.1037/0022-3514.69.5.797

Steele, C. M., Spencer, S. J., & Aronson, J. (2002). Contending with group image: The psychology of stereotype and social identity threat. *Advances in Experimental Social Psychology, 34*, 379–440. doi.org/10.1016/S0065-2601(02)80009-0

Stephens, N. M., Hamedani, M. G., & Destin, M. (2014). Closing the social-class achievement gap: A Difference-Education intervention improves first-generation students' academic performance and all students' college transition. *Psychological Science, 25*(4), 943–953. doi.org/10.1177/0956797613518349

U.S. Census Bureau. (2015). American Community Survey, 2014 American Community Survey 1-Year Estimates, Table S0201. Retrieved from factfinder2.census.gov

U.S. Census Bureau. (2016). *Public Education Finances: 2014.* G14-ASPEF. Washington, DC: U.S. Government Printing Office.

U.S. Commission on Civil Rights. (2003). *A quiet crisis: Federal funding and unmet needs in Indian country.* Retrieved from www.usccr.gov/pubs/na0703/na0204.pdf.

Walpole, M. (2003). Socioeconomic status and college: How SES affects college experiences and outcomes. *The Review of Higher Education, 27*(1), 45–73. doi.org/10.1353/rhe.2003.0044

Walter, M., & Andersen, K. (2013). *Indigenous statistics: A quantitative research methodology.* Walnut Creek, CA: Left Coast Press.

Wigfield, A., & Eccles, J. S. (2000). Expectancy-value theory of achievement motivation. *Contemporary Educational Psychology, 25*, 68–81. doi.org/10.1006/ceps.1999.1015

Yeager, D. S., & Dweck, C. S. (2012). Mindsets that promote resilience: When students believe that personal characteristics can be developed. *Educational Psychologist, 47*(4), 302–314. doi.org/10.1080/00461520.2012.722805

CHAPTER 10

More Than Nuance

Recognizing and Serving the Diversity of the Latinx Community

Desiree D. Zerquera, Jasmine Haywood,
and Martín De Mucha Flores

Latinxs hold a variety of racial and ethnic identities, they have no homogeneous culture, and have a variety of different experiences. In *Visible Identities*, Alcoff (2008) argues that it is a metaphysical and political mistake to think of Latinxs as a monolithic racial or ethnic group that shares a set of intrinsic physical features and a common culture. Aspects of heterogeneity among Latinxs result in a diversity of in-group lived experiences (Haywood; 2017; Torres, 2003). Thus, in developing policy and practice to appropriately serve Latinx populations, particularly within educational contexts, we must better understand and address heterogeneity.

The purpose of this work is to complicate the heterogeneity that exists within the Latinx community, centering around the influences of ethnicity, U.S. geographic differences, and race. We further seek to highlight the implications of overlooking Latinx heterogeneity within educational research, policy, and practice, focusing in particular on the higher education context. To do so, we draw connections between research conducted by historians, anthropologists, sociologists, and interdisciplinary scholars focused on the study of race, ethnicity, and Latinx communities. We supplement this existing work with analysis of public data that provides the opportunity for presenting a more nuanced picture of Latinxs.

In this chapter, we first present the evolution of a panethnic Latinx category and the ways in which this homogenization has contributed to the silencing of identities that are situated within this broader community. This section serves to trace historical and sociopolitical rationale as to how the homogenization of the Latinx community has evolved, highlighting the lasting tensions of this evolution. From this context, we next consider the complexity within these identities and draw from educational research and data to further clarify the implications of homogenous perspectives and to highlight the richness offered by a more heterogeneous way of understanding Latinxs. We center this exploration on three key facets of Latinx heterogeneity: geographical residence within the U.S., ethnicity, and race and associated phenotype. Finally, we pose recommendations for how better to serve this population through awareness of this in-group diversity.

Throughout this chapter, we employ the term *Latinx* to refer to individuals of all genders and gender nonconforming individuals who ethnically and/or culturally have origins within the Spanish-speaking regions of the Caribbean, South America, Central America, Mexico, and what is today the southwestern region of the United States. This definition arguably invokes a heritage-based definition of individual and group identity; however, we advance the sociological concept of racial and ethnic identity as being socially constructed and not fixed (Haney Lopez, 1994; Valdez, 2013). The concept of a Latinx identity surely varies (Torres, 2003; Torres et al., 2012). As such, we center this chapter within the complexities of the Latinx community. We use Latinx as an alternative to other terms such as *Hispanic, Latino,* or even *Latina/o* or *Latin@*. The terminology seeks to reject the colonial history invoked by the term *Hispanic* and breaks the gender binary imposed by the grammatical constructs of the Spanish language. Though the usage has invoked some controversy, it provides a broader view encompassing trans* and gender nonconforming Latinxs' identification (Pastrana, Battle, & Harris, 2017; Reichard, 2015).

THE BOUNDARIES OF A UNIFIED "HISPANIC" EXPERIENCE

The development of a panethnic identity emerged from Latinxs' need to have a political platform and national presence during the Civil Rights Movement (Omi & Winant, 1994). The coalescing of Latinx subgroups aimed to mobilize resources to support the needs of Latinxs in the United States. However, the long-term effect was a lasting homogenizing of the many different groups that comprise the Latinx community.

Through the 1960s and much of the early 1970s, African American activists had mobilized a political platform attracting national attention and resources. Similarly, Latinxs at the time—specifically Chicanos in California and the Southwest, and Puerto Ricans in New York—were in search of federal and foundation resources to support job training, access to health care and other social services, and called government attention to the injustices facing Latinxs (Gómez-Quiñones, 1990). However, lack of a unified identity made it difficult for Latinx communities around the country to be heard and seen on a national platform. It became clear to Latinx activists that a political identity that connected all Latinx groups in the United States was necessary (Humes et al., 2011). Policymakers during the 1960s and 1970s thought Latinx demands for greater equity from the U.S. government would eventually be resolved over time, either through assimilation of Latinxs into majority culture or via immigration policy (Acuña, 2011). Missed in these assumptions was that, unlike previous immigrants to the United States, Latinxs kept a strong affinity for their home country of origin and connected deeply with their mixed racial identity and ancestry (Novak, 1973).

During the mid-1970s to late 1980s the largest Latinx subgroups were Mexican Americans (including those who identified as Chicano/a, a political identity shaped by civil rights leaders) in the Southwest, Puerto Ricans along the East Coast, and growing numbers of Cubans in Florida (Humes, Jones, & Ramirez, 2011). These communities were actively organized by the National Council of La Raza (NCLR) to use the term *Hispanic* to unite their political concerns. The use of the term centers on a political need to push back against moves by the Johnson administration to categorize the emerging Latinx national agenda as pertaining solely to individuals who were "Spanish Speaking" or of "Spanish Origin" (Humes et al., 2011). NCLR, the League of United Latin American Citizens (LULAC), and other developing national advocacy groups saw the use of the term *Hispanic* as their only way to unite all of the disparate and diverse experiences into one political voice, while balancing the need and ability to organize mass protests of Latinxs that would draw national attention to the inequities they experienced across the country (Fergus, 2004).

The terms "Spanish speaking" and "Spanish origin" were too narrow. The focus on linguistic use and Spanish connection left out a number of Latinx communities who did not speak Spanish but identified as Latinx. Shadowing the use of these terms is the rejection of colonial ties to Spain and embrace of indigenous and African ancestry; this ideology was particularly advanced within the movements of the growing number of Chicana/o nationalists and Puerto Rican Young Lords activists (Marquez, 1993; Thomas, 2010). Using *Hispanic American* or *Hispanic* was broad enough to encompass the entire Latinx American diaspora in the United States without disenfranchising large subgroups of Latinxs (Hayes-Bautista, 1983).

Hayes-Bautista (1983) calls the 1980s the "Decade of the Hispanic" (p. 276). There were clear benefits to being identified as a panethnic group during a decade when resources for research were scarce. It afforded the Latinx population greater recognition within economic and social policies, and inclusion in the lengthy, broad-ranging legal history relative to civil rights (Humes, Jones & Ramirez, 2011). Some argue that the benefits of panethnicity are still realized today, and that without a panethnic identification the Latinx community would be perceived as disparate subgroups whose needs could be met via individualized legislation rather than civil rights policy (Omi & Winant, 1994). Yet the heterogeneity of the Latinx population must be taken into account, especially considering the difference among Latinx subgroups. It was not until the 1970 census that the U.S. government collected data on Latinx ethnicity, allowing for consideration at a national level of the representation of this community within the United States (United States Commission on Civil Rights, 1974). While the U.S. Census Bureau needed to provide an accurate account of all the Latinx communities to make claims for federal resources, it was complicated by the need to also expose inequity.

While the term *Hispanic* and later terms such as Latinx are broad enough to encompass the Latinx diaspora in the United States, the panethnic identity has not been embraced without challenge. The Latinx identity is defined by a diversity of experiences related to race, language, religion, immigration, and ethnicity (Portes & MacLeod, 1996). While the panethnic identity offers the political platform and leverage to speak from a unified experience, it does so while masking other areas of diversity. Though the umbrella term *Hispanic* served a political purpose for three decades, recent implications from census data have proven that the broad identity moniker of *Hispanic* has possibly outlived its purpose (Humes et al., 2011). The following section seeks to deepen our understanding of the heterogeneity of Latinxes.

UNPACKING NUANCES WITHIN THE LATINX POPULATION

While generalizing and labeling the Latinx experience can be a meaningful practice in terms of politics and providing unity, it should be explicit, purposeful, and done deliberately. Taking into consideration the full heterogeneity of the Latinx population mandates "that we define complex experiences as closely to their full complexity as possible and that we not ignore voices at the margin" (Grillo, 2013, p. 22), rather than essentializing this population. In contrast to what an essentialist perspective might advance, there is no singular, monolithic Latinx experience (Harris, 1997). Nuñez and colleagues (2013) offer a comprehensive overview of key dimensions of the demographic diversity of Latinx students in higher education, including ethnicity and immigration status. We build on their work, examining the heterogeneity of experiences among Latinxs and the implications of a heterogeneous perspective. In the following section, we consider three important aspects of heterogeneity within the Latinx community: where Latinxs live in the United States; the contours of ethnicity; and the ways in which race and phenotype vary and impact Latinx communities.

GEOGRAPHIC HETEROGENEITY WITHIN THE LATINX POPULATION

While Latinxs are not a new population within the United States context, the growth of the population in the past two decades has drawn much attention from the public and policymakers. As of the latest census population estimates, there are 56.6 million Latinxs in the United States, comprising over 17% of the total population (U.S. Census Bureau, 2016). Considering Latinxs made up just 9% and 12% of the U.S. population in 1990 and 2000, respectively (Guzman, 2001), this growth is significant. And while the United States had experienced steep Latinx growth before, what makes the growth within the past decade particularly interesting is where it has occurred.

Differences in Growth and Responses

While traditional areas of large Latinx populations such as Los Angeles and Miami hold strong, historically homogeneous states and counties in the South and Midwest are becoming key sites of settlement and growth for Latinxs (Stepler & Lopez, 2016). These regions are responding in different ways. Many Spanish-language radio stations and radio programs have emerged in growing Latinx centers in recent years in response to these market changes (Khemlani, 2014). The health care industry has enhanced outreach to target Latinxs in particular to address barriers presented by high rates of uninsurance, language and cultural barriers, and rurality (Casey, Blewett, & Call, 2003). Among the general public, the emergence of hate groups and anti-Latinx rhetoric has accompanied the rapid growth within some regions (Lacy & Odem, 2009). As compared to states with long histories of significant Latinx populations, where these types of services and general public responses have long been present, within these new regions reactions to the Latinx population are still forming. This undoubtedly shapes Latinx experiences differently in these states.

Implications of Differences in Geography

Some studies have worked to contribute to a more heterogeneous perspective of Latinxs with regards to where these populations are situated. The seminal book *Apple Pie and Enchiladas* (Chapa & Millard, 2004) drew significant attention to the Midwest as a distinct space of Latinx experiences. The work of Gross and colleagues (Gross, Torres, & Zerquera, 2013; Gross, Zerquera, Berry, & Inge, 2014; Zerquera & Gross, 2017) builds on this notion of distinction of experiences and complicates understandings of what shapes Latinx college student success. Their work, situated within Indiana, shows how the Latinx population in a state that historically has had smaller or more transient Latinx communities, but that has experienced considerable Latinx population growth in recent decades, is shaped by some influences notably different from those experienced by Latinxs in other states. For instance, they found that (contrary to what has emerged in other work) Latinx students in Indiana have higher rates of success at regional state institutions than at more selective universities (Zerquera & Gross, 2017).

Additionally, some work has offered a national perspective with attention to state-by-state differences in an effort to unpack national data trends that may mask differences by state context. Zerquera, Acevedo-Gil, Flores, and Maranthal (2015) compare state-by-state portraits of Latinx community college enrollment to challenge national discourse around Latinx college-going. Analysis shows that nationally over 42% of Latinxs enrolled in higher education were enrolled in community colleges (compared to 39% of non-Latinxs), 36% in public 4-year colleges (compared to 38% of non-Latinxs), 16% at private 4-year colleges (compared to 17% of non-Latinxs), and 9% in for-profits (compared to 8% of non-Latinxs). The state-by-state comparison challenges a simple conclusion about the likeliness of Latinxs to attend community colleges. Latinxs in more than half of the United States are enrolled in 4-year colleges at higher rates, primarily within states in the southeast and northeast. Further, there were only six states in which Latinx enrollment was concentrated in community colleges and non-Latinxs enrolled in greater proportions in other sectors—Minnesota, Virginia, Colorado, Oklahoma, Kentucky, and Connecticut. The disconnect between national averages and state-by-state comparisons may be in part explained simply by numbers—over 15 million Latinxs live in California alone, a state with a well-developed community college system and large enrollments in 2-year institutions. The distortion provided by national enrollment averages has dangerous potential to misinform decisions that can affect the educational trajectories of our nation's largest minoritized group. These data trends indicate that greater attention must be paid to the context of where Latinxs in the United States live, and suggest the implications of failing to do so.

LATINX ETHNIC HETEROGENEITY

The ethnic diversity within the Latinx community has become increasingly complex in this time of population growth in which Latinxs now make up the second largest population group (Colby & Ortman, 2015). Latinxs include not just immigrants born abroad, but children and grandchildren of immigrants as well as those who identify with the proclamation "the border crossed us" (see Cisneros, 2013). Nevertheless, ethnicity plays out significantly and reflects diversity of culture, customs, privilege, and oppression (Nuñez et al., 2013. The following section provides a review of the ethnic heterogeneity within the Latinx population.

Varying Ethnicities Within the Latinx Population

Although those of Mexican and Puerto Rican descent make up the majority of Latinxs, these groups decreased their proportion of all Latinxs between

2000 and 2010. According to calculations based on data from the Integrated Public Use Microdata Series (IPUMS), Mexicans made up more than three percentage points less and Puerto Ricans almost two percentage points less of the total Latinx population in 2010 than they had in 2000. Among Dominicans and Cubans—other historically large ethnic subgroups in the United States—smaller but similar decreases were observed.

Though a small change, this decrease among larger, longstanding groups indicates a growing heterogeneity among Latinx subgroups living in the United States Notable growth occurred among those of Central American descent in particular, with Guatemalans (1.4% to 2.3%), Hondurans (0.8% to 1.5%), and Salvadorans (2.9% to 3.7%) making up larger proportions of the Latinx population in the United States than they had 10 years before. While the ethnic communities of backgrounds connected to the countries of Venezuela, Panama, Bolivia, Uruguay, and Costa Rica, among many others, are smaller in number, they still comprise nearly 20% of the over 15 million Latinxs living in the United States. Their numbers are not to be ignored, and how we as a nation serve them requires a perspective that accounts for their distinct experiences.

Analysis of Educational Differences Among Latinx Ethnicities

Educational attainment rates provide a key area for uncovering the masking of differences. As of 2014, just 15.5% of Latinxs age 25 or older had earned a bachelor's or higher degree, lagging behind the general population by more than half (32.5% of total U.S. population) (Ryan & Bauman, 2016). However, disaggregating by ethnicity, there are key trends that highlight educational attainment differences within the Latinx community. For instance, just about 10% of Mexican, Honduran, and Salvadoran populations hold bachelor's degrees or higher. At the same time, Venezuelans and Argentinians hold bachelor's or higher degrees at rates higher than that of the overall U.S. population (50% and 40%, respectively). These differences reflect varied experiences of privilege, oppression, and immigration histories of these different groups (Nuñez et al., 2013). However, this illuminates the ways that drawing from an overall picture might serve to further deepen inequities within the Latinx community.

LATINX RACIAL HETEROGENEITY

An important yet overlooked aspect that exemplifies Latinx heterogeneity is racial identity. Fewer Latinxs identify as White today than did in years past—from 64% in 1980, to 54% in 1990, to just below 50% in 2000 (Haney-López, 2005). At the same time, the number of Latinxs who identify as Black has increased from just below 400,000 in 1980 to more than

900,000 in 2000 (Haney-López, 2005). According to the 2000 U.S. Census, 2.7% of Latinxs self-identified as Black and 47.9% as White (Logan, 2004); more recent findings from the 2014 National Survey of Latinxs show that the proportion of Latinxs who identify as Afro-Latino has increased to 24% (Pew Research Center, 2015). Further, according to a recent survey by the Pew Research Center (2015), over 16% of Latinx adults identify as multiracial, reflecting the mixed racial backgrounds of the Latinx community. In this way, Latinxs are also linked to the histories of indigenous peoples and can display indigenous physical traits (Lipsitz, 1998). Historically, the Taínos in Puerto Rico and Hispaniola, the Caribs of the Lesser Antilles, and the Guanahatabeys of Western Cuba engaged in racial mixing or mestizaje with the Spanish (Rouse, 1992). While much of the mixing was through marriage, it typically occurred through violent rape (Acuña, 2011. In Mexico and some countries in Latin America *mestizo/a* is a broad term that upholds the notion that Latinxs are all one single race descended from Europeans and indigenous populations. While an indigenous ancestry is acknowledged among many Latinx subgroups, it is still stigmatized (Hunter, 2007). However, African ancestry is most frequently ignored while phenotypical characteristics suggesting African descent are instead attributed to an indigenous heritage (Daniel, 2002).

Racial Identification Among Latinx Subgroups

Racial identities differ across ethnicities. As far as national origin goes, Black Latinx identification is most prevalent among Dominicans at 12.7%, followed by Puerto Ricans at 8.2% and Cubans at 4.7% (Logan, 2004). While Dominicans hold the highest proportion of self-identified Afro-Latinxs, the highest number, more than a quarter million, of Afro-Latinxs are Puerto Rican, the second-largest Latinx subgroup in the United States (Brown & Lopez, 2013; Logan, 2004). For Latinx populations, racial identity evolved over generations through racial mixing among Europeans, Africans, and indigenous peoples. The Spanish presence throughout the Americas and the associated class divide, the trade of enslaved Africans, and enslavement and conquests of indigenous peoples fostered the creation of deeply complex bloodlines, each associated with different forms of power and oppression within racialized societies.

Being asked to racially self-identify as either White or Black is an unfamiliar concept to many Latinxs. The primary factor that impacts Latinxs' racial self-identification is their experience with racism. Scholars have empirically linked skin color and experiences with discrimination, such that darker-skinned Latinos experience discrimination more frequently than lighter-skinned Latinos (Araujo & Borrell, 2006; Frank, Akresh & Lu, 2010; Haywood, 2017; Telles & Murguia, 1990). Discriminatory experiences have been found to be more prevalent among darker-skinned

Mexicans, Cubans, Puerto Ricans, and Dominicans (Araujo Dawson, 2015; Golash-Boza & Darity, 2008). A socially constructed generic Latinx phenotype has evolved, prioritizing a Eurocentric prototype of Latinxs, shifting to become lighter over time (Dávila, 2002). Latinidad, or Latinx identity, is socially constructed in that it "is revealed as historically contingent, socially mediated systems of meaning that attach to elements of an individual's morphology and ancestry" rather than an individual's biology (Haney-López, 1994, pp. 38–39).

Considerations and Implications of Race in Latinx Educational Research

More recently, scholars have delved into Latinx ethnic subgroups in higher education (Hurtado, Saenz, Santos, & Cabrera, 2008; Nuñez & Crisp, 2012; Nuñez et al., 2008) and Latinx racial identification within higher education (Dache, Haywood, & Mislán, 2019; Haywood, 2017). Still, the literature on Latinx college students presents a narrow, monolithic view of Latinx identity that insinuates that race and ethnicity are one and the same. The fields of psychology and sociology provide insight into the role of skin color in Latinxs' educational experiences. Murguia and Telles (1996) found that Mexican Americans who phenotypically looked White had higher levels of educational attainment than Mexican Americans with darker skin, even when controlling for family background. Darker-skinned Mexicans in the United States are more likely to confront racism based on their ethnicity and skin color. Arce, Murguia, and Frisbie (1987) had similar findings in their examination of Mexican Americans' skin color and education; however, they incorporated a variable regarding facial characteristics. They discovered that dark skin combined with indigenous facial characteristics (rather than White) was correlated with decreased education levels. Other scholars (Bonilla-Silva & Dietrich, 2008) have also found that educational attainment levels among racially White-identified Latinxs are higher than among their dark-skinned counterparts. Relatedly, Telzer and Vazquez-Garcia (2009) examined how the skin color of immigrant Latina college students and U.S.-born Latina college students impacts their self-perceptions, focusing primarily on Mexican, Puerto Rican, and Dominican students. As the researchers expected, they found that darker skin was a factor in negative self-perceptions among non-U.S.-born Latinas. Interestingly, the researchers found that only darker-skinned immigrant participants had poorer self-perceptions, whereas darker-skinned U.S.-born participants did not. In sum, these studies highlight the differing and negative experiences of darker-skinned Latinxs throughout their educational experiences.

While Latinx skin color and phenotype has seldom been taken into account in empirical studies within the field of education, there are a few exceptions that demonstrate the significance of considering Latinx phenotype. Fergus (2009) examined whether skin color variation had an effect on the educational journeys of 17 Mexican and Puerto Rican high school students. He sought to understand how students described their own racial/ethnic identity, as compared to how they believed other students defined it. He calls attention to "the omission of skin color as a variable in the construction of a racial/ethnic identification" (p. 343). Most notably, Fergus records the students' ethnic self-identification, how others racially or ethnically perceive them, in addition to how the researcher racially or ethnically defines them. The findings focus on the ways in which the students were racialized in school and how the participants identified versus how others might identify them. Students whom Fergus classified as displaying phenotypically Latinx and Black characteristics spoke of instances of racism in relation to their racial identity, whereas more European-looking students did not share similar experiences. Similarly, Haywood (2017) found that Afro-Latinx college students experienced colorism, social exclusion from panethnic Latinx groups, and a questioning of their Latino authenticity. Fergus (2009) concludes that "racializing is moderated by skin color among Latinos/Latinas" (p. 369). He calls for larger studies on the role that racialization plays in Latinx student engagement and for further exploration of how skin color is bound to identification. He asserts, "We need to understand who gets to be Black, White, and Hispanic and how such social constructs operate as a lens for setting the conditions for learning and navigating and engaging the school context" (p. 371). While limited work from the field of education has centered within this area, it is imperative we consider the links between racial/ethnic identity, mental health, and educational attainment to address the role of skin color and phenotype in educational settings (Codina & Montalvo, 1994; Montalvo & Codina, 2001; Telzer & Vazquez-Garcia, 2009).

RECOMMENDATIONS FOR RESEARCH, POLICY, AND PRACTICE

Despite the great heterogeneity within the Latinx population, much of research, policy, and practice employs a homogeneous lens to understand Latinxs. As researchers, policymakers, administrators, and practitioners, there is more we can and must do to understand and account for heterogeneity of the Latinx community in our work.

Cultural Fluency Within Our Work

Policymakers, administrators, and practitioners need a critical awareness that takes into account the diversity within and across geopolitical contexts and Latinx communities. Even when there is Latinx representation within these levels of decisionmaking, education surrounding the specific needs and experiences of the diverse Latinx subgroups within the state are essential. Trainings provided by local community-based organizations and Latinx Studies departments and centers may enhance the awareness of these needs. For higher education administrators and others working on college campuses, drawing from the rich resources of the cultural centers and ethnic studies departments on campus may provide insight. Resources should be allocated specifically for the development of a campus community that better understands Latinx issues as being complex and multifaceted. Established and emerging scholars across the nation are working to draw more attention to the diversity within the Latinx community with regards to race (e.g., Dache, Haywood, & Mislán, 2019; Fergus, 2004, 2009; Haywood, 2017) and state contexts (Duany, 2011) and may offer insights into these experiences that can benefit a campus community through sharing this understanding.

Structuring and Using Data to Capture Complexity

To make better decisions, we need better tools. While tools like *The Equity Scorecard* provide a model for how to structure and use data to illuminate and address educational inequities at campus and system levels (Bensimon, Hao, & Bustillos, 2006), scorecards need to consider more than just the five standard racial demographic groups typically captured by colleges and universities. Intake forms during matriculation should account for detailed student demographics, and analysis of student outcomes should systematically create intersectional subgroup comparisons. For instance, matriculation information should be revised to ask students questions about ethnicity in addition to race and "Hispanic/Latino, yes or no?" so that institutions can use this information in analyses of student outcomes to better understand which Latinx subgroups may be better or less well served by policies and practices. Though it can be difficult within standard practices to disaggregate already small numbers of individuals into even smaller groups, it is important to keep in mind the voices at the margins that can be lost through these gross overgeneralizations (Zuberi, 2001).

Additionally, tools to examine Latinx outcomes through a more heterogeneous lens are present. Latinx ethnicity has been separated out from racial categories in dominant data collection efforts as a result of 2010 U.S. Census Bureau changes. Still, researchers rarely disaggregate data collected from Latinx populations, in turn treating this population as a monolithic group. Disaggregating demographic data on Latinxs by race and ethnicity would allow for more thorough analyses, and in turn inform higher education stakeholders as to how to best support Latinx subgroups like Afro-Latinx students. Ignoring race in the study of Latinx collegians pushes the experiences of African descendant Latinxs to the margins.

CONCLUSION

Latinx experiences in the United States are greatly shaped by where they reside, whether that be within a densely Latinx area or a region where Latinxs have only recently began to settle, and to where they trace their ethnic and racial heritage. Without a heterogeneous lens through which to understand Latinxs, researchers, educators, and policymakers risk a grave disservice. As the Latinx population continues to gain traction and attention within political- and marketing-based spheres in efforts to tap into the potential profits from the "sleeping giant," higher education reserachers and policymakers must also center on understanding the complexity of this population.

The power of a collective voice in the realm of politics and decision-making is not to be understated. It was a necessary move in the fight for civil rights and social justice, and continues to provide a collective platform for the Latinx community. However, the cost of the homogenization of the Latinx population is the perpetuation of White supremacist and colonial ideology. It masks the ways differences play out within state contexts with differing influences and histories. It also masks the various ethnicities and racial identities that exist under the broad Latinx umbrella. Approaching the Latinx population through a lens of homogeneity can perpetuate inequitable outcomes facing different Latinx populations, even with the best of intentions. The heterogeneity highlighted in this chapter serves to raise awareness so that decisions to consider a heterogeneous or homogenous perspective in shaping policies, practices, and perspectives can be strategic and intentional, and not made out of ignorance or disregard.

REFERENCES

Acuña, R. (2011). Occupied America. In R. Delgado & J. Stefancic (Eds.), *The Latino/a Condition: A Critical Reader* (pp. 61–64). New York, NY: New York University Press.

Alcoff, L. M. (2008). Mapping the boundaries of race, ethnicity, and nationality. *International Philosophical Quarterly, 48*(2), 231–238.

Araújo, B. Y., & Borrell, L. N. (2006). Understanding the link between discrimination, mental health outcomes, and life chances among Latinos. *Hispanic Journal of Behavioral Sciences, 28*(2), 245–266.

Araújo-Dawson, B. (2015). Understanding the complexities of skin color, perceptions of race, and discrimination among Cubans, Dominicans, and Puerto Ricans. *Hispanic Journal of Behavioral Sciences, 37*(2), 243–256.

Arce, C.H., Murguia, E., & Frisbie, W. P. (1987). Phenotype and life chances among Chicanos. *Hispanic Journal of Behavioral Sciences, 9*(1), 19–32.

Bensimon, E. M., Hao, L., & Bustillos, L. T. (2006). Measuring the state of equity in public higher education. In P. Gandara, G. Orfield, C. L. Horn (Eds.),

Expanding opportunity in higher education: Leveraging promise (pp. 143–165). Albany, NY: SUNY Press.

Bonilla-Silva, E., & Dietrich, D. R. (2008). The Latin Americanization of racial stratification in the US. In R. E. Hall (Ed.), *Racism in the 21st century* (pp. 151–170). New York, NY: Springer.

Brown, A., & Lopez, M. H. (2013, August). *Mapping the Latino population, by state, county and city*. Washington, DC: Pew Research Center. Retrieved from www.pewhispanic.org/2013/08/29/mapping-the-latino-population-by-state-county-and-city/

Casey, M., Blewett, L., & Call, K. (2003). *Response of local health care systems in the rural Midwest to a growing Latino population.* Twin Cities, MN: University of Minnesota Rural Health Research Center.

Chapa, J., & Millard, A.V. (2004). *Apple pie and enchiladas: Latino newcomers in the rural Midwest.* Austin, TX: University of Texas Press.

Cisneros, J. D. (2013). *The border crossed us: Rhetorics of borders, citizenship, and Latina/o identity.* Tuscaloosa, AL: The University of Alabama Press.

Codina, G. E. & Montalvo, F. F. (1994). Chicano phenotype and depression. *Hispanic Journal of Behavioral Sciences, 16*(3), 296–306.

Colby, S. L., Ortman, J. M. (2015). *Projections of the size and composition of the U.S. population: 2014 to 2060.* Current Population Reports, P25-1143, U.S. Census Bureau, Washington, DC, 2014. Retrived from: www.census.gov/content/dam/Census/library/publications/2015/demo/p25-1143.pdf.

Dache, A., Haywood, J., & Mislán, C. (2019). A badge of honor, not shame: An AfroLatina theory of Black-imiento for U.S higher education research. *The Journal of Negro Education, 88*(2), 130–145.

Daniel, G. R. (2002). *More than Black: Multiracial identity and the new racial order.* Philadelphia, PA: Temple University Press.

Dávila, A. (2002). Talking back: Spanish media and U.S. Latinidad. In M. Habell-Pallan and M. Romero (Eds.), *Latino/a Popular Culture* (pp. 25–37) New York, NY: New York University Press.

Duany, J. (2011). *Blurred borders: Transnational migration between the Hispanic Caribbean and the United States.* Chapel Hill, NC : University of North Carolina Press.

Fergus, E. (2004). *Skin color and identity formation: Perceptions of opportunity and academic orientation among Mexican and Puerto Rican youth.* New York, NY: Routledge.

Fergus, E. (2009). Understanding Latino students' schooling experiences: The relevance of skin color among Mexican and Puerto Rican high school students. *Teachers College Record, 111*(2), 339–375.

Frank, R., Akresh, I. R., & Lu, B. (2010). Latino immigrants and the U.S. racial order how and where do they fit in? *American Sociological Review, 75*(3), 378–401.

Golash-Boza, T., & Darity, W. (2008). Latino racial choices: the effects of skin colour and discrimination on Latinos' and Latinas' racial self-identifications. *Ethnic and Racial Studies, 31*(5), 899–934.

Gómez-Quiñones, J. (1990). *Chicano politics: Reality and promise, 1940–1990.* Albuquerque, NM: University of New Mexico Press.

Grillo, T. (2013) Antiessentialism and Intersectionality: Tools to dismantle the master's house. *Berkeley Journal of Gender, Law & Justice, 10*(1), 16–30.

Gross, J., Torres, V., & Zerquera, D. (2013). Financial aid and attainment among students in a state with changing demographics. *Research in Higher Education, 54*(4), 383–406.

Gross, J., Zerquera, D., Berry, M. S., & Inge, B. (2014). Latino associate degree completion: Effects of financial aid over time. *Journal of Hispanic Higher Education, 13*(3), 177–190.

Guzman, B. (2001, May). *The Hispanic population: Census 2000 brief.* Washington, DC: U.S. Census Bureau.

Haney-López, I. F. (1994). Social construction of race: Some observations on illusion, fabrication, and choice. *Harvard Civil Rights-Civil Liberties Law Review, 29*, 1.

Haney-López, I. (2005). Race on the 2010 census: Hispanics & the shrinking white majority. *Daedalus, 134*(1), 42–52.

Harris, A. P. (1997) Race and essentialism in feminist legal theory. In A. K. Wing (Ed.), *Critical race feminism: A reader* (pp. 11–18). New York: New York University Press.

Hayes-Bautista, D. E. (1983) On comparing studies of different Raza populations. *American Journal of Public Health, 73*(3), 274–276.

Haywood, J. M. (2017). 'Latino spaces have always been the most violent': Afro-Latino collegians' perceptions of colorism and intragroup marginalization. *The International Journal of Qualitative Studies in Education, 30*(8), 759–782.

Humes, K., Jones, N., & Ramirez, R. (2011). *Overview of race and Hispanic origin: 2010.* Washington, DC: U.S. Department of Commerce, Economics and Statistics Administration, U.S. Census Bureau.

Hunter, M. (2007). The persistent problem of colorism: Skin tone, status, and inequality. *Sociology Compass 1*(1), 237–254. doi: 10.1111/j.1751-9020.2007.00006.x

Hurtado, S., Santos, J. L., Sáenz, V. B., & Cabrera, N. L. (Eds.). (2008). *Advancing in higher education: A portrait of Latina/o college freshmen at four-year institutions, 1975–2006.* Los Angeles, CA: Higher Education Research Institute.

Khemlani, A. (2014, July). More FM radio stations broadcast in Spanish in response to growing Latino populations. *Latin Post.* Retrieved from www.latinpost.com/articles/17624/20140720/more-fm-radio-stations-broadcast-spanish-response-growing-latino-populations.htm

Lacy, E., & Odem, M. E. (2009). Popular attitudes and public policies: Southern responses to Latino immigration. In M. E. Odem & E. Lacy (Eds.), *Latino immigrants and the transformation of the U.S. south* (pp. 143–164). Athens, GA: University of Georgia Press.

Lipsitz, G. (1998). *The possessive investment in whiteness: How white people profit from identity politics.* Philadelphia, PA: Temple University Press.

Logan, J. R. (2004). How race counts for Hispanic Americans. *Sage Race Relations Abstracts, 29*(1), 7–19.

Marquez, B. (1993). *LULAC: The evolution of a Mexican American political organization.* Austin, TX: University of Texas Press.

Montalvo, F. F., & Codina, G. E. (2001). Skin color and Latinos in the United States. *Ethnicities, 1*(3), 321–341.

Murguia, E., & Telles, E. E. (1996). Phenotype and schooling among Mexican Americans. *Sociology of Education, 69*(4), 276–289.

Novak, M. (1973). *The rise of the unmeltable ethnics: Politics and culture in the seventies.* New York, NY: Macmillian.

Nuñez, A. M., & Crisp, G. (2012). Ethnic diversity and Latino/a college access: A comparison of Mexican American and Puerto Rican beginning college students. *Journal of Diversity in Higher Education*, 5(2), 78–95.

Nuñez, A. M., Hoover, R. E., Pickett, K., Stuart-Carruthers, A.C., & Vazquez, M. (2013). Latinos in higher education and Hispanic-Serving Institutions: Creating conditions for success (ASHE Higher Education Report: Volume 39, Number 1). Hoboken, NJ: Wiley Periodicals, Inc.

Nuñez, A. M., McDonough, P., Ceja, M., & Solórzano, D. (2008). Diversity within: Latino college choice and ethnic comparisons. In C. Gallagher (Ed.), *Racism in post-race America: New theories, new directions* (pp. 267–284). Chapel Hill, NC: Social Forces Publishing.

Omi, M., & Winant, H. (2014). *Racial formation in the United States* (3rd ed.). New York, NY: Routledge.

Pastrana, A., Battle, J., & Harris, A. (2017). *An examination of Latinx LGBT populations across the United States: Intersections of race and sexuality.* New York, NY: Palgrave Macmillan.

Pew Research Center (2015, April). *Multiracial in America: Proud, diverse and growing in numbers.* Washington, D.C. Retrieved from www.pewsocialtrends.org/wp-content/uploads/sites/3/2015/06/2015-06-11_multiracial-in-america_final-updated.pdf

Portes, A., & MacLeod, D. (1996). What shall I call myself? Hispanic identity formation in the second generation. *Ethnic and Racial Studies*, 19, 523–547.

Reichard, R. (2015, August). Why we say Latinx: Trans and gender non-conforming people explain. *Latina Magazine.* Retrieved from www.latina.com/lifestyle/our-issues/why-we-say-latinx-trans-gender-non-conforming-people-explain

Rouse, I. (1992). *The Tainos: Rise and decline of the people who greeted Columbus.* New Haven, CT: Yale University Press.

Ryan, C. J., & Bauman, K. (2016). *Educational Attainment in the United States: 2015.* Current Population Reports, P20-578, U.S. Census Bureau, Washington DC, 2015. Retrieved from: www.census.gov/content/dam/Census/library/publications/2016/demo/p20-578.pdf

Stepler, R., & Lopez, M. H. (2016, September). *U.S. Latino population growth and dispersion has slowed since onset of the Great Recession.* Washington, DC: Pew Research Center.

Telles, E., & Murguia, E. (1990). Phenotype discrimination and income differences among Mexican Americans. *Social Science Quarterly*, 71, 682–696.

Telzer, E. H., & Vasquez-Garcia, H. A. (2009). Skin color and self-perceptions of immigrant and US-born Latinas: The moderating role of racial socialization and ethnic identity. *Hispanic Journal of Behavioral Sciences*, 31, 357–374.

Thomas, L. (2010). *Puerto Rican citizen: History and political identity in twentieth-century New York City.* Chicago, IL: University of Chicago Press.

Torres, V. (2003). Influences on ethnic identity development of Latino college students in the first two years of college. *Journal of College Student Development*, 44(4), 532–547.

Torres, V., Martinez, S., Wallace, L. D., Medrano, C. I., Robledo, A. L., & Hernandez, E. (2012). The connections between Latino ethnic identity and adult experiences. *Adult Education Quarterly*, 62(1), 3–18.

U.S. Census Bureau (2016, June). *Annual estimates of the resident population by sex, age, race, and Hispanic origin for the United States and states: April 1, 2010 to July 1, 2015*. Washington, DC: Author.

United States Commission on Civil Rights. (1974). *Counting the forgotten: The 1970 Census count of persons of Spanish speaking background in the United States: A report*. Washington, DC: U.S. Government Printing Office.

Valdez, Z. (2013, February). Ethnicity is a social construction too. *Racism Review: Scholarship and Activism Toward Racial Justice*. Retrieved from www.racismreview.com/blog/2013/02/24/ethnicity-is-a-social-construction-too/

Zerquera, D., Acevedo-Gil, N., Flores, E., & Maranthal, P. (2015, April). *Repositioning trends of Latino enrollments in community colleges*. Paper presented at the annual meeting of the American Education Research Association, Chicago, IL.

Zerquera, D., & Gross, J. P. K. (2017). Context matters: A critical consideration of Latino student success outcomes within different institutional contexts. *Journal of Hispanic Higher Education, 16*(3), 209–231. doi.org: 10.1177/1538192715612915.

Zuberi, T. (2001). *Thicker than blood: How racial statistics lie*. Minneapolis, MN: University of Minnesota Press.

CHAPTER 11

Data Quality in the Evaluation of Latino Student Success

Stella M. Flores, Brian Holzman, and Leticia Oseguera

The year 2010 marked the beginning of what demographers call "the tipping point" of demographic changes in America's racial and ethnic population (Dougherty & Jordan, 2012), in which Latinos played a major role. Three key demographic developments have contributed to the current state of Latino educational attainment in the United States. The first is the growing number of majority-minority states/jurisdictions. For example, in five states or jurisdictions—Hawaii, California, New Mexico, Texas, and Washington, DC—non-Whites now comprise the majority of the population, and in ten others—Arizona, California, Washington, DC, Florida, Georgia, Hawaii, Maryland, Nevada, New Mexico, Texas—the minority population under age 15 outnumbers the White population. As a point of reference, Latinos comprise the majority racial and ethnic groups in six of these ten "youth states" —Arizona, California, Florida, New Mexico, Nevada, Texas—which are also among the ten states with the largest Latino populations. While it is now well known that Latinos have become the largest minority group in the nation (16.3%, compared to 12.6% Black and 4.8% Asian; Ennis, Rios-Vargas, & Albert, 2011), their growing majority status across multiple states and, more importantly for this discussion, in the U.S. education system provides, a new demographic platform from which to assess, construct, and forecast education policy.

The second development has to do with Latinos' immigrant identity. We know that, by 2010, foreign-born individuals accounted for 13% of the U.S. population, or about 40 million people (Grieco et al., 2012). More than half of the 40 million were from Latin America (53%). In comparison, Asian-origin individuals comprised 28% of the foreign-born U.S. population in 2010. The majority of the foreign-born U.S. population resided in four states—California, Texas, New York, Florida—although 14 states and the District of Columbia had immigrant populations exceeding the 13% national average. This growing foreign-born population is seen most vividly in the public schools, where nearly a quarter of all student are now the children of immigrants (Migration Policy Institute, 2014). Immigration has been part of the Latino story in the United States, which includes sensitive issues such as who owned borders, the role of treaty promises, how people entered the country once borders were established, what social and economic capital adults brought to their new location, and the role of language. Understanding these issues is important to public schools and critical to knowing how to serve, learn from, and build with these populations.

While detailing the evolution of Latino immigration to the United States is not within the scope of this chapter, we note that differences in relationships with various Latin American countries have shaped where and how populations have entered the United States. A majority of the Latino population is Mexican-origin (64%), followed by individuals of Puerto Rican (10%), Salvadoran (4%), Cuban (4%) and Dominican (3%) descent (Stepler & Brown, 2016). While the Mexican story dominates Latin American migration, individuals of Dominican origin are a fast-growing Caribbean immigrant group to the United States (Levitt, 2007) and are primarily concentrated in the cities of New York and northern New Jersey, Miami-Ft. Lauderdale, and Boston. Immigrants from Central America, whose largest migration came after civil wars in the 1980s, are largely in San Francisco, Los Angeles, and most recently Washington, DC, where Salvadorans made up the plurality of the Latino population (Menjívar, 2007). In sum, there is a substantial amount of Latino heterogeneity across state contexts that is often a result of relationships between the United States and other nations.

The third demographic development has occurred in higher education institutions, entities that are supported and regulated by state, federal, and, in the case of community colleges, municipal policies: the increased college enrollment of Latino students, which has a complex relationship with population growth. For example, a nationwide increase in college enrollment in 2010 took Latino enrollment to a record level; in fact, Latino students represented the majority of the increase over 2009 (Fry & Lopez, 2012). Moreover, by 2011, Latinos comprised the largest racial and ethnic minority enrolled in the nation's 2- and 4-year postsecondary institutions. That year, the nation also saw record high school graduation rates for Black and Latino students, including both the traditional diploma and the GED. Thus, the increase in college enrollment for both groups is likely explained by the increased number of high school graduates. However, despite the higher number of Latino students attending U.S. colleges and universities, complex issues surround Latinos' educational attainment. While these demographic accounts are noteworthy, they do not account for the increased number of Latino people who are eligible to enroll in college but have not opted to do so. Despite a numeric increase in college enrollment, the average cohort of Latino students in some states actually shows a decrease in the percentage of that population that enrolls in college (Flores & Park, 2013; Harris & Tienda, 2012). Accounting for the higher percentage of high school graduates thus yields a different picture of demographic success for Latinos in U.S. colleges and universities (Harris & Tienda, 2012). We direct our review to this complicated outcome.

EXAMINING THE RELIABILITY OF CURRENT DATASETS FOR MEASURING LATINO OUTCOMES

Given the changing demographics of the U.S., increased immigration from Latin America, and the challenges facing Latino college access and success, the purpose of this chapter is to determine whether current datasets can measure Latino students' educational outcomes, as well as the existing and increasing variation among this population. We do this by analyzing Latino students' representation in federal, state, and metropolitan datasets, and in some cases at the district level. We argue that the datasets for each of these jurisdictions offer both advantages and disadvantages in examining Latino student educational progress based on the particular strengths and challenges of each dataset. Strengths include attention to details of identity and generational characteristics, country of origin, or legal status, or a sample representation of respondents at the state level, as contained in federal census datasets. Another strength is the universal representation of students in a state as captured by longitudinal administrative data, including student pathways from preschool through college and into the workforce (referred to as the P–20w pathway throughout this chapter), which can include important details on curriculum options that are relevant in assessing students' educational success.

The datasets discussed in this chapter are not meant to be a comprehensive list, and each one we examine has tradeoffs that are critical to understand, based on the question of interest and purpose of inquiry. We seek to provide that knowledge through this analysis of the data sources that can be used to explore Latino student achievement through the kindergarten-to-labor force pipeline. The ultimate goal of this chapter is twofold. First, we aim to provide a unique assessment of how to use the reliable data sources available to design more effective and accurate educational interventions for Latino students. Our second aim is to provide a foundation for improving existing and future data sources so they will capture critical information on what is now the most diverse demographic era the nation has experienced in its public schools across the P–20w educational pipeline. The Appendix lists the studies reviewed in this chapter as well as others conducted by university research centers that may be of interest to scholars interested in studying Latino heterogeneity.

FEDERAL DATASETS

A number of federal data sources have been used to study education among the Latino population (e.g., Flores, 2010a, 2010b; Hirschman, 2001; Kao & Tienda, 1998; Reardon & Galindo, 2009). Although the National Center for Education Statistics (NCES) collects most of the information on educational achievement and attainment, the Bureau of Labor Statistics (BLS) and the Census Bureau also administer surveys commonly used in education research. These latter two datasets provide information that is representative at a state level, and the sampling design enables researchers to test questions of state policy.

National Center for Education Statistics

Table 11.1 provides a summary of the studies conducted by NCES, including information that may be relevant to research on Latino students. NCES studies, which are nationally representative, contain detailed information on family background and educational experiences. The National Assessment of Educational Progress (NAEP) and the early childhood and high school longitudinal studies also administer cognitive assessments commonly used by school districts as well as not-for-profit and governmental entities. One key advantage of these federal datasets is that they are much more likely than state datasets to provide information on the heterogeneity of Latinos. While all studies ask participants whether they identify as Latino, most federal surveys also disaggregate by ethnicity, usually Mexican, Puerto Rican, and Cuban. Some surveys offer other ethnic group options that are country-specific (e.g., Dominican) or region-specific (e.g., Central American); otherwise there is typically an "Other Latino" option. These distinctions are important for the states that are likely to serve populations with Latin-Caribbean origins, whose residents may have different reasons for and experiences with immigration than individuals from Central and South America (e.g., Cuban immigrants are more likely to be political refugees and come from highly educated families, while Mexican immigrants are more likely to be poor, in search of economic opportunity, and, at times, undocumented). While many NCES datasets do provide these ethnic group breakdowns, they still suffer from small sample size problems, so rigorous statistical analyses of Latino subgroups may have insufficient power.

Federal data are also more likely to provide information related to immigration, such as asking students (or their parents) which country they were born in or if they are U.S. citizens or residents. While no federal dataset to date asks specifically if an individual is undocumented due to ethical concerns, and legal rulings such as *Plyler v. Doe* that protect individuals in schools, categories such as "foreign-born noncitizen" have been used as a

Table 11.1. Commonly Used NCES Student-Level Datasets

Study	Description	Years	Information Relevant to Latino Children
Early Childhood Longitudinal Study, Birth Cohort (ECLS-B)	Longitudinal study of children born in the U.S. in 2001 who are followed through kindergarten entry. Parents, teachers, and non-parental care and education providers surveyed. Information on family background, early childhood education and school experiences, and cognitive assessments.	Follow-up surveys in 2001–02 (~9 months old), 2003–04 (~2 years old), 2005–06 (~4 years old), and fall 2006 or fall 2007 (kindergarten).	Ethnic group (broad categories); whether mother and father were born in U.S.; native language; how often spoke non-English language with primary caregiver as child; language proficiency.
Early Childhood Longitudinal Study, Kindergarten Class of 1998–99 (ECLS-K)	Longitudinal study of kindergarten students in 1998–99 who are followed through 8th grade. Parents, teachers, and school administrators surveyed. Information on family background, school experiences, and cognitive assessments.	Follow-up surveys in fall and spring of kindergarten (1998–99), fall and spring of 1st grade (1999–2000), spring of 3rd grade (2002), spring of 5th grade (2004), and spring of 8th grade (2007).	Ethnic group (broad categories); whether student, mother, and father were born in U.S.; citizenship status; native language; how often spoke non-English language with primary caregiver as child; language proficiency.
Early Childhood Longitudinal Study, Kindergarten Class of 2010–11 (ECLS-K:2011)	Longitudinal study of kindergarten students in 2010–11 who are followed through 5th grade. Parents, teachers, school administrators, and before- and after-school care providers surveyed. Information on family background, school experiences, and cognitive assessments.	Follow-up surveys in spring of kindergarten (2010–11), fall and spring of 1st grade (2011–12), fall and spring of 2nd grade (2012–13), spring of 3rd grade (2014), spring of 4th grade (2015), and spring of 5th grade (2016).	Ethnic group (broad categories); whether student, mother, and father were born in U.S.; citizenship status; native language; how often spoke non-English language with primary caregiver as child; language proficiency.

National Assessment of Educational Progress (NAEP)	Nationally representative assessment of academic performance among 4th, 8th, and 12th grade students. Students, teachers, and school administrators surveyed. The Main NAEP has tested students in a variety of subjects since 1969. The content changes over time to reflect changes in curricula. The NAEP Long-Term Trend has tested students in mathematics and reading using the same test roughly every 4 years since the 1970s. In some years, the National NAEP samples are drawn so they are representative of each state.	Data available most years since 1969. The grade and subject tested varies by year.	Ethnic group (in more recent administrations; broad categories); language spoken at home.
National Household Education Surveys (NHES)	Cross-sectional study of the educational activities of the U.S. population. Includes surveys of adult education, before- and after-school programs and activities, early childhood program participation, parent and family involvement in education, civic involvement, household library use, school readiness, and school safety and discipline. The adult education, school programs and activities, early childhood, parent and family involvement, and school readiness surveys are regularly administered. The surveys administered vary by year.	Surveys in 1991, 1993, 1995, 1996, 1999, 2001, 2003, 2005, 2007, 2012, 2016, and 2019.	Whether student, mother, and father were born in U.S.; native language; language proficiency.

Table 11.1. Commonly Used NCES Student-Level Datasets

Study	Description	Years	Information Relevant to Latino Children
National Longitudinal Study of the H.S. Class of 1972 (NLS-72)	Longitudinal study of high school seniors in spring 1972. Students, school counselors, and school administrators surveyed. Information on family background, high school and college experiences, test scores, and high school and college transcripts.	Follow-up surveys in 1973, 1974, 1976, 1979, and 1986.	Ethnic group (broad categories); native language.
High School and Beyond (HS&B)	Longitudinal study of high school sophomores and seniors in spring 1980. Students, parents, teachers, and school administrators surveyed.	Follow-up surveys in 1982, 1984, 1986, and 1992 (sophomore cohort only).	Ethnic group (broad categories); whether student, mother, and father were born in U.S.; native language; language proficiency.
National Education Longitudinal Study of 1988 (NELS:88)	Longitudinal study of 8th graders in spring 1988. Students, parents, teachers, and school administrators surveyed.	Follow-up surveys in 1990, 1992, 1994, and 2000.	Ethnic group (broad categories); whether student, mother, and father were born in U.S.; native language; language proficiency.
Education Longitudinal Study of 2002 (ELS:2002)	Longitudinal study of high school sophomores in spring 2002. Students, parents, teachers, and school administrators surveyed.	Follow-up surveys in 2004, 2006, and 2012.	Ethnic group (broad categories); whether student, mother, and father were born in U.S.; native language; language proficiency.
High School Longitudinal Study of 2009 (HSLS:09)	Longitudinal study high school sophomores in fall 2009. Students, parents, teachers, school counselors, and school administrators surveyed. Study has a strong focus on science, technology, engineering, and math.	Follow-up surveys in 2012, 2013, 2016, and 2021.	Ethnic group (broad categories); whether student, mother, and father were born in U.S.; native language.

National Postsecondary Student Aid Study (NPSAS)	Nationally representative study of students in postsecondary institutions with a focus on college costs and financial aid. Sample includes students enrolled in undergraduate, graduate, and professional education programs. NPSAS provides baseline data for two longitudinal studies, Beginning Postsecondary Students (BPS) and Baccalaureate and Beyond (B&B).	Data collected in 1986–1987, 1989–1990, 1992–1993, 1995–1996, 1999–2000, 2003–2004, 2007–2008, and 2011–2012, 2015–2016, 2017–2018, and 2019–2020. BPS data are drawn from the 1990, 1996, 2004, and 2012 samples while B&B data are drawn from the 1993, 2000, 2008, and 2016 samples.	Ethnic group (broad categories); whether student, mother, and father were born in U.S.; citizenship status; native language; how often spoke non-English language with primary caregiver as child.
Beginning Postsecondary Students Longitudinal Study (BPS)	Longitudinal, nationally representative study of first-time college students surveyed at the end of their first year and three and six years after entering college.	Data drawn from NPSAS. Four cohorts available: 1990 (surveyed through 1994), 1996 (surveyed through 2001), 2004 (surveyed through 2009), and 2012 (surveyed through 2017).	Ethnic group (broad categories); whether student, mother, and father were born in U.S.; citizenship status; native language; how often spoke non-English language with primary caregiver as child.
Baccalaureate and Beyond (B&B)	Longitudinal, nationally representative study of students graduating from baccalaureate institutions.	Data drawn from NPSAS. Three cohorts available and one underway: 1993 (surveyed through 2003), 2000 (surveyed through 2001), 2008 (surveyed through 2018), and 2016 (surveyed through 2017, with additional follow-ups in 2020 and 2026).	Ethnic group (broad categories); whether student, mother, and father were born in U.S.; citizenship status; native language; how often spoke non-English language with primary caregiver as child.

proxy (although usually with appropriate disclaimers) to determine if an individual is likely to be undocumented. While some surveys do not ask directly about generational status, questions about the country of birth may enable researchers to generate measures of immigrant generation (i.e., first, second, third, and higher). Some surveys do ask respondents when they arrived in the United States, which facilitates more detailed measures, like 1.5 or 1.75 immigrant generations. The age at which a student is assessed, however, may produce different information on citizenship. Citizenship items in early childhood studies tend to be binary, while those in postsecondary studies are more detailed, usually asking students if they are resident aliens, eligible noncitizens, or foreign students with visas. Finally, data on language use and proficiency varies by study, but respondents usually at least report whether English was their first or primary language as a child.

One challenge of national data on English language proficiency and progress, however, is the lack of information on the number of years spent in a language program, the type of language program, or when a student was reclassified to English-language status. State and district data provide more capacity to ask these questions, which will be discussed. While a majority of Latino students are not English learners, a majority of English learners are U.S. citizens, which highlights the complex interplay between ethnicity and citizenship status for students whose first language is not English (Gándara & Rumberger, 2009).

While most federal datasets like the NCES studies are nationally representative and/or longitudinal, they are not universe studies but samples, and are often too small to make generalizations to the state level. Many of these studies have limited panels, surveying individuals in a select number of years (e.g., for ELS, in 2002, 2004, 2006, and 2012). On the other hand, federal datasets contain thousands of variables and may collect information from survey and administrative data from parents, teachers, and schools in addition to students, enabling robust analyses that may range from the role of families and teachers in educational achievement to how financial aid impacts college choice.

National Longitudinal Studies

While the U.S. Department of Labor's Bureau of Labor Statistics (BLS) has been administering longitudinal studies since the late 1960s, it first began asking respondents to identify as Latino with the National Longitudinal Study of Youth 1979 (NLSY79). NLSY79 is a study of men and women who were between ages 14 and 22 in 1979. The study provides detailed information on individuals' educational and labor market activities and on significant events like family formation. Respondents were surveyed annually from 1979 to 1994, and biannually from 1996 to the present. The survey collects information on primary, secondary, and postsecondary schooling (academic and vocational), as well as high school transcripts and cognitive test scores from the Armed Services Vocational Aptitude Battery. In 1986, the BLS began following the children born to female participants of NLSY79. This study is ongoing and data are collected every other year. The most recent longitudinal survey administered by the BLS is the National Longitudinal Study of Youth 1997 (NLSY97). It began in 1997 with youth aged 12–16 and surveyed them annually until 2011 and biannually since then. Like NLSY79, the study provides detailed information on family background, academic performance, educational attainment, occupation and income, and other life experiences.

These three studies all contain information on ethnic group (Mexican/Chicano, Cuban, Puerto Rican, Other Spanish), citizenship, and language. NLSY97 also asked interviewers to code the respondents' skin tone, using a color card with a scale from 1 (lightest) to 10 (darkest). The NLS studies, which today are either annual or biannual, may be useful to researchers interested in understanding changes over time or in analyzing participants' event history. Scholars have used the 1979 and 1997 NLSY studies to examine changes in higher educational attainment over time; they also often focus on income (Bailey & Dynarski, 2011) and in some cases compare Black and White populations (Bound, Lovenheim, & Turner, 2012; Fryer & Greenstone, 2010).

Current Population Survey

The CPS is a monthly survey of American households sponsored by the U.S. Census Bureau and the Bureau of Labor Statistics. It is most widely known for providing the data used to calculate the monthly unemployment rate, and it has been used in numerous studies of immigration and state policy evaluations. Although it is not a universe survey, the CPS is useful in that it is administered monthly and has sufficient sample size to generalize to state and national levels. While the CPS primarily focuses on labor market experiences and earnings, it includes a number of items on educational attainment and whether an individual is enrolled in school or college. Each month, the CPS asks respondents age 16 and older questions on various topics (e.g., volunteering, voting). The October CPS supplement focuses on school enrollment; it asks respondents to report not only whether they are attending school but also what grade they are in, if they attend part- or full-time, and are enrolled in a 2- or 4-year public or private institution. In addition, parents are asked to report if their children are attending school, including early childhood education such as nursery school or part- or full-time kindergarten.

CPS respondents are asked if they identify as Latino and, if so, their group identity in five broad categories: Mexican, Puerto Rican, Cuban, Central/South American, and Other Spanish. There are also numerous items on immigration, specifically the country of birth of the respondent and the respondent's parents, as well as their citizenship status (i.e., native-born in U.S., native-born in U.S. territories, native but born abroad to American parents, foreign-born but naturalized, foreign-born noncitizen). The foreign-born noncitizen category has been used as a proxy for undocumented status for Latino and Mexican populations in recent studies linking immigration policy and school and college enrollment (e.g., Flores, 2010a, 2010b; Flores & Chapa, 2009; Kaushal, 2008). Although the CPS does not collect information on language proficiency, there is a binary indicator of whether Spanish is the primary language of the household.

U.S. Census Bureau

The Census Bureau administers two major surveys, the decennial census (census; every 10 years) and the American Community Survey (ACS; every year). They employ various sampling methods, such as a yearly and 3-year average strategy, and can be used to examine educational attainment. They are particularly useful in studies of Latinos because they have large sample sizes, which allow state-level analyses, and they ask respondents to report their ethnic group beyond the broad categories typically used in NCES studies. The census and ACS also ask respondents where they were born and, if outside the United States, when they arrived in this country; they also request a self-assessment of their language proficiency. The detail of the census is unmatched in terms of information on race, ethnicity, and mixed-race status. This will become increasingly important, as it gives new populations more categories to choose from as they move through their education and labor trajectories. Finally, despite the advantages the census datasets offer, their sampling does undercount important populations, namely minority men, some immigrants, and institutionalized populations, including people who are incarcerated or in the military. These populations are important, in part because they will include some Latinos above a certain age, and without them researchers will not have the most accurate information on this group's outcomes during or after high school. Such a limitation, therefore, may lead researchers to underestimate educational and occupational attainment gaps between Latino and other racial and ethnic groups.

STATE ADMINISTRATIVE DATASETS

In 2002, the U.S. Department of Education launched the Statewide Longitudinal Data Systems grant program, which was authorized by the Educational Technical Assistance Act of 2002 to help states design, develop, and implement the expansion of P-20w (early learning to workforce) longitudinal data systems (Garcia & L'Orange, 2010; NCES, n.d.). The State Higher

Education Executive Officers have since monitored the increasing number of states participating in this program and have documented state higher education entities that provide data on student trajectories from prekindergarten to high school completion, college enrollment to completion, and workforce activity through unemployment insurance records collected by state entities (Garcia & L'Orange, 2012). As of 2016, State Higher Education Executive Officers analysts had documented that 29 states had access to both K–12 and labor/workforce agency data, although this count is rapidly changing as states update their systems (Armstrong & Whitfield, 2016).

Across states, the range of elements in these data systems varies widely. Table 11.2 provides a summary of general elements across the various states by sector, from kindergarten to workforce. Texas and Florida, two high-Latino population states, offer the most comprehensive data warehouses, while California, Colorado, New Mexico, and Nevada, states with sizeable Latino populations, have made important strides in connecting the K–12 data warehouse to higher education and labor force data. While state data systems are still under development in many places, several large school districts have formed data sharing agreements and researcher–practitioner partnerships (RPPs) with universities or nonprofit organizations. RPPs exist in Arizona (Phoenix and Tucson), California (San Francisco and Los Angeles), Florida (Miami-Dade), Georgia (Atlanta), Illinois (Chicago), Louisiana (New Orleans), and Texas (Houston) and provide researchers with an opportunity to construct novel studies, interventions, and measures to study educational pathways and school effectiveness.

As for specific issues related to Latino student achievement, state data warehouses offer the most promise in assessing English learners' course-taking and progress in schools, access to a curriculum likely to lead to college readiness and success through coursework, and the role of labor force participation during and after schooling. Previous work by Bachmeier and Bean (2011) documented Mexican-origin students' propensity to work while in high school and to continue to work after graduation, rather than to attend college, due to financial and family reasons. Flores and Park (2013) found that the first postsecondary choice for Latino students eligible to enroll in college immediately after high school is in fact to work, rather than to enroll in college at all, regardless of their level of academic achievement. Given Latino students' work history and choices made throughout their educational trajectory, states with labor force participation data are likely to provide the most comprehensive information on the U.S. Latino student experience. That is, in assessing the trajectory of Latino students in the U.S., the most comprehensive evaluations will be those that account for work history throughout the educational pipeline. For many students, work will be the most important competitor to college enrollment. State and national datasets that include these experiences will more accurately capture the road to college completion. It will be especially informative for states to have

Table 11.2. General Variables by Sector, State Administrative Unit Record Data Systems Across 28 States (2012)

Sector	Variables
K–12 ELEMENTS	
Demographic	Student name or K–12/IHE ID, DOB, gender, race/ethnicity, SSN, citizenship, state residency status, free and reduced-price lunch, economic disadvantage status, language spoken at home
HS Background	High school attended, district/school code, student resident county-district code
HS Academic Activity	Date student enrolled, course type (regular, honors, AP), course title, course grade
HS Completion	HS GPA, graduation date, K–12 assessment scores
POSTSECONDARY ELEMENTS	
Demographic	Student name, DOB, gender, race/ethnicity, student ID, citizenship (limited), state residency status
Academic History	Admissions scores, placement scores, prior college(s) attended, transfer credit, enrollment
Enrollment Status	Degree-seeking, full/part-time, first term of academic history, program/major
Financial Aid	Dependency status, family income, federal, state, institutional, merit, need-based, other type of aid, FAFSA fields
Academic Activity	Course title, mode of instruction, grade, term/credit hours, completion, academic history, transfer, remediation eligibility, course-level info, financial aid, program inventory, noncredit instructional activity, faculty/staff, finance, facilities, capital projects, institutional characteristics
Academic Attainment	Degree awarded, degree date, cumulative hours/credits earned, cumulative GPA
Labor/Workforce Elements	Employer ID, employer size, wages earned, wage type code, hours worked, employment quarter code, employment year, date student/employee applied for Unemployment Insurance and date of UI check, U.S. Census Industry classification system (NAICS), U.S. Department of Labor Standard Occupational Classification code and title

Source: Data generated from Garcia & L'Orange, 2010, 2012.

these data given the heterogeneity of Latino populations across the U.S. Labor markets in New York City with larger Dominican-origin populations are likely to differ from the Mexican-origin labor market in Texas. Unfortunately, even the most comprehensive databases fall short in providing detail on the heterogeneity of the Latino population—country of origin, citizenship status, generational status, and parental education. This latter element is relevant in understanding a student's family's social and human capital, even when limited information on poverty status is provided at the time of the interview.

SURVEYS OF MAJOR METROPOLITAN AREAS: THE IMMIGRATION DATASETS

Over the past couple decades, sociologists have taken a keen interest in studying the assimilation and acculturation of first- and second-generation immigrants (e.g., Kasinitz, Mollenkopf, Waters, & Holdaway, 2008; Portes & Rumbaut, 2001). To understand these populations, they have conducted several studies of the children of immigrants in specific metropolitan areas. All these studies collect detailed information on country of origin (although the ethnic groups sampled differ by study), generational status, years living in the United States, and language proficiency. They also ask respondents to report information on their social experiences as immigrant children in the United States. The three most well-known studies in this group are the Children of Immigrants Longitudinal Study (CILS), the Immigrant Second Generation in Metropolitan New York (ISGMNY), and the Immigration and Intergenerational Mobility in Metropolitan Los Angeles (IIMMLA). CILS was a longitudinal survey of 8th- and 9th-grade students living in the Miami/Fort Lauderdale (FL) and San Diego (CA) metropolitan areas, while ISGMNY and IIMMLA were cross-sectional surveys of adults in the New York City (1999) and Los Angeles (2004) metropolitan areas. All three studies focused on how the children of immigrants experienced school and the transition to the labor market, offering many opportunities to study different facets of immigrant integration.

CONCLUSION AND RECOMMENDATIONS

The representation of Latinos in state and national datasets has evolved considerably since this population was first comprehensively captured in the 1970 U.S. Census and in longitudinal datasets in 1972. Advances in data have provided a greater opportunity to track students in some states across their entire education and labor trajectories, although the detail with which Latino students are captured varies by state. Moreover, deeper evaluations of Latinos from different ethnic groups are less available than they perhaps should be, given this group's demographic presence in U.S. schools and across the nation. To that end, we offer our recommendations on how to improve data analyses of Latino students, based on experiences and outcomes that are represented in their historical incorporation and current presence in U.S. schools.[1]

Our main messages for this chapter appear below, followed by our detailed recommendations for documenting and surveying the Latino student populations.

Message 1: Encourage agencies to engage in and/or continue more data-sharing and multijurisdictional discussion of the advantages and challenges of their respective data warehouses. States such as Texas and California have bountiful datasets at the state and district level (e.g., Houston, San Diego). Understanding how these states and districts have developed successful, collaborative relationships with one another to share data and work toward shared goals will serve as important examples to other states. Some researchers have begun to document this process; further translation and dissemination of this experience to other state policymakers and their intermediaries should also be encouraged (Turley & Stevens, 2015).

Message 2: Join advanced data-sharing practices with the appropriate expertise to interpret and recommend better educational practices that address the heterogeneity of the Latino student population. Latinos represent a new population in many districts and states. Ensuring that there are trained experts who understand how to interpret experiences relevant to this population—migration, citizenship, language—among the collaborators in the data partnership will likely improve the effectiveness of educational diagnoses as well as intervention designs.

In light of these key messages, we offer the following recommendations for a more comprehensive evaluation of Latino students in U.S. schools.

Recommendation 1: Disaggregating Latino student groups by state context is likely to increase the efficacy of interventions in areas with diversified Latino populations. Although Mexicans, Puerto Ricans, and Cubans are three of the largest Latino groups and they are often disaggregated in national and state data, groups that are growing in size (e.g., Dominicans, Latinos from Central America) are typically missing or grouped into broad "other" categories. More detailed categories are common in census data and studies focused on the children of immigrants, which lack information on educational experiences or are narrowly focused on immigrants in certain metropolitan areas. Aggregating ethnic groups in education datasets may do a disservice to practitioners and policymakers interested in understanding the heterogeneous Latino population and in identifying the most effective interventions for students. Disaggregating these groups into more nuanced categories is, of course, a matter of sample size and will likely require additional government or outside funding.

Recommendation 2: State data should reflect opportunities to collect complex yet ethical information on the growing number of children of immigrants, as differences in legal status within families will continue to be an issue of both demographic and psychological adjustment for Latino students. Approximately one in four American schoolchildren is an immigrant or the child of an immigrant (Migration Policy Institute, 2014). Given the growing number of immigrants and the increasing focus on immigration policy, it is heartening to see that a number of studies have included measures of immigration status and language. Most studies ask respondents to report their place of birth and that of their parents, which allows for immigrant generation variables. Only a minority of studies probe into legal status, but the subject is worth exploring further, given the political rhetoric surrounding unauthorized immigration. Recent studies also suggest that legal status is an important area of social stratification among immigrants and may have long-lasting intergenerational effects (Bean, Brown, & Bachmeier, 2015; Gonzales, 2016).

Recommendation 3: Improve tracking of the English learner trajectory at the federal level and seek greater ethnic and generational detail at the state level, including teachers' qualifications to teach students by state context. Understanding English learner program participation by school and state context is especially important, given differences in state policy that allow or ban English learner instruction in schools or that have different rules and regulations regarding which teachers are qualified to teach non-native English speakers. In addition, states in the South, such as North Carolina, that are new to the Latino diaspora are in a unique position to collect data on their new populations. Data collection should be done in conjunction with those who have the appropriate expertise to interpret student experiences within these new learning contexts.

Recommendation 4: State and national data should include measures of stratification increasingly used in social science that may have profound impacts on Latino educational opportunity. Aside from the primary measures of Latino heterogeneity discussed in this chapter—ethnic group, immigrant generation, citizenship, and language—there are many other ways in which Latinos differ. Two of the more novel measures examined in social science, which may be considered controversial and require more invasive data collection, are skin tone and geography. Latinos descend from indigenous, European, and African populations and, within the same ethnic group, skin tone may vary widely, leading to different experiences with discrimination. Hersch (2011) finds that among immigrants, controlling for racial and ethnic group, individuals with darker skin tones earn lower wages than their lighter-skinned compatriots. Latino opportunities also appear to also vary by where they live. Hillman finds that Latinos often live in communities with little access to colleges, specifically 4-year institutions (2016). It is possible supply-side constraints impact some Latino groups more than others. As the Latino population becomes increasingly diverse and spreads across the country, gathering information on additional axes of stratification may need to be considered in state and national data collection efforts.

Studies on Latino educational attainment provide multiple narratives. The population has reached a critical demographic turning point in terms of its presence in U.S. schools and the nation. However, that presence has not translated in the numbers expected into such outcomes as representation in 4-year institutions, selective institutions, college completion more broadly, or certain sectors of the labor market. Advances in data systems are beginning to reveal just how underrepresented this population is in these sectors. The measures available in the existing data sources are, of course, not perfect and may not adequately capture the intersectional nature of Latino identity with other cultural and social markers. However, in education and policy research, we need quantifiable variables and some level of representation of individuals. The alternative is not using data at all. Clearly, improvements in data construction and data use are still needed in order to understand the causes and consequences of Latino (under)representation in higher education. A key purpose of this chapter is to recommend a path to better data collection and use so that researchers, practitioners, and policymakers make more effective decisions about interventions intended to increase educational attainment for Latinos, and for other groups requiring a more nuanced perspective and understanding of their experiences in the U.S. education system.

Appendix: Links to Information on Study Design, Codebooks, and Questionnaires

Study	Type	Agency	Links
Early Childhood Longitudinal Study, Birth Cohort (ECLS-B)	Federal	National Center for Education Statistics	nces.ed.gov/ecls/birth.asp
Early Childhood Longitudinal Study, Kindergarten Class of 1998–99 (ECLS-K)	Federal	National Center for Education Statistics	nces.ed.gov/ecls/kindergarten.asp
Early Childhood Longitudinal Study, Kindergarten Class of 2010–11 (ECLS-K:2011)	Federal	National Center for Education Statistics	nces.ed.gov/ecls/kindergarten2011.asp
National Assessment of Educational Progress (NAEP)	Federal	National Center for Education Statistics	nces.ed.gov/nationsreportcard/
National Household Education Surveys (NHES)	Federal	National Center for Education Statistics	nces.ed.gov/nhes/
National Longitudinal Study of the H.S. Class of 1972 (NLS-72)	Federal	National Center for Education Statistics	nces.ed.gov/surveys/nls72/
High School and Beyond (HS&B)	Federal	National Center for Education Statistics	nces.ed.gov/surveys/hsb/

Appendix, continued

Study	Type	Agency	Links
National Education Longitudinal Study of 1988 (NELS:88)	Federal	National Center for Education Statistics	nces.ed.gov/surveys/nels88/
Education Longitudinal Study of 2002 (ELS:2002)	Federal	National Center for Education Statistics	nces.ed.gov/surveys/els2002/
High School Longitudinal Study of 2009 (HSLS:09)	Federal	National Center for Education Statistics	nces.ed.gov/surveys/hsls09/
National Postsecondary Student Aid Study (NPSAS)	Federal	National Center for Education Statistics	nces.ed.gov/surveys/npsas/
Beginning Postsecondary Students Longitudinal Study (BPS)	Federal	National Center for Education Statistics	nces.ed.gov/surveys/bps/
Baccalaureate and Beyond (B&B)	Federal	National Center for Education Statistics	nces.ed.gov/surveys/b&b/
National Longitudinal Study of Youth 1979 (NLSY79)	Federal	National Longitudinal Studies, Bureau of Labor Statistics	www.bls.gov/nls/nlsy79.htm www.nlsinfo.org/content/cohorts/nlsy79
National Longitudinal Study of Youth 1979 Children and Young Adults (NLSY79 Child/YA)	Federal	National Longitudinal Studies, Bureau of Labor Statistics	www.bls.gov/nls/nlsy79ch.htm www.nlsinfo.org/content/cohorts/nlsy79-children

Data Quality in the Evaluation of Latino Student Success

Study	Type	Agency	Links
National Longitudinal Study of Youth 1997 (NLSY97)	Federal	National Longitudinal Studies, Bureau of Labor Statistics	www.bls.gov/nls/nlsy97.htm www.nlsinfo.org/content/cohorts/nlsy97
Current Population Survey (CPS)	Federal	Bureau of Labor Statistics	www.bls.gov/cps/
Decennial Census	Federal	Census Bureau	www.census.gov/2010census/
American Community Survey (ACS)	Federal	Census Bureau	www.census.gov/programs-surveys/acs.html
The Freshman Survey	Institutional Research Centers	Higher Education Research Institute, University of California, Los Angeles	www.heri.ucla.edu/cirpoverview.php www.heri.ucla.edu/researchersToolsCodebooks.php
Your First College Year Survey	Institutional Research Centers	Higher Education Research Institute, University of California, Los Angeles	www.heri.ucla.edu/yfcyoverview.php www.heri.ucla.edu/researchersToolsCodebooks.php
College Senior Survey	Institutional Research Centers	Higher Education Research Institute, University of California, Los Angeles	www.heri.ucla.edu/cssoverview.php www.heri.ucla.edu/researchersToolsCodebooks.php
Diverse Learning Environments Survey	Institutional Research Centers	Higher Education Research Institute, University of California, Los Angeles	www.heri.ucla.edu/dleoverview.php www.heri.ucla.edu/researchersToolsCodebooks.php

Appendix, continued

Study	Type	Agency	Links
Beginning College Survey of Student Engagement (BCSSE)	Institutional Research Centers	Center for Postsecondary Research, Indiana University, Bloomington School of Education	bcsse.indiana.edu/
National Survey of Student Engagement (NSSE)	Institutional Research Centers	Center for Postsecondary Research, Indiana University, Bloomington School of Education	nsse.indiana.edu/
National Longitudinal Study of Freshman (NLSF)	Institutional Research Centers	Office of Population Research, Princeton University	nlsf.princeton.edu/
Texas Higher Education Opportunity Project (THEOP)	Institutional Research Centers	Office of Population Research, Princeton University	theop.princeton.edu/
New Immigrant Survey (NIS)	Institutional Research Centers	Office of Population Research, Princeton University	nis.princeton.edu/
Longitudinal Survey of American Youth/Life (LSAY/LSAL)	Institutional Research Centers	Institute for Social Research, University of Michigan	lsay.org/

Study	Type	Agency	Links
National Longitudinal Study of Adolescent to Adult Health (Add Health)	Institutional Research Centers	Carolina Population Center, University of North Carolina at Chapel Hill,	www.cpc.unc.edu/projects/addhealth
Project Talent	Institutional Research Centers	American Institutes for Research	www.projecttalent.org/
University of Washington-Beyond High School (UW-BHS)	Institutional Research Centers	Department of Sociology and Center for Studies in Demography and Ecology, University of Washington	depts.washington.edu/uwbhs/
Children of Immigrants Longitudinal Study (CILS)	Major Metropolitan Areas	Center for Migration and Development, Princeton University	www.princeton.edu/cmd/data/cils-1/
Immigrant Second Generation in Metropolitan New York (ISGMNY)	Major Metropolitan Areas	Researchers at the City University of New York and Harvard University	www.icpsr.umich.edu/icpsrweb/RCMD/studies/30302
Immigration and Intergenerational Mobility in Metropolitan Los Angeles (IIMMLA)	Major Metropolitan Areas	Researchers at the University of California, Irvine and the University of California, Los Angeles	www.russellsage.org/research/Immigration/IIMMLA www.icpsr.umich.edu/icpsrweb/DSDR/studies/22627

Source: Authors' compilation.

NOTE

1. See Appendix of this chapter for a working list of links to information on study design, codebooks, and questionnaires.

REFERENCES

Armstrong, J., & Whitfield, C. (2016). *Strong foundations 2016: The state of state postsecondary data systems*. Boulder, CO: State Higher Education Executive Officers. Retrieved from https://files.eric.ed.gov/fulltext/ED569332.pdf

Bachmeier J., & Bean, F. D. (2011). Ethnoracial patterns of schooling and work among adolescents: Implications for Mexican immigrant incorporation. *Social Science Research, 40*, 1579–1595.

Bailey, M. J., & Dynarski, S. M. (2011). Gains and gaps: A historical perspective on inequality in college entry and completion. In R. J. Murnane & G. J. Duncan (Eds.), *Whither opportunity? Rising inequality and the uncertain life chances of low-income children* (pp. 117–132). New York, NY: Russell Sage Foundation Press.

Bean, F. D., Brown, S. K., & Bachmeier, J. D. (2015). *Parents without papers: The progress and pitfalls of Mexican American integration*. New York, NY: Russell Sage Foundation.

Bound, J., Lovenheim, M. F., & Turner, S. E. (2012). Increasing time to baccalaureate degree in the United States. *Education Finance and Policy, 7*(4), 375–425.

Dougherty, C., & Jordan, M. (2012, May 17). Minority births are new majority. *Wall Street Journal*. Retrieved from online.wsj.com/article/SB10001424052702303879604577408363003351818.html

Ennis, S. R., Rios-Vargas, M., & Albert, N. G. (2011). *The Hispanic population: 2010*. 2010 Census Briefs C2010BR-04. Washington, DC: U.S. Census Bureau.

Flores, S. M. (2010a). The first state Dream Act: In-state resident tuition and immigration in Texas. *Educational Evaluation and Policy Analysis, 32*(4), 435–455.

Flores, S. M. (2010b). State Dream Acts: The effect of in-state resident tuition policies and undocumented Latino students. *The Review of Higher Education, 33*(2), 239–283.

Flores, S. M., & Chapa, J. (2009). Latino immigrant access to higher education in a bipolar context of reception. *Journal of Hispanic Higher Education, 8*(1), 90–109.

Flores, S. M., & Park, T. J. (2013). Race, ethnicity, and college success: Examining the continued significance of the minority-serving institution. *Educational Researcher, 42*, 115–128.

Fry, R., & Lopez, M. (2012). Now largest minority group on four-year college campuses, Hispanic student enrollments reach new highs in 2011. Retrieved from www.pewresearch.org/hispanic/2012/08/20/hispanic-student-enrollments-reach-new-highs-in-2011/

Fryer, R. G., Jr., & Greenstone, M. (2010). The changing consequences of attending historically Black colleges and universities. *American Economic Journal: Applied Economics, 2*, 116–148.

Gándara, P., & Rumberger, R. (2009). Immigration, language, and education: How does language policy structure opportunity? *Teachers College Record, 111,* 750–782.

Garcia, T. I., & L'Orange, H. P. (2010). *Strong foundations: The state of state postsecondary data systems.* Boulder, CO: State Higher Education Executive Officers.

Garcia, T. I., & L'Orange, H. P. (2012). *Strong foundations: The state of state postsecondary data systems: 2012 Update on data sharing with K–12 and Labor.* Boulder, CO: State Higher Education Executive Officers. Retrieved from files.eric.ed.gov/fulltext/ED540260.pdf

Gonzales, R. G. (2016). *Lives in limbo: Undocumented and coming of age in America.* Oakland, CA: University of California Press.

Grieco, E. M., Trevelyan, E., Larsen, L., Acosta, Y. D., Gambino, C., de la Cruz, P., & Walters, N. (2012). *The size, place of birth, and geographic distribution of the foreign-born population in the United States: 1960 to 2010* (No. 96). Washington, DC: U.S. Census Bureau.

Harris, A. L., & Tienda, M. (2012). Hispanics in higher education and the Texas Top Ten Percent Law. *Race and Social Problems, 4*(1), 57–67.

Hersch, J. (2011). The persistence of skin color discrimination for immigrants. *Social Science Research, 40*(5), 1337–1349.

Hillman, N. W. (2016). Geography of college opportunity: The case of education deserts. *American Educational Research Journal, 53*(4), 987–1021.

Hirschman, C. (2001). The educational enrollment of immigrant youth: A test of the segmented-assimilation hypothesis. *Demography, 38*(3), 317–336.

Kao, G., & Tienda, M. (1998). Educational aspirations of minority youth. *American Journal of Education, 106*(3), 349–384.

Kasinitz, P., Mollenkopf, J. H., Waters, M. C., & Holdaway, J. (2008). *Inheriting the city: The children of immigrants come of age.* New York, NY: Russell Sage Foundation.

Kaushal, N. (2008). In-state tuition for the undocumented: Education effects on Mexican young adults. *Journal of Policy Analysis and Management, 27*(4), 771–792.

Levitt, P. (2007). Dominican Republic. In M. C. Waters & R. Ueda (Eds.), *The new Americans: A guide to immigration since 1965* (pp. 399–411). Cambridge, MA: Harvard University Press.

Menjívar, C. (2007). El Salvador. In M. C. Waters & R. Ueda (Eds.), *The new Americans: A guide to immigration since 1965* (pp. 412–420). Cambridge, MA: Harvard University Press.

Migration Policy Institute. (2014). *Children in U.S. immigrant Families: Number and share of total child population, by age group and state, 1990–2012.* Retrieved from www.migrationpolicy.org/programs/data-hub/charts/children-im-migrant-families

National Center for Education Statistics. (n.d.) *Statewide longitudinal data system grant program.* Retrieved from nces.ed.gov/programs/slds/about_SLDS.asp

Pew Research Center (2015). *Modern immigration wave brings 59 million to U.S., driving population growth and change through 2065: Views of immigration's impact on U.S. society mixed.* Washington, DC: Pew Research Center. Retrieved from www.pewresearch.org/hispanic/2015/09/28/

modern-immigration-wave-brings-59-million-to-u-s-driving-population-growth-and-change-through-2065/

Portes, A., & Rumbaut, R. G. (2001). *Legacies: The story of the immigrant second generation.* Berkeley, CA: University of California Press.

Reardon, S. F., & Galindo, C. (2009). The Hispanic-White achievement gap in math and reading in the elementary grades. *American Educational Research Journal, 46*(3), 853–891.

Stepler, R., & Brown, A. (2016). Hispanics in the United States Statistical Portrait. Washington, DC: Pew Research Center. Retrieved from www.pewresearch.org/hispanic/2016/04/19/2014-statistical-information-on-hispanics-in-united-states/

Turley, R. N. L., & Stevens, C. (2015). Lessons from a school district-university research partnership: The Houston Education Research Consortium (HERC). *Educational Evaluation and Policy Analysis, 37*,6S–15S.

CHAPTER 12

Conclusion

Robert T. Teranishi

Race remains an inextricable aspect of American politics, policies, and laws. At the same time, it is a social and political concept that is malleable and can fluctuate as the context through which it is operationalized changes (Omi & Winant, 2014). Thus, how race is conceptualized and represented through data can and should evolve to define, measure, and report a more accurate rendering of social groups. The boundaries defining people and relationships are significant because they are associated with a broader structure of resources, which stratify opportunities racially (Omi & Winant, 2014). On an organizational and structural level, how race is operationalized in our educational system has significant implications for the distribution of opportunities and resources, which is directly correlated with education outcomes and social mobility.

This book began with the question: *Can institutions address educational inequality if the beliefs they hold about students—based on current racial categorizations—are inaccurate?* As we had speculated at the forefront, the answer is that they cannot. Beyond establishing that broad racial categories render imprecise understandings of gaps in academic experiences and outcomes, the chapters in this volume extend our understanding of those gaps between and within racial groups to paint a clearer picture of our system of education. In other words, the contributors in this book conjecture: In what ways do the assumptions we hold about racial groups in contemporary society broadly affect what we know about individual subgroups specifically? In these concluding remarks, I discuss the key themes that address this question in this volume, in addition to offering some recommendations for research, practice, and policy in education. Namely, I focus on the importance of 1) the conceptualization and operationalization of race, 2) issues with data and measurement, and 3) promoting collaboration among researchers, advocates, practitioners, and policymakers.

THE CONCEPTUALIZATION AND OPERATIONALIZATION OF RACE AND ETHNICITY MATTER

While there have been calls for disaggregated data to represent the different experiences and outcomes of students by ethnicity—and a movement to create data systems to provide this level of information—there remains a lack of information about subgroups that comprise larger racial categories (Teranishi, Lok, & Nguyen, 2013). The result of the homogenization of vast within-group diversity is that it renders some subgroups invisible, which can lead to a misrepresentation of the barriers that inhibit some students from succeeding. The educational system's reliance on broad race groups as a categorical distinction for making decisions, rationing support, and giving attention relies on the transparency of the stories told by categories. In this book and elsewhere, it is plain to see that relying on broader racial categories alone can obscure complex realities.

There are many examples of the consequences of aggregation. In Shotton's chapter, for instance, she tells us that the Native American population is inclusive of 567 federally recognized tribes in the United States, each accounting for a diverse set of histories, cultures, and identities. She also points out that there are over 200 different Native languages spoken, with each tribe having its own linguistic tradition (Faircloth, Alcantar, & Stage, 2015; Shotton, 2016). These are distinctions between subgroups that are masked by the treatment of the population as a homogenous group. Of course, it is not simply about differences between smaller groupings of people. As Ladson-Billings establishes, it is the fluctuating complexity of race that must be captured to more precisely examine how inequality is maintained, and obscured.

The concealment of inequality facing Asian Americans, for example, has historical roots that can be traced to contemporary racial debates, such as affirmative action, as Omi, Nguyen, and Chan write in their chapter. Although they are a population comprised of 48 different ethnic subgroups, Asian Americans have been used as a group to advance the efforts of maintaining White domination in college access (Garces & Poon, 2018). Why has this been possible? The treatment of the population in the aggregate is masking the significant differences in educational attainment, and opinions, among varying groups. While a high proportion of Taiwanese (74.1%), Asian Indians (71.1%), and Koreans (52.7%) in the United States have a bachelor's degree or higher, subgroups such as Lao (12.4%), Cambodians (14.1%), and Hmong (14.7%) are much less likely to obtain the same level of education (Teranishi, Lok, & Nguyen, 2013). These distinctions are not representative of the "model minority myth," and also demonstrate the significance of uncovering the complexities of race that undergird the maintenance of inequality.

In addition to the implications of race in laws and policies, broad racial categories also mask the changes that are occurring within groups and thus the forces that are having a disproportionate impact on these changes. For example, while immigration has been and will continue to be a significant factor in the numerical and proportional increase of the groups that make up the U.S. population, the impact weighs on groups in different ways. Conceptually, our society has relegated immigration to a "Latino issue." We do not recognize that it is also a formidable factor in the heterogeneity of the Black population. As Griffin and George Mwangi highlight in their chapter, while the U.S. Black population overall increased by approximately 15% between 2000 and 2010, the Black immigrant population increased by more than 300%. The Black immigrant population is far from being a monolithic group; it includes peoples from Africa and the Caribbean, as well as Central and South America.

In combination, these brief examples are portraits of complex and diverse groups of people that comprise broad racial categories, which reach into vast areas of education, from who has access to college to which students fill our classrooms, and how they are supported or otherwise ignored. Unfortunately, the treatment of groups at the level of broad racial categories can render many of these groups invisible and fail to reflect their unique needs and challenges. Moreover, these new, emerging subgroups are often inclusive of the most marginalized and vulnerable individuals, who are not gaining access to resources and opportunities because they are hidden through a process of conceptual omission.

DATA AND MEASUREMENT MATTER

The conceptualization and operationalization of race is often enacted through its treatment in data systems. This is important because data has become an increasingly important factor in how decisions are made in education. There is a surge of activity to create more robust datasets, as well as establish a stronger culture of inquiry and decisionmaking processes driven by evidence, rather than by intuition, anecdotes, and hunches (McClenney, McClenney, & Peterson, 2007; New England Resource Center for Higher Education Publications, 2008). The widespread use of data is furthered by technologies that are making data more accessible than ever. The inquiry movement in education is driven by the belief that data is critical for gauging more accurately who our students are, how they are performing, and how institutions can adapt to be more effective and efficient with their resources. Moreover, data has become a tool for informing the work of practitioners and policymakers in education systems that are increasingly concerned with accountability. Thus, data systems are not just a factor in the enumeration of racial groups, but in our ability to represent the trajectory and outcomes of groups and to distribute resources to address inequity in education.

With the increased importance of data in education, it is important to also raise awareness about the quality and reliability of data. Jencks and Phillips (1998) discuss the importance of considering "labeling bias" in educational research, which refers to the mismatch between what an indicator claims to measure and what it is actually measuring. Attention to this distinction raises awareness of important, but often misunderstood, problems in the application of data in research, practice, and policy. Simply put, increasing the amount of data does not automatically improve the quality of assessment; data needs to be tailored to respond to specific needs. The Data Quality Campaign, a national advocacy organization that promotes the development and effective use of data in education, says, "We need a new paradigm in education where data is in context, reliable, timely, portable and flows in all directions" (Data Quality Campaign, 2011).

It is imperative that data be able to provide a more accurate rendering of our increasingly complex and heterogeneous student populations. To this point, Johnston-Guerrero and Ford's chapter notes that we also need to gain a deeper understanding of students who identify as or are categorized by more than one racial group, a growing population that lacks representation in policy and in the creation and facilitation of services and support in education. In other words, how do we create data that can address heterogeneity within multiraciality? Additionally, Flores, Holzman, and Oseguera look across federal, state, and local datasets to examine the extent to which there is variability in the ability of data to measure Latino student experiences and outcomes throughout the educational pipeline from preschool through college and into the workforce. They conclude that while there have been significant advances in the ability of data to track educational outcomes for individuals and groups, there is a great deal of variability among datasets in their ability to represent the heterogeneity within the Latino population.

Aggregated data are providing a misleading statistical portrait of a heterogeneous racial groups that consists of subgroups that experience divergent trends in educational outcomes. This is particularly problematic when it conceals significant disparities in opportunities and outcomes for some subgroups. Thus, the use of disaggregated data is not only a powerful tool for measuring and reporting on the changing demography of students and the population generally; it is an essential tool for enabling stakeholders to mitigate disparities and inequality on a more granular level—placing resources where they are needed most and can address the more specific needs of particular student groups. For the study of Native people, according to Shotton, it means recognizing the difference between federally recognized vs. state recognized, tribal citizenship vs. ancestry, and acknowledging the difference between racial categorization and political and legal recognition.

Ultimately, better data results in more reflection and better insight. Data should be collected in a manner that reflects the heterogeneity of different racial populations. This has been an evolving project for the U.S. Census Bureau, which has revealed useful insight from which other government agencies can learn. New data categories that reflect the increasingly diverse national demography will be critical for education policy and practice. Disaggregated data should be consistent across schools within districts, and between K–12 and higher education within states, and there should be a movement to make this consistent between states and at the national level.

COLLABORATION BETWEEN RESEARCHERS, ADVOCATES, PRACTITIONERS, AND POLICYMAKERS MATTERS

While several implications emerge from the research in this book, it is important to recognize that political will is a key element of change in how racial subgroups are reflected in education research, practice, and policy. We need a call to action to establish momentum for change, which is inclusive of a broad set of constituents interested in and working on advancing equity in education. The civil rights community and other advocacy efforts, for example, should be aware of and advocate for a more nuanced perspective of racial minority groups. This is important groundwork for establishing awareness about the unique needs and challenges of particular subpopulations, and can build a foundation for better data that can reflect the opportunities, experiences, and outcomes of these groups.

Thus, a common theme raised in this volume is the importance of bridging the gap between raising awareness about the need for disaggregated data and creating conditions through which change can occur. While research can bring attention to the need for change, it must be coupled with efforts by advocates, practitioners, and policymakers to ensure that these issues are adequately addressed. Omi, Nguyen, and Chan provide useful case studies of how this has occurred within the AAPI community, which has been at the forefront of advocating for disaggregated data for many years. As Hafoka, Vaughn, Aina, and Alcantar point out, for the AAPI community, this is not just a political issue; "it is a visibility issue, a civil rights issue, and an issue of better serving this population" (p. 77). Data is not just a tool for practitioners and policymakers who work within education institutions and systems; it is an essential tool for advocacy and social justice, shedding light on ways to mitigate disparities in educational outcomes and improve support for the most marginalized and vulnerable populations.

Thus, it is essential for advocacy groups, direct support providers, and others outside of the systems of education to have input on the data that is being collected about their communities. Additionally, it is equally important for these constituents to have access to the data. These partnerships that revolve around data are important for ensuring that information about specific communities is more reflective of and responsive to these communities. This type of collaboration may involve difficult conversations, but they are necessary steps toward fundamental change that can occur through concrete actions.

In order to establish momentum—or in some cases, even a starting point for data reform—there is a dire need for more proof points. Research that utilizes disaggregated data, and their subsequent results, should be shared widely to demonstrate the utility of this data for informing practice, policy, and advocacy, especially for subgroups that are particularly marginalized and vulnerable.

In order for this research to occur, disaggregated data must be accessible for use by researchers engaged in the assessment and evaluation of services and programs. Data should also be shared across institutions within systems or consortia, across sectors (e.g., K–12 and higher education), as well as across political boundaries (e.g., states and territories), which enables tracking students throughout the educational pipeline.

It is through these steps that momentum can be established to result in change. The movement to disaggregate data needs to be built on a shared rationale that change is important and necessary and that a collaborative effort between a broad set of constituents is an important foundation for ongoing work. Discussions between these constituents about the collection, reporting, and use of disaggregated data can be facilitated through partnerships and working groups. These efforts should be supported by philanthropy, which can help offset the cost associated with changing systems and being a part of a broader network of support. The U.S. Department of Education can also play a role in providing guidance and technical assistance to institutions, and more importantly, collecting and reporting disaggregated student population data.

CONCLUSION

This book reveals how aggregated data can provide a misleading statistical portrait of heterogeneous racial groups. This is particularly problematic when it conceals significant disparities in opportunities and outcomes for particular student subgroups. This book also provides examples for effectively utilizing disaggregated data and the extent to which it can be a powerful tool for measuring and reporting on the changing demography of particular student groups. This more nuanced perspective on particular student groups is critical for measuring participation and representation in different sectors of education, as well as for enabling stakeholders to mitigate disparities and inequality that exist between subgroups.

In the preface, Walter Allen says "the future of our nation literally hangs in the balance." As our education system serves an increasingly complex and heterogeneous constituency, we must bring to bear a deeper and more thoughtful understanding of who our students are, what their needs are, and how we can best serve them. Thus, the goal of inclusive diversity must be rooted in making sure that individual students and broader community groups are not rendered invisible in how we talk about education practice and policy. Moreover, we must enable students and communities to see themselves in the data, which is unfortunately not currently the case for many marginalized and vulnerable groups. Overcoming this deficit is essential for addressing the real consequences that come with the conceptualization and operationalization of race and ethnicity in education systems throughout the United States.

REFERENCES

Data Quality Campaign. (2011). *Data is power*. Washington, DC: Author.

Faircloth, S. C., Alcantar, C. M., & Stage, F. K. (2015). Use of large-scale data sets to study educational pathways of American Indian and Alaska Native students, *New Directions for Institutional Research*, 5, 24.

Garces, L. M, & Poon, O. A. (2018). *Asian Americans and race-conscious admissions: Understanding the conservative opposition's strategy of misinformation, intimidation & racial division*. Los Angeles, CA: The Civil Rights Project.

Jencks, C., & Phillips, M. (1998). *The Black-White test score gap*. Washington, DC: Brookings Institution Press.

McClenney, K., McClenney, B., & Peterson, G. (2007). *A culture of evidence: What is it? Do we have one?* Ann Arbor, MI: Society for College and University Planning.

New England Resource Center for Higher Education Publications. (2008). *Brief 18: Creating a culture of inquiry*. Boston, MA: Author.

Omi, M., & Winant, H. (2014). *Racial Formation in the United States* (3rd ed.). New York, NY: Routledge.

Shotton, H. (2016). *Beyond reservations: Exploring diverse backgrounds and tribal citizenship among Native college students*. Los Angeles, CA: Racial Heterogeneity Project.

Teranishi, R. T., Lok, L., & Nguyen, B. M. (2013). *iCount: A data quality movement for Asian Americans and Pacific Islanders in higher education*. New York, NY: CARE Project.

About the Editors and Contributors

Iosefa Aina is the associate dean and interim director of the Draper Center at Pomona College. Sefa is a longtime advocate for social justice for the Asian American and Pacific Islander community as evidenced by his position as Board Chair of Empowering Pacific Islander Communities (EPIC). Sefa also served on President Obama's Advisory Commission on Asian American and Pacific Islanders for 4 years.

Cynthia Maribel Alcantar is an assistant professor of Higher Education Leadership at the University of Nevada, Reno. Her research focuses on the factors that impact the social mobility and integration of racial/ethnic minority and immigrant populations in the United States, particularly on the influence of schools (i.e., K–12 schools, community colleges, and minority-serving institutions) on the educational pathways and civic participation of racial/ethnic minority and immigrant students. She earned her PhD in Social Science and Comparative Education at the University of California, Los Angeles.

Walter Allen is a Distinguished Professor and Allan Murray Cartter Professor of Higher Education at the University of California, Los Angeles. He is an expert on the sociology of race, ethnicity, and diversity in education and has written extensively on these topics.

Laura M. Brady is an associate research scientist in the Department of Psychology at the University of Michigan. Her research leverages cultural and social psychological theories to understand and eliminate inequalities rooted in race, social class, and gender, particularly in the domain of education.

Jason Chan is the fellowship and career advisor and assistant director of the Center for Career and Professional Advising at Haverford College. His research interests are in race and diversity in higher education, with a focus on environmental and contextual influences on college students' understanding of race and racial identity. Jason's professional background is in the higher education and educational nonprofit sectors.

About the Editors and Contributors

Edward R. Curammeng is an assistant professor in the College of Education at California State University, Dominguez Hills. His research examines the relationship between ethnic studies and education in shaping the experiences of students and teachers of color. He earned his BA and MA in Asian American Studies from San Francisco State University and his doctorate in Social Science and Comparative Education from University of California, Los Angeles.

Martín De Mucha Flores is a doctoral student at University of San Francisco and works at Berkeley City College as Associate Dean of Educational Success and Equity.

Stella M. Flores is an associate professor of Higher Education at the Steinhardt School of Culture, Education, and Human Development NYU. She is also Director of Access and Equity at the Steinhardt Institute for Higher Education Policy at NYU. In her research, she employs large-scale databases and quantitative methods to investigate the effects of state and federal policies on college access and completion rates for low-income and underrepresented populations.

Karly Sarita Ford is an assistant professor in the Education Policy Studies department at The Pennsylvania State University. Her research focuses on the relationship between education and social stratification. Ford's research interests are Higher Education, Sociology of Education, International Comparative Education, and the social processes of collecting and representing demographic (race, gender, class) data.

Luis Ricardo Fraga is Reverend Donald P. McNeill, C.S.C., Professor of Transformative Latino Leadership, Joseph and Elizabeth Robbie Professor of Political Science, Director of the Institute for Latino Studies, and fellow at the Institute for Educational Initiatives at the University of Notre Dame. His primary interests in American politics where he specializes in the politics of race and ethnicity, Latino politics, immigration policy, educational politics, voting rights policy, and urban politics.

Stephanie A. Fryberg is an professor of Psychology at the University of Michigan. She is a member of the Tulalip Tribes of Washington State. Her research explores how social representations of race, culture, and social class influence the development of self, psychological well-being, and educational attainment.

Kimberly A. Griffin is an associate professor in the Higher Education, Student Affairs, and International Education Policy Program (Student Affairs Area of Specialization) at the University of Maryland. Dr. Griffin's research interests are primarily focused in three areas: diversity in graduate education and the professoriate; diversity within the Black higher education community; and mentoring and career development.

'Inoke Hafoka is a doctoral candidate in Social Science and Comparative Education at the University of California, Los Angeles. He is currently an associate instructor of Ethnic Studies at The University of Utah. His research focuses on the mobility of communities of color, with a specific interest on Tongans and (more broadly) Pacific Islanders, within the U.S. context, forms of education beyond tertiary institutions, Pacific Studies, Indigenous Studies, sport, and documentary film.

Jasmine Haywood is a program officer at Lumina Foundation. She leads Lumina's work around the metrics, strategic learning, and evaluation of progress toward the foundation's goals. Previously, she was a visiting faculty member in the Department of Educational Leadership at Indiana State University and the Managing Editor for the International Journal of Qualitative Studies in Education (QSE). Jasmine earned her master's and PhD in higher education and student affairs from Indiana University. She has published scholarship in the areas of Afro-Latino student experiences, racial microaggressions, and faculty of color.

Brian Holzman is a research scientist at Rice University. In his research, Dr. Holzman bridges sociological literature and college choice theory to examine racial and socioeconomic stratification in educational attainment. He seeks to illuminate potholes in the postsecondary pathway and use quasi-experimental techniques to identify interventions and policies that ease educational transitions for traditionally underrepresented youth.

Marc P. Johnston-Guerrero is an associate professor in the Higher Education and Student Affairs (HESA) program at The Ohio State University and is also affiliated faculty with the Asian American Studies program. Johnston-Guerrero's research interests focus on diversity and social justice issues in higher education and student affairs, with specific attention to college students negotiating and making meaning of race and racism and multiracial/mixed race issues.

Gloria Ladson-Billings is the Kellner Family Distinguished Professor in Urban Education in the Department of Curriculum and Instruction and is Faculty Affiliate in the Departments of Educational Policy Studies, Educational Leadership and Policy Analysis and Afro American Studies at the University of Wisconsin-Madison. Ladson-Billings' research examines the pedagogical practices of teachers who are successful with African American students. She also investigates Critical Race Theory applications to education.

About the Editors and Contributors

Chrystal A. George Mwangi is an associate professor and program coordinator in the higher education program at University of Massachusetts Amherst. Her scholarship broadly centers on (1) structures of opportunity and educational attainment for underrepresented populations along the P-20 education pipeline; (2) impacts of globalization and migration on U.S. higher education at the student, institution, and policy levels; and (3) African and African Diaspora populations in higher education.

Bach Mai Dolly Nguyen is an assistant professor of education at Oregon State University. Her research examines how categorization reveals, maintains, and mitigates inequality in education, with particular attention to racial and organizational classifications. In combination, these areas of research have manifested in studies on minority-serving institutions (MSIs), ethnic stratification, and organizational behavior and change.

Mike Hoa Nguyen is an assistant professor of higher education at the University of Denver's Morgridge College of Education. His research examines the benefits and consequences of public policy instruments in expanding or constraining the academic operations of colleges and universities, with a specific focus on federal diversity initiatives. This agenda falls into two policy strands: (1) how the federal Minority Serving Institution (MSI) program serves as a vehicle for academic institutions to enhance student success by advancing the political agendas of communities of color and (2) the influence of the judicial branch, as a policymaking body, in regulating the role of racial diversity at colleges and university.

Michael Omi is an associate professor of Ethnic Studies and Asian American and Asian Diaspora Studies at the University of California, Berkeley. He the coauthor of *Racial Formation in the United States* (3rd Edition, 2014) and coeditor of *Japanese American Millennials: Rethinking Generation, Community, and Diversity* (2019).

Leticia Oseguera is an associate professor in the Higher Education Program and Research Associate in the Center for the Study of Higher Education at The Pennsylvania State University. Her area of research focuses on educational policies around college access and admissions, including standardized testing, financial aid, and percent plans in college admissions.

Nicole Perez is a postdoctoral research associate in the Office for Research on Student Success at the University of Illinois at Chicago. Her research interests lie at the intersection of immigration, race and ethnicity, education and social inequality. Throughout her research endeavors she has examined the importance of place, context of reception, access to social institutions, and localized constraints and opportunities young Latinx encounter in forging their (im)mobility pathways.

Heather J. Shotton is is an associate professor in Educational Leadership and Policy Studies and Director of Indigenous Education Initiatives at the University of Oklahoma. Shotton is a citizen of the Wichita and Affiliated Tribes. Shotton's academic areas of interest include Indigenous women, Indigenous leadership, and Indigenous higher education.

Zoe Higheagle Strong (Nez Perce Tribe) is an assistant professor of educational psychology and directs the Center for Native American Research and Collaboration (CNRC) at Washington State University. She researches social, emotional, and environmental factors that shape adolescent development and educational outcomes.

Robert T. Teranishi is professor of Social Science and Comparative Education, the Morgan and Helen Chu Endowed Chair in Asian American Studies, and codirector for the Institute for Immigration, Globalization, and Education (IGE) at the University of California, Los Angeles (UCLA). He is also a senior fellow with the Steinhardt Institute for Higher Education Policy at New York University and principal investigator for the National Commission in Asian American and Pacific Islander Research in Education (CARE). His research examines the causes and consequences of the stratification of college opportunities, with a particular interest in the impact of higher education practice and policy on the mobility of marginalized and vulnerable communities.

Kēhaulani Vaughn is an assistant professor in Education, Culture, and Society at the Universty of Utah. Her research explores Pacific Island Studies, Native American Studies, Indigenous epistemologies, Indigenous education, and decolonial practices and pedagogies. She has taught numerous courses including: Pacific Islander Indigenous Education, Community Studies, Decolonial Education, Race and Ethnicity in the United States, Indigeneity in Hawaiʻi, Asian American Studies, Native American Studies and Research Methodology.

Desiree D. Zerquera is an associate professor for Higher Education and Student Affairs in the Department of Leadership Studies at the University of San Francisco. Her research focuses on how inequalities structure the experiences of underrepresented students in accessing and succeeding in higher education, with expertise in the areas of organizational theory, public policy, financial aid, research methodology, and Latino student experiences.

Index

NAMES

Abumrad, J., 59
Acevedo-Gil, N., 159
Acosta, Y. D., 170
Acuña, R., 156, 161
Adkins, N., xvi
Aguilera, D., 75
Aina, Iosefa, 8–9, 67–83, 199
Akresh, I. R., 161
Alba, R., 32
Albert, N. G., 170
Alcantar, Cynthia M., 5, 8–9, 67–83, 71, 72, 124, 127, 196, 199
Alcoff, L. M., 30, 154
Alito, Samuel, 61–62
Allen, Walter R., xiii–xxii, xv, xvii, xix, 200–201, xxn
Alo, K. M. B. C., 78
Alvarez, L., ix
Andersen, K., 131, 133, 145
Anderson, G. M., 109, 110
Anderson, M., viii, x, 104–107
Aoki A., 50n2
Araújo, B. Y., 161
Araújo-Dawson, B., 161–162
Arce, C. H., 162
Arenson, K. W., 103–104
Armstrong, E. A., 2
Armstrong, J., 181
Aronson, J., 131, 132
Asad, A., 104, 105
Austin, B., 146
Awokoya, J., 110
Azalea, Iggy, 25–26

Bachmeier, J. D., 181, 185
Bai, M., 15
Bailey, M. J., 179
Balutski, B. J. N., 69, 70
Banaji, M. R., 93
Banks, C. A. M., viii
Banks, James A., vii–xii
Barmer, A., 1
Barrett, T., 16
Basquiat, 26
Batalova, J., viii, 105

Battle, J., 155
Bauman, K., 160
Bean, F. D., 30, 31, 181, 185
Beastie Boys, 25–26
Bell, Derrick, 18
Bennett, P. R., 107–108
Bensimon, Estella Mara, ix, 164
Benson, J. E., 4–5
Berry, M. S., 158
Beyoncé, 17, 27
Biden, Joe, 16
Bilge, S., xx
Binning, K. R., 132
Bishundat, D., 51
Black, E., 87
Bland, Sandra, 22
Blewett, L. A., 133, 158
Blum, Edward, 59–60
Blumenbach, Johannes, 87
Bonilla-Silva, E., xviii, 4, 30, 162
Bonta, Rob, 55–56
Borrell, L. N., 161
Bouck, E. C., 138
Bound, J., 179
Brady, Laura M., 9, 131–153
Brayboy, B. M. J., 119–120, 122–124, 126, 127–129, 148
Brown, A., 161, 171
Brown, E. G. (Jerry), 46–47, 56, 57, 62
Brown, F., 112
Brown, H., 34, 48–49
Brown, S. K., 185
Brunn-Bevel, R. J., 107–108, 111–112
Brunsma, D. L., 86, 88
Bullock, J., 88
Bullock Mann, F., 1
Burack, J. A., 131
Burrell, J. O., 111
Bustillos, L. T., 164
Byrd, A., 51
Byrd, W. C., 107–108, 111–112

Cabrera, N. L., 5, 162
Cajete, Gregory, 79
Calderón, J., 4
Caldwell, J. Y., 5
Caldwell, L. D., 109, 110
Call, K. T., 133, 158
Camarota, S. A., viii
Capitelli, S., ix
Carbonneau, K. J., 146
Carey, Maria, 24
Casey, M., 158
Castagno, A. E., 119–120, 122–124, 127–129, 148
Cate, L., 89
Ceja, M., 162
Celious, A., 5
Chan, Jason, 8, 46–66, 51, 71, 196–199
Chan, K. S., 3
Chandler, K. L., xvii, 68, 77
Chang, E. T., 3
Chang, M. J., xvii, xviii, 58, 59, 68, 77
Changamire, N., 109, 110
Chapa, J., 158, 180
Charity Hudley, A. H., ix
Charles, C. Z., vii, xiv, 107–108, 112
Chaudhari, P., 90
Chessman, H., xvi, xxn
Chickering, A. W., xvii
Childs, John Brown, 25
Chisholm, Shirley, 16
Chua, A., 103
Cisneros, J. D., 159
Claire, T., 132
Clarke, C. A., 3
Clinton, Bill, 15, 17
Coates, Ta-Nehisi, 17
Cockburn, M., 3
Codina, G. E., 163
Cohen, G. L., 132
Cohn, D., 1, 2
Colby, S. L., 1, 2, 159
Collins, P. H., xx
Common, 26

207

Conchas, G. Q., ix
Conrad, C., xv
Contreras, Frances, ix
Cookson, P. W., Jr., ix
Corcos, A., 87
Cornell, S. E., 32
Covarrubias, R., 131, 134
Crenshaw, Kimberlé W., xviii, 18, 104
Crisp, G., 162
Croizet, J.-C., 132
Crosby, J. R., 132
Cullors, Patrisse, 25
Cunningham, E. L., 5, 110–112

Dache, A., 162, 164
Dache-Gerbino, A., 104, 110, 113–114
DaCosta, K. M., 93
Daniel, G. R., 161
Danta, R., 4
Daoud, N., 108, 110
Darity, W., 161–162
Darling-Churchill, K. E., 121, 131
Davidson, L., 69
Davies, P. G., 132, 133
Dávila, A., 162
Davis, F. J., 86
Davis, J. D., 5
Dead Prez, 26
De Brey, C., 1, 131, 134, 145
de la Cruz, P., 170
de la Garza, R. O., 36
Delgado, D. J., 86, 88
Delgado, Richard, 18
Deloria, Vine, Jr., 122–123, 126
del Pilar, W., 108, 109
De Mucha Flores, Martin, 9
DeSipio, L., 36
Destin, M., 145
DeVoe, J. F., 121, 131
Deyhle, D., xv
Diaz, V., 76
Dietrich, D. R., 162
Diliberti, M., 1
Dillow, S. A., 131
Dinh, Q., 70
Ditlmann, R., 132
Dixon, D. L., 69
Dizon, J. P. M., 55
Dodoo, F. N. A., 4
Dolezal, Rachel, 17–18
Dougherty, C., 170
Dowd, Alicia C., ix
Dowling, J. A., 4
Dowrick, P. W., 67, 78

DSegura, G. M., 34–35, 38
D'Souza, D., 87
Duany, J., 4, 164
Du Bois, B., 5
Du Bois, W. E. B., 25
Dunlop Velez, E., 1, 134
Duster, T., 87
Dweck, C. S., 141
Dynarski, S. M., 179

Eccles, J. S., 141
Echeverria-Estrada, C., 105
Echo-Hawk, H., 5
Eck, Diana L., ix
Elam, M., 86, 87
Eminem, 25–26
Endo, R., 3
English, S., 108–110
Ennis, S. R., 170
Erikson, E., xviii
Erisman, B. W., 103, 109, 112, 113
Espinosa, L. L, xvi, xxn
Espiritu, Y. L., 4, 34, 48, 50n2, 57, 61
Estrella, R., 71

Faircloth, S. C., 5, 124, 127, 131, 196
Falcon, A., 36
Fang, J., 57
Fann, A. J., 119–120, 122–124, 127–129
Farley, R., 31
Feliciano, C., 4
Fergus, E., 156, 162–164
Fiasco, Lupe, 26
Fleming, L., 111
Flores, E., 159
Flores, Martín De Mucha, 154–169
Flores, Stella M., 9, 170–194, 171, 173, 180, 181, 198
Flores-González, N., 38–39
Ford, A., 91–93
Ford, Karly Sarita, 9, 84–99, 89
Fordham, S., 30
Fraga, Luis Ricardo, 8, 29–45, 34–35, 38
Frank, R., 161
Fredericks, A. C., 111
Frederickson, George M., 31
Freitas, A. K., 69, 70
Fries-Britt, S. L., 104, 109–112
Frisbie, W. P., 162
Fry, R., 171
Fryberg, Stephanie A., 9, 131,

131–153, 133, 134, 145
Fryer, R. G., Jr., 179
Fuchs, C., 57
Fujikane, C., 74

Galindo, C., 173
Gambino, C., 170
Gándara, P., ix, 178
Garces, L. M., 196
Garcia, F. C., 36
Garcia, J. A., 34–35, 36, 38, 132
Garcia, N. M., xvii
Garcia, T. I., 180–182
Garvey, Marcus, 25
Garza, Alicia, 25
Gasman, M., xv
Gates, Henry Louis, Jr., 103
George Mwangi, Chrystal A., vii, 4, 5, 9, 103–104, 103–118, 108–112, 114, 197
Gerhardstein, R., 132
Ghosh, A., 52
Gleeson, S., 33
Glover, K. S., 4
Glover, S. H., 138
Golash-Boza, T., 161–162
Goldsmith, P. A., 31
Gomes, Peter, 23
Gomez, S. L., 3
Gómez-Quiñones, J., 155
Gonzales, R. G., 33, 185
González, G., xvii
Goodyear-Ka'ōpua, N., 76
Gorski, P. C., ix
Gould, S. J., 87
Graham, Susan, 88
Gramzow, R. H., 132
Grandmaster Flash and the Furious Five, 26
Green, Linda, 18
Greenstone, M., 179
Grieco, E. M., 170
Griffin, A., 108, 109
Griffin, Kimberly A., vii, xv, 9, 103–118, 108–112, 197
Grillo, T., 157
Gross, J. P. K., 158
Gryn, T., 170
Guinier, Lani, 26, 103
Guzman, B., 158

Hafoka, 'Inoke, 8–9, 67–83, 69, 199
Hafoka, M. P., 69
Hahn, J., 25–26
Hall, W. D., 111
Hallock, J., viii
Hamedani, M. G., 145

Index

Hamilton, L. T., 2, 6
Hamm, Mia, 27
Haney-López, I. F., 155, 160–162
Hannaford, I., 21
Hao, L., 164
Harper, C. E., 90, 94
Harper, S., xvii
Harris, A, 155
Harris, A. L., 171–172
Harris, A. P., 157
Harris, C. I., xviii
Harris, D., xv
Harris, J. C., 86, 89, 94–95
Hartmann, D., 32
Hartson, K. A., 132
Hau'ofa, E., 68, 69, 74–75
Hayes-Bautista, D. E., 156
Haynie, A. C., 4–5, 108, 109
Haywood, Jasmine M., 9, 154, 154–169, 161–164
Hepler, B. B., 68
Hernandez, D. J., 105, 107
Hernandez, E., 155
Hero, R. E., 34–35, 38
Hersch, J., 185–186
Heuer, R., 146
Higheagle Strong, Z., 146, 148
Hill, Lauryn, 26
Hillman, N., 186
Hirschman, C., 173
Hixon, L., 68
Ho, A. K., 93
Hochschild, J. L., xv
Hoeffel, E. M., 120, 125
Hoffman, C. M., 139, 146–147
Holdaway, J., 183
Hollinger, D.A., 87
Holzman, Brian, 9, 170–194, 198
Honda, Mike, 52
Hong, S., 3
Hoopes, M. J., 133
Hoover, R. E., 157, 159, 160
Hopkins, M., ix
Horn-Ross, P. L., 3
Howard-Hamilton, M. F., xvii–xviii
Howe, K. R., 74
Hsu, H., 15–16
Huffer, E., 76
Hughes, K., 2
Humes, K. R., 84, 86, 155–157
Hune, S., 3, 72
Hunter, M., 93
Hurtado, S., xv, 162

Hussar, W., 1, 131, 134, 145

Immortal Technique, 26
Inge, B., 158
Inouye, T. E., 71
Iserman, E. C., 133
Ishibashi, K., 75
Ishikawa, H., 3
Itzigsohn, J., 4

Jackson, James, 18
Jackson, Jesse, 16
Jackson, Michael, 17
Jacobs, P., 103
James, LeBron, 27
Jasiri X., 26
Jayakumar, U. M., xix
Jay-Z, 26
Jeantel, Rachel, 22
Jefferson, Thomas, xv
Jegatheesan, B., 148
Jencks, C., 30, 198
Jimenez, T., 33
John, A., 103
Johnson, Lyndon, 156
Johnson, P. J., 133
Johnston, M. P., 90
Johnston-Guerrero, Marc P., 9, 84, 84–99, 86–87, 88–89, 91–93, 198
Jones, C., xv, xix, xxn
Jones, J. A., 34, 48–49
Jones, N. A., 84, 86, 88, 155–157
Jones-Correa, M., 4, 34–35, 38
Jordan, M., 170
Jordan, Michael, 17
Joshi, H., 57

Kalt, J. P., 123–125
Kana'iaupuni, S. M., 69, 70, 75
Kang, J. C., viii, 3
Kao, G., 2, 3, 31, 173
Kasinitz, P., 104, 105, 183
Kauanui, J. K., 72, 76
Kaushal, N., 180
Keller, U., 107, 109
Kelley, M., 89
Kellogg, A. H., 94
Kena, G., 1, 134
Kent, M. M., 103–107
KewalRamani, A., 1
Keys, Alicia, 24
Khemlani, A., 158
Kiang, P. N., 51
Kim, C., 30
Kim, M. O., 3, 68

King, Martin Luther, Jr., 25
Kitano, H. H. L., 72
Kodama, C., xvii–xviii, 51
Kēpa, M., 76
Kravitz, Lenny, 24
Kristoapovich, P., 1
Krogstad, J. M., 70
KRS-One, 26
Krupnick, M., 55
Kupo, V. L., 77
Kweli, Talib, 26

Lacy, E., 158
Ladson-Billings, Gloria, xiv, xvi, 8, 15–28, 20n2
Lamar, Kendrick, 26
Lambert, B., 19
Larsen, L., 170
Larson, K. A., 31
LaVerne, A. B., 109, 110
Leal, D. L., 4
LeCompte, M. D., 75
Lee, C., 55
Lee, C. D., ix
Lee, E., 34
Lee, J., 30, 31, 109, 110, 114
Lee, S., xvii–xviii
Lee, S. S., 51
Lee, Stacey J., 47, 51
Levin, D. T., 93
Levitt, P., 171
Levitt, William, 19–20
Liang, C. T., xvii–xviii
Liddell, D. L., 94
Liebler, C. A., 70, 147
Liem, J. H., 112
Linnaeus, Carolus, 87
Lipsitz, G., 161
Logan, J. R., 161
Logel, C., 132, 133
Lok, L., 196
Lombardo, P. A., 87
Longoria, Eva, 23
Looney, S., 103, 109, 112, 113
Lopez, C., 34
Lopez, D., 4
Lopez, G., 105, 106
Lopez, I. H., 21
Lopez, K., 133
Lopez, M. H., 158, 161, 171
L'Orange, H. P., 180–182
Lovenheim, M. F., 179
Low, V., xv
Lowe, S. C., 119, 120, 125, 127–129
Lu, B., 161
Lunceford, C. J., 89–90
Lutz, A., 107–108
Lynch, M., 94

Lytle, C. M., 122–123, 126

MacLeod, D., 157
Madrid, E. M., 31
Maeda, D. J., xviii, xix
Mahiri, J., x
Major, B., 132
Malcolm X, 25
Mallinson, C., ix
Malone, N., 75
Manning, E., 1
Mantle, L., 55
Manu'atu, L., 76
Manzano, L., 51
Maranthal, P., 159
Markle, Meghan, 95–96
Markus, H. R., 131–133, 145
Marquez, B., 156
Mars, Bruno, 27
Marsh, J., 6
Martin, A., 94
Martin, Trayvon, 22, 25
Martinez, S., 155
Martinez-Ebers, V., 34–35, 38
Massey, D. S., vii, 107–108, 112
Maynard, A. E., 67, 78
Mayo, C., ix
Mayorga, O. J., xvii
McCain, John, 16
McClenney, B., 197
McClenney, K., 197
McDonough, P., 162
McEwen, M. K., xvii–xviii
McFarland, J., 1, 131, 134, 145
McGavin, K., 50n2
McGregor, D., 73
McIntosh, K. L., 108, 109, 111–112
McLewis, C., xv, xix, xxn
Medrano, C. I., 155
Menjívar, C., 171
Mickelson, R. A., 30
Millard, A. V., 158
Minthorn, R. S., 119, 126, 128–129
Mislán, C., 104, 110, 113–114, 162, 164
Model, S., 108
Mollenkopf, J. H., 183
Montagu, A., 87
Montalvo, F. F., 163
Mooney, M., vii, 107–108, 112
Moore, C. G., 138
Moore, I., 111
Mora, G. Cristina, 31, 38
Morning, A. J., 30–31, 87
Morrison, Toni, 15, 17, 20

Mos Def (Yasmin Bey), 26
Moses, M. S., xviii, xix
Mosselson, J., 109, 110
Motha, Suhanthie, ix
Moy, E., 73
Mr. Freeze, 25–26
Murguia, E., 161, 162
Murphy, M. C., 132
Museus, S. D., 50n3, 51
Musu-Gillette, L., 1, 131, 134, 145

Nagel, J., 32
Nakanishi, D., 50n2, 51
Neidert, L. J., 31
Newby, C. A., 4
Ngai, M., 34
Ngo, B., 51
Nguyen, Bach Mai Dolly, xvi, 1–12, 71, 72, 196
Nguyen, Mike Hoa, xvii, 8, 46–66, 68, 71, 77, 196, 199
Nguyen, T-L. K., 50n3, 51
Noguera, P., xvi
Norris, T., 120, 125
Novak, M., 156
Nuñez, A. M., 157, 159, 160, 162

Obama, Barack, 15–16, 24
Obgu, J. U., 30
Oboler, S., 4
O'Brien, P., ix
O'Connor, Barbara, 56
Odem, M. E, 158
Ogbu, J., 30
Okamoto, D. G., 34
Okamoto, M., 55
Okonofua, B. A., 106
Omi, Michael, xiv, 6–8, 21, 46–66, 48, 49, 155, 156, 195, 196, 199
Ong, P. M., 3
Onyenekwu, I., 103–104, 114
Ortiz, V., 31
Ortman, J. M., 1, 2, 159
Osborne, J. W., 132
Oseguera, Leticia, 9, 170–194, 198
Osei-Twumasi, Olivia, ix
Oyserman, D., 5, 133, 145
Ozaki, C. C., 90

Padilla, A., 89
Page, C., 103
Paguyo, C. H., xviii, xix
Palin, Sarah, 16
Pane, J., 6
Park, J. J., xvi, xvii, xix

Park, R. E., 86
Park, T. J., 171, 181
Parker, Tony, 23
Pascarella, E. T., 2
Pascoe, P., 86
Pastrana, A., 155
Patterson, A., 89
Patterson, K. S., 91–93
Patterson, S. M., 110
Patton, L. D., xv, xvii–xviii
Peralta, A. M., 104, 109, 110
Perez, Nicole, 8, 29–45, 33
Pérez, William, ix
Petersen, P., 133
Peterson, G., 197
Pham, J. T., 3
Phillips, M., 30, 198
Pickett, K., 157, 159, 160
Pizzolato, J. E., 90
Ponce, N., 3
Poon, O. A., 51, 55, 196
Porter, J. N., 30
Portes, A., 30, 33, 157, 183
Poston, W. S. C., 86
Preston, M., 16
Probst, J. C., 138
Public Enemy, 26
Purdie-Vaughns, V., 132

Qalo, R., 76
Quach, T., 3
Quinn, D. M., 132, 133

Raimon, E. A., 86
Ramirez, R. R., 84, 86, 155–157
Rathbun, A., 1
Reardon, S. F., 173
Redmond, M. A., 3
Reese, W. J., xv, xix
Reichard, R., 155
Reid, Harry, 16
Reisser, L., xvii
Rendón, L. I., xvii–xviii, 2
Renn, Kristen A., 84, 86–90, 92, 94
Rice, C., 109, 110, 114
Rice, Tamir, 22
Ricourt, M., 4
Rimer, S., 103–104
Rios-Vargas, M., 170
Roberts, D., 87
Robledo, A. L., 155
Robles, R. A., 52
Rockquemore, K. A., 86, 88
Rodriguez, C. E., 30–31, 34
Roediger, D. R., 87
Rojas, L. B., 69
Rong, K. L., 112
Root, M. P. P., 86

Index

Ross, T., 1
Rouse, I., 161
Rubenfield, J., 103
Rumbaut, R. G., 33, 183
Rumberger, R. W., 31, 178
Ryan, C. J., 160

Sáenz, V. B., 162
Sakaki, Judy, 54
Samuels, M. E., 138
Sanders, J., 32
Santos, J. L., 162
Schmader, T., 132
Schor, P., 7
Scovronick, N., xv
Segura, G. M., 34–35, 38
Sekaquaptewa, D., 132
Sexton, P. R., 107–108, 111–112
Sharpton, Al, 16
Shotton, Heather J., 9, 119, 119–130, 120, 126, 127–129, 196
Shyong, F., 56
Sidanius, J., 93
Small, C. A., 69
Smedley, A., 87
Smith, Jaden, 27
Smith, Linda Tuhiwai, 71
Smith, Will, 27
Snowden, F. M., 21
Snyder, T. D., 121, 131, 139, 146–147
Solórzano, D. G., xix, 162
Solyom, J. A., 119–120, 122–124, 127–129
Sonnenberg, W., 131, 145
Sorto, G., 103
Spencer, S. J., 132, 133
Spickard, Paul, 93–94
Squire, D., 51, 55
Stage, F. K., 5, 124, 127, 196
Steele, C. M., 131–133
Steele, D. M., 131–133
Stephens, N. M., 145
Stepler, R., 158, 171
Stevens, C., 184
Stone, J. M., 133, 145
Stonequist, E. V., 86
Strong, Zoe Higheagle, 9, 131–153
Stuart-Carruthers, A. C., 157, 159, 160
Stullich, S., 146
Suarez-Orozco, C., 105
Suarez-Orozco, M., 105
Sue, S., 72
Suh, S. A., xvii
Sussman, R. W., 20
Swisher, K., xv

Taborsky-Barba, S., 132
Tachine, A. R., 5, 127
Takagi, D. Y., 57
Takeuchi, D., 3, 72
Tan, A. G., 139, 146–147
Tatum, B. D., xvi, xviii
Tauriac, J. J., 112
Taylor, M., xvi, xxn
Taylor, V. J., 132
Telles, D., 161
Telles, E. E., 162
Telles, E. M., 31
Telzer, E. H., 162, 163
Teranishi, Robert T., ix, xvi, xvii, xviii, 1–12, 51, 71, 72, 195–201, 196
Terenzini, P. T., 2
Thai, X., 16
Thaman, K. H., 67, 79
Third Base, 25–26
Thomas, L., 156
Thomas, S. L., 69, 70
Thompson, J. S., 2
Thompson, M., 132
Tienda, M., 31, 171–173
Tillman, K. H., 107, 109
Timberlake, Justin, 27
Tippeconnic, J. W., III, 131
Todorova, I., 105
Tometi, Opel, 25
Torres, G., 26
Torres, K. C., vii, 107–108, 112
Torres, V., 154, 155, 158
Townsend, S. S. M., 133, 145
Trask, H.-K., 69, 73–74, 77
Trevelyan, E., 170
Truth, Sojourner, 25
Tubman, Harriet, 25
Tucker, Judge, 21
Turk, J. M., xvi, xxn
Turley, R. N. L., 184
Turner, S. E., 179

'Ulu'ave, M. F., 69
Um, K., 3
Utsey, S. O., 109, 110

Vakalahi, H. F. O., 76
Valdés, G., ix
Valdez, M. F., 67, 78
Valdez, Z., 155
Vasquez-Garcia, H. A., 162, 163
Vaughn, Kēhaulani, 8–9, 67–83, 199
Vazquez, M., 157, 159, 160
Velez, W., 31
Vigil, J. D., ix
Vines, P. L., 120, 125

Vinson, E., 133
Vue, R., 50n3

Walker, C., 132
Wallace, L. D., 155
Walpole, M., 146
Walter, M., 131, 133, 145
Walters, N., 170
Wang, F. K., 52
Wang, X., 1, 134
Wanger, S., 128
Washington, Booker T., 25
Waterman, S. J., 119, 120, 127–129
Waters, M. C., 4–5, 32, 104, 105, 183
Watt, J J., 27
West, Kanye, 26
Whitfield, C., 181
Wigfield, A., 141
Wijeyesinghe, C. L., 86
Wilkinson-Flicker, S., 1, 131, 145
Williams, K. M., 86, 88
Williams, Patricia, 18
Williams, Serena, 27
Williamson, S. Y., 111
Wilson, K. L., 30
Winant, Howard, xiv, 6–7, 21, 23–24, 48, 49, 155, 156, 195
Wise Intelligence, 26
Wong, P., 50
Woods, Tiger, 17
Wu, F., 57

Yam, K., 62
Yamano, T., 51
Yancey, G. A., 30
Yang, J., xvii
Yeager, D. S., 141
Yellow Bird, E., 5
Yeo, J. J., 3
Yeung, F., 50n3
Yosso, T. J., xix
Younger, T. K., 111

Zacher, M., 147
Zerquera, Desiree D., 9, 154–169, 158, 159
Zhang, C., 56–57
Zhang, J., 1
Ziegler, K., viii
Zimmerman, George, 22, 25
Zong, J., viii
Zuberi, T., 87, 164

SUBJECTS

AAPI. *See* Asian Americans and Pacific Islanders (AAPI)
Achievement gap
   Black-White, 30–31
   White/Asian students and all other groups, 137–138, 196
Administration for Native Americans (ANA), 123
Affirmative action
   Asian American, 57–61
   challenges to, vii, xviii
   panethnicity in, 57–61
   positions of opponents, 58–60
   positions of proponents, 60–61
   unintended consequences of, vii–viii
African Americans. *See* Black/African Americans
African immigrants. *See* Black immigrants
Afro-Latinos, 160–163, 164
Alaska Natives. *See* American Indians and Alaska Natives
American Community Survey (ACS), 106, 134–135, 139–141, 180, 189
American Indians and Alaska Natives, 119–129, 131–149
   as Census category, 2–3, 5
   data disaggregation, 134–143, 144, 146–148, 198
   demographic trends, viii, 120–122
   educational outcomes, 1–2, 125–126, 134–143
   identity safety/identity threat and, 9, 131–134, 144–145
   invisibility, 119, 127, 128–129
   panethnicity/lumping, 133–134, 144–145
   reclassification of Native Hawaiian and Pacific Islanders (NHPI) and, 73
   residential patterns, 120–122
   school location, 138–139, 140, 146–147, 149
   self-identification, 126–127
   socioeconomic indicators, 135–138, 141–143, 145, 146
   tribal affiliation/citizenship, 5, 124–128, 139–141, 147
   tribal nations, 119–120, 122–125
   within-group heterogeneity, 5, 119, 124, 131, 133–145
Annie E. Casey Foundation, viii
Apple Pie and Enchiladas (Chapa & Millard), 158
Armed Services Vocational Aptitude Battery, 179
Asian American Civil Rights, 60
Asian American Coalition for Education (AACE), 58–59
Asian Americans, 46–63
   achievement gap with other groups, 137–138, 196
   affirmative action, xviii–xix, 57–61
   Asian Americans and Pacific Islanders (AAPI) as subcategory, 1, 46–47, 52, 53–57, 60, 61, 72
   as Census category, 2–3
   data disaggregation, 3–4, 46–47, 51–57, 61, 72–73, 74, 77–80, 199
   demographic trends, viii, 1, 170
   educational outcomes, vii–viii, 1–2, 51
   ethnoracialization, 48–49
   exclusion as underrepresented minority (URM), xvi
   hidden opportunity gaps, 3–4
   immigrant generation, 30–31
   as label, 49–50
   model minority myth, vii, xvii, xviii, 47, 51, 58, 60
   panethnicity/lumping, 47, 48–50, 55–61, 68–72, 77
   racial formation theory, 48–49
   racial identity issues, 20
   within-group heterogeneity, xvi, 3–4, 50, 60
Asian Americans Advancing Justice (AAAJ), 3, 51, 60–61, 68–72, 77
Asian Americans and Pacific Islanders (AAPI), 1, 46–47, 52, 53–57, 60, 61, 72. *See also* Asian Americans; Native Hawaiian and Pacific Islanders (NHPI)
Asian and Pacific Islander American Health Forum (API-AHF), 73
Asian and Pacific Islander Institute on Domestic Violence (APIIDV), 71
Asian Pacific Coalition, 54–55
AYPAL, 52

Baccalaureate and Beyond (B&B), 177, 188
Beginning College Survey of Student Engagement (BCSSE), 190
Beginning Postsecondary Students Longitudinal Study (BPS), 177, 188
Black/African Americans, 15–27
   Afro-Latinos, 160–163, 164
   Black immigrants vs., 4–5, 103–104, 106–112, 113. *See also* Black immigrants
   Black Lives Matter, 22–23, 25, 26
   Black-White achievement gap, 30–31
   as Census category, 2–3
   Civil Rights movement, 25, 155–157
   Critical Race Theory (CRT) and, 18–20
   data disaggregation, 18
   demographic trends, viii, 1, 170, 197
   educational outcomes, vii, 1–2, 103–104, 106–112
   generational status, 4–5
   hip hop culture/musical performers, 17, 24, 25–27
   housing segregation, 19–20

Index

police violence, 22–23, 25, 26
race as concept and, 20–23
racial identity issues, 15–18
in sports, 23, 27
Black immigrants, 103–115
Black/African Americans vs., 4–5, 103–104, 106–112, 113. *See also* Black/African Americans
cultural adjustment, 109–110
data disaggregation, 113
demographic trends, x, 104–107, 197
educational outcomes, vii, 103–104, 106–112
identity development, 110
perceptions of racism and campus climate, 110–112
as potential new "model minority," 103
recommendations, 112–115
socioeconomic indicators, 106–107
within-group heterogeneity, 105–106
Black Lives Matter, 22–23, 25, 26
Brazil, fluidity of race in, 24
Brown v. Board of Education (1954), xv
Bureau of Indian Education (BIE), 121, 125
Bureau of Labor Statistics (BLS), 107, 173, 178, 179–180
Bureau of the Census. *See* U.S. Census Bureau

California
affirmative action ban by voters, xviii
data disaggregation of Asian Americans and Pacific Islanders (AAPI) by ethnic group, 46–47, 52, 53–57, 61, 72
data disaggregation of Native Hawaiian and Pacific Islanders (NHPI), 72
Immigration and Intergenerational Mobility in Metropolitan Los Angeles (IIMMLA), 183, 191
State Assembly Bills 176 and 1726, 55–57
California Department of Education (CDE), 95
Campaign for College Opportunity, 72
CARE (National Commission on Asian American and Pacific Islander Research in Education), 3, 51–52, 54–55, 72
Caribbean immigrants. *See* Black immigrants
Census Bureau. *See* U.S. Census Bureau
Center for Migration Studies, viii–ix
Children of Immigrants Longitudinal Study (CILS), 183, 191
Chinese Exclusion Act (1882), 57, 58
City University of New York (CUNY), xvi
Civil Rights movement, 25, 155–157
College Board, 1–2
College Senior Survey, 189
Colonial legacy
for American Indians and Alaska Natives, 124, 126
for Latinos/Latinx, 156
for Native Hawaiian and Pacific Islanders (NHPI), 67–68, 71, 73–76, 78–80
Colorism, 93

Common Application, The, 90, 91
Complexity, 164
of race and ethnicity, 23–25, 39
Congressional Asian Pacific American Caucus, 52
Cooperative Institutional Research Program (CIRP) Freshman Survey, 90
"Count Me In" Campaign, University of California, Los Angeles (UCLA), 54–55
Critical Legal Studies (CLS), 18
Critical Race Theory (CRT), 18–20
Current Population Survey (CPS), 179–180, 189

Data Quality Campaign, 198
Decennial Census, 180, 189
Deficit perspective
on American Indians and Alaska Natives, 131, 135, 139, 144
on Black/African Americans, 24
data aggregation and, vii
development of, xvii
on Native Hawaiian and Pacific Islanders (NHPI), 77, 79
Disaggregation of data
American Indians and Alaska Natives, 134–143, 144, 146–148, 198
Asian American and Pacific Islander (AAPI), 3–4, 46–47, 51–57, 61, 72–73, 74, 77–80, 199
Black/African American, 18
Black immigrant, 113
Latinos/Latin, 184–185, 198
multiracial people, 88–89, 93–94, 198
Native Hawaiian and Pacific Islanders (NHPI), 70, 72–73, 74, 77–80, 198
need for, xvii–xviii, 72–73, 197–200
Diverse Learning Environments Survey, 189
Diversity
American Indian and Alaska Native, 5, 119, 124, 131, 133–145
Asian American, xvi, 3–4
Black immigrant, 105–106
in higher education, vii–x
of immigrant population, viii
language and religious, viii–ix
Latino/Latinx, 154, 156–163
of schools, viii
trends in U.S., 1–2
within-group, vii–viii, xvi

Early Childhood Longitudinal Studies, 174, 187
Educational outcomes
American Indian and Alaska Native, 1–2, 125–126, 134–143
Asian American, vii–viii, 1–2, 51
Black/African American, vii, 1–2, 103–104, 106–112
Black immigrants, vii, 103–104, 106–112
Latino/Latinx, 1–2, 31, 159, 160, 170, 171–186

Educational outcomes, *continued*
  Native Hawaiian and Pacific Islander (NHPI), 1–2, 72, 78
Educational Technical Assistance Act (2002), 180
Education Longitudinal Study of 2002 (ELS:2002), 176, 188
80-20 National Asian American PAC, 59
Empowering Pacific Islander Communities (EPIC), 3, 51, 68–72, 77
English learners, 178, 181, 185
Equity Scorecard, The, 164
Ethnic Labels, Latino Lives (Oboler), 4
Ethnoracial hierarchy
  Latinos, 29, 34, 37–39
  nature of, 29
  uses of, 84
  White dominance, xiii–xviii, 30–34, 84, 196
Ethnoracialization model
  ethnoracialization, defined, 48–49
  nature of, 34

Federal Register, 119
Fisher v. District Court (1976), 126
Fisher v. University of Texas at Austin (2016), xviii, xix, 57–58, 59, 61–62
Fluidity, 94
  of race and ethnicity, 23–25, 32
Freshman Survey (CIRP), 90
Freshman Survey (UCLA), 189

Gratz v. Bollinger (2003), xviii
Grutter v. Bollinger (2003), xviii

Haitians. *See* Black immigrants
Harvard University, vii–viii, xviii–ix, 23, 57, 103
Hawaii Natives. *See* Native Hawaiian and Pacific Islanders (NHPI)
Heterogeneous race model (Celious & Oyserman), 5
Higher Education Act (1965), xv–xvi
Higher Education Research Institute (HERI), 90
High School and Beyond (HS&B), 176, 187
High School Longitudinal Study of 2009 (HSLS:09), 176, 188
Hip hop culture, 25–27
Hispanics. *See* Latinos/Latinx
Hispanic-Serving Institutions (HSIs), xv–xvi
Historically Black Colleges and Universities (HBCUs), xvi, 18
History Matters, 20
Housing segregation, 19–20
Ho v. SFUSD (1994), 52
Hudgins v. Wright (1806), 21
Hybridity, of race and ethnicity, 23–25

iCount (data disaggregation project), 51–52

Identity safety/identity threat
  American Indian and Alaska Native, 9, 131–134, 144–145
  identity safety, defined, 131, 132
  identity threat, defined, 9, 132
Immigrant Second Generation in Metropolitan New York (ISGMNY), 183, 191
Immigration
  of Asian Americans, 30–31
  of Blacks. *See* Black immigrants
  datasets, 183, 185, 191
  of Latinos/Latinx, 30–31, 33, 36–37, 170–171, 183, 185, 191, 197
  of Native Hawaiian and Pacific Islanders (NHPI), 69–70, 76, 77
  sources of immigrants, viii
Immigration Act (1990), 104–105
Immigration and Intergenerational Mobility in Metropolitan Los Angeles (IIMMLA), 183, 191
Immigration and Nationality Act (1965), 104
Indigenous people. *See* American Indians and Alaska Natives; Native Hawaiian and Pacific Islanders (NHPI)
Integrated Postsecondary Education Data System (IPEDS), 89, 90
Integrated Public Use Microdata Series (IPUMS), 159–160
Invisibility
  of American Indians and Alaska Natives, 119, 127, 128–129
  of multiracial people, 84, 92, 95–96
Islam, ix

Jamaicans. *See* Black immigrants
Japanese American incarceration, 57, 58

Labeling bias, 198
Lamar University, 93
Latino National Survey (LNS), 34–35, 38–39
Latinos/Latinx, 29–42, 154–165, 170–191
  Afro-Latinos, 160–163, 164
  alternative terminology for, 155–157
  in Black-White dichotomy, 30–34, 37–38, 160–163
  as Census category, 2–3, 156–158, 161, 164
  colonial legacy, 156
  cultural affinity, 36
  data disaggregation, 184–185, 198
  demographic trends, viii, 1, 30, 158, 159, 170–172
  educational outcomes, 1–2, 31, 159, 160, 170, 171–186
  ethnic and racial identities, 29, 32, 33–34
  ethnic heterogeneity, 156, 159–160
  in ethnoracial hierarchy, 29, 34, 37–39
  federal datasets, 173–180, 187–189
  geographic heterogeneity, 157–159

Index

immigrant generation status, 30–31, 33, 36–37, 170–171, 183, 185, 191, 197
major metropolitan area datasets, 183, 191
national origin identification, 34–37, 38–39, 40–42
panethnicity/lumping, 4, 29, 32, 33–37, 39, 154, 155–156
racial heterogeneity, 160–163
racial vs. ethnic groups, 29, 32, 33–34, 156, 159–163
recommendations, 163–164, 183–186
socioeconomic indicators, 185–186
state administrative datasets, 180–183
within-group heterogeneity, 154, 156–163
League of United Latin American Citizens (LULAC), 156
Learning Race in the U.S. Context (LRUSC), 110
Levittown, 19–20
Longitudinal Survey of American Youth/Life (LSAY/LSAL), 190
Loving v. Virginia (1967), 86

Michigan, affirmative action ban by voters, xviii
Migration Policy Institute, 170, 185
Model minority
  Asian Americans as, vii, xvii, xviii, 47, 51, 58, 60
  Black immigrants as, 103
  concept of, 51
Monolithic monotone (Lee), 47
Morton v. Mancari (1974), 126
Multicultural education, nature of, ix
Multiracial people, ix–x, 84–96
  contemporary notions of multiraciality, 86–89
  data disaggregation, 88–89, 93–94, 198
  demographic trends, 84
  fluidity of, 94
  invisibility/erasure of, 84, 92, 95–96
  monoracial categorization vs., 84–86, 95–96
  racial category vs. racial identity vs. racial identification, 86, 88
  racial data representation, 90–92
  racial demographic data collection, 89–90
  reclassifying/erasure and, 84, 92, 95–96
  recommendations, 94–95
  self-identification vs. observer identification, 92–93, 95–96
  terminology and, 86n1
  Two or More Races vs. multiracial, 88–89, 95

National Advisory Committee on Racial, Ethnic and Other Populations, 32
National Assessment of Educational Progress (NAEP), 134–143, 173, 175, 187
National Association for the Advancement of Colored People (NAACP), 17–18, 52
National Center for Education Statistics (NCES), viii, xv, 1, 92, 125, 135, 149, 173–178, 180
National Commission on Asian American and Pacific Islander Research in Education (CARE), 3, 51–52, 54–55, 72
National Congress of American Indians (NCAI), 123
National Council of La Raza (NCLR), 156
National Education Longitudinal Study of 1988 (NELS:88), 176, 188
National Household Education Surveys (NHES), 175, 187
National Indian Education Study (NIES), 134, 141–143
National Longitudinal Study of Adolescent to Adult Health (Add Health), 191
National Longitudinal Study of the H.S Class of 1972 (NLS-72), 176, 187
National Longitudinal Study of Youth 1979 (NLSY79), 178–179, 188
National Longitudinal Study of Youth 1979 Children and Young Adults (NLSY79 Child/YA), 188
National Longitudinal Study of Youth 1997 (NLSY97), 179, 189
National Longitudinal Survey of Freshmen (NLSF), 108, 190
National Origins Act (1924), 87
National Postsecondary Student Aid Study (NPSAS), 177, 188
National School Lunch Program (NSLP), 135–138, 141–143, 146
National Survey of Latinx, 161
National Survey of Student Engagement (NSSE), 190
National Urban Indian Family Council, 138, 147
Native Americans. *See* American Indians and Alaska Natives
Native Hawaiian and Pacific Islanders (NHPI), 67–80
  as Census category, 2–3, 5
  colonial legacy, 67–68, 71, 73–76, 78–80
  data disaggregation, 70, 72–73, 74, 77–80, 198
  deficit perspective and, 77, 79
  demographic trends, viii, 1, 68
  educational outcomes, 1–2, 72, 78
  ethnic groups within, 70
  Eurocentric models of schooling, 67–68
  importance of Indigenous education, 67–69, 79
  migration to U.S. mainland, 69–70, 76, 77
  "Pacific Islander" as term, 74–75
  panethnicity/lumping with Asian American and Pacific Islanders (AAPI), 68–72, 77
Nativism, 110

New England Resource Center for Higher Education Publications, 197
New Immigrant Survey (NIS), 190
New York, Immigrant Second Generation in Metropolitan New York (ISGMNY), 183, 191
NHPI. *See* Native Hawaiian and Pacific Islanders (NHPI)

Oakland Unified School District, data disaggregation of Asian Americans, 52
Oceania, 68, 69. *See also* Native Hawaiian and Pacific Islanders (NHPI)

Pacific Islanders. *See* Native Hawaiian and Pacific Islanders (NHPI)
Panethnicity
  in affirmative action programs, 57–61
  American Indian and Alaska Native, 133–134, 144–145
  Asian American, 47, 48–50, 55–61, 68–72, 77
  challenges of, ix–x
  defined, 48
  Latino/Latinx, 4, 29, 32, 33–37, 39, 154, 155–156
  Native Hawaiian and Pacific Islander (NHPI), 68–72, 77
  racialization vs., 33–34
People of the Pacific. *See* Native Hawaiian and Pacific Islanders (NHPI)
Pew Research Center, 3, 51, 84, 86, 92, 94, 104, 161
Plyler v. Doe (1982), 173–178
Police violence, 22–23, 25, 26
Predominantly Black Institutions (PBIs), xvi
Predominantly White Institutions (PWI), xvi, 109–110
Project Talent, 191

Race and ethnicity. *See also* Multiracial people *and specific racial and ethnic groups*
  ambiguity of, 21–23
  biological distinctions between races, 87–88
  categorization by U.S. Census Bureau, xvi, 2–3, 5–6, 7, 25, 31–32, 48–49, 52–53, 120–122, 125, 156–158, 161, 164, 198–199
  categorization in education, xv–xvii, xix, 196–197
  categorization in education policy, xviii–ix, 144–145, 199–200
  categorization in education research, xvii–xviii, 197–199
  complexity and, 23–25
  conceptualization and operationalization of, 20–23, 196–197
  development of, 32
  disaggregation of data concerning. *See* Disaggregation of data
  early classification systems, 87–88
  ethnicity, defined, 31
  fluidity and, 23–25, 32
  history and power of categorization in education, xix
  hybridity and, 23–25
  importance of race, 20–23
  as problem in U.S. democracy, xiii, xix–xx, 20
  race, defined, 31
  racial determination tests, 21
  racial formation theory and, xiv, 6–7
  racial identity issues, 15–18
  racial projects, 48
  reclassification of categories, 73, 84, 92
  role of, 20
  White dominance and, xiii–xviii, 30–34, 84, 196
Racial democracy, xiii, 20
Racial essentialism, xvi
Racial formation theory, xiv, 6–7, 48–49
Racial Heterogeneity Project (RHP), viii, 7–8
Racial projects, 48
RAND, 6
Rearticulation (Omi & Winant), 49, 56–57, 62
Refugee Act (1980), 104–105
Regents of the University of California v. Bakke (1978), xviii
Residential patterns
  of American Indians and Alaska Natives, 120–122
  Black/African American housing segregation, 19–20

San Francisco Unified School District (SFUSD), data disaggregation of Asian Americans, 52
School location, of American Indians and Alaska Natives, 138–139, 140, 146–147, 149
Self-identification
  by American Indians and Alaska Natives, 126–127
  by Latinos/Latinx, 161–162
  by multiracial people, 92–93, 95–96
Smart technologies, 27
Socioeconomic indicators
  for American Indians and Alaska Natives, 135–138, 141–143, 145, 146
  for Black immigrants, 106–107
  for Latinos/Latinx, 185–186
South Africa, fluidity of race in, 23–24
State Higher Education Executive Officers, 180–181
Student identity development models, xvii–xviii
Students for Fair Admissions (SFFA), 59–60
Students for Fair Admissions (SFFA) v. the President and Fellows of Harvard College (2018), vii–viii, xviii–ix

Index

Tennessee Department of Education, 84, 85, 87–88
Texas Higher Education Coordinating Board, 93
Texas Higher Education Opportunity Project (THEOP), 190
Thomas Theorem, xix
Tribal affiliation/citizenship, American Indian and Alaska Native, 5, 124–128, 139–141, 147
Tribal Colleges and Universities (TCU), 125

Underrepresented minority (URM) students, xvi
United Kingdom, fluidity of race in, 24
United Nations, 76
United States
 American Indian tribal nations, 119–120, 122–125
 colonial presence in Pacific, 75–76
 fluidity of race in, 24–25
 housing segregation, 19–20
 immigration and. See Immigration
 as "postracial" society, 15–16, 114
U.S. Census Bureau, 139, 146, 156–158, 161, 164
 American Community Survey (ACS), 106, 134–135, 139–141, 180, 189
 categories used by, xvi, 2–3, 5–6, 7, 25, 31–32, 48–49, 52–53, 120–122, 125, 156–158, 161, 164, 198–199
 Census as tool of White domination, xiv–xv
 Current Population Survey (CPS), 179–180, 189
 databases of, 134–135
 Decennial Census, 180, 189
 ethnicity of Black people (2020), 114
 heterogeneity within categories, 2–6
 limitations of aggregated data, 2–6
 multiracial people and, 86–87, 88
 stereotypic classifications of race, xvi
U.S. Commission on Civil Rights, 131, 156–157
U.S. Department of Education, 52–53, 127, 134, 200
 Integrated Postsecondary Education Data System (IPEDS), 89, 90
 Statewide Longitudinal Data Systems, 180–183
U.S. Department of the Interior, Bureau of Indian Affairs, 119, 123, 124

U.S. Executive Office of the President, 121, 125
U.S. Office of Management and Budget (OMB), 70, 127
 Directive 15, 72–73, 88–90, 94
U.S. v. Bhagat Singh Thind (1923), 20
University of California, Los Angeles (UCLA), 3
 "Count Me In" Campaign, 54–55
 Freshman Survey, 189
 Racial Heterogeneity Project (RHP), viii, 7–8
University of California Office of the President (UCOP), xvi
University of California (UC) system, xvi, xviii
University of North Carolina, xix
University of Oklahoma, 128
University of Texas, xviii, xix, 57–58, 59, 61–62
University of Washington-Beyond High School (UW-BHS), 191
URM (underrepresented minority) students, xvi

Virginia Racial Integrity Act (1924), 87
Visible Identities (Alcoff), 154

Washington state
 data disaggregation of Asian Americans and Pacific Islanders by ethnic group, 52, 72
 data disaggregation of Native Hawaiian and Pacific Islanders (NHPI), 72
 Washington Student Achievement Council, xvi
White House Initiative on AAPIs (WHIAAPI), 51–52
Whites
 achievement gap with other groups, 137–138, 196
 as Census category, 2–3
 educational outcomes, 1–2
 racial hierarchy and, xiii–xviii, 30–34, 84, 196
 racial identity issues, 17–18
World is a Ghetto, The (Winant), 23–24
World War II, 19, 23, 50, 57–59

Xenophobia, 110

Your First College Year Survey, 189